Elegant Glassware of the Depression Era

Revised 5th Edition

By Gene Florence

COLLECTOR BOOKS

A Division of Schroeder Publishing Co., Inc.

Searching For A Publisher?

We are always looking for knowledgeable people considered to be experts within their fields. If you feel that there is a real need for a book on your collectible subject and have a large comprehensive collection, contact us.

COLLECTOR BOOKS
P.O. Box 3009
Paducah, Kentucky 42002-3009

748.2911
FLO

DEDICATION

This book is dedicated to my wife, Cathy. She has been my editor and critic for the forty-three books I have written in the last twenty one years. Without her, there would be no rhyme nor reason. Without her, there would be no books!

FOREWORD

"Elegant" glassware, as defined in this book, refers to the handmade and acid etched glassware that was sold in the department stores and jewelry stores during the Depression era through the 1950's as opposed to the dime store and give-away glass that is known as Depression Glass.

The rapid growth of collecting "Elegant" glassware has been phenomenal and many dealers who wouldn't touch that crystal stuff a few years ago are stocking up on as much "Elegant" as basic Depression Glass. Depression glass shows used to be stocked with only 15% to 20% "Elegant" glass, but now there is more than 50% "Elegant" glassware at most shows.

The success of the first four books has precipitated this fifth. Nine new patterns and an additional thirty-two pages await you. "Elegant" has become standard terminology for glass collectors and dealers to describe handmade glassware.

I hope you enjoy this book, and I hope you will feel the years of effort to give you the best book possible on "Elegant" glassware were well spent.

PRICING

ALL PRICES IN THIS BOOK ARE RETAIL PRICES FOR MINT CONDITION GLASSWARE. This book is intended to be only **A GUIDE TO PRICES.** There are regional price differences which cannot be reasonably dealt with herein.

You may expect dealers to pay from thirty to sixty percent less than the prices quoted. My personal knowledge of prices comes from my experience of selling glass in my Grannie Bear Antique Shop in Lexington, from my traveling to and selling at shows in various parts of the United States, and (immediately prior to the pricing of this book) from setting up as a dealer at the National Heisey and Cambridge Glass shows. I readily admit to soliciting price information from persons I know to be expert in these various fields so as to provide you with the latest, most accurate pricing information possible. However, final pricing judgment is mine; so, for any errors (or praises), the buck stops here.

MEASUREMENTS AND TERMS

All measurements and terms in this book are from factory catalogues or actual measurements from the piece. It has been my experience that actual measurements vary slightly from those listed in catalogues; so don't get unduly concerned over slight variations. For example, Fostoria always measured plates to the nearest inch, but you will find that most Fostoria plates are never exact inches in measurement.

ACKNOWLEDGMENTS

The photography sessions for this book were spread over a two year period with one session lasting five days. A special thanks to Dick and Pat Spencer for their glass and work at the photography sessions and their information and pricing help in this book. Dick has been hard at work on a glass animal book that will be out in the fall of 1992, but still took the time to help with Heisey's rising prices. Pat is due extra credit for the flower arranged Plantation photograph.

There are so many other people behind the scenes in the production of a book like this that it's hard to believe! Some have lent glass, some, their precious time; others lent their talents and expertise. Many of these people have become friends (and most still are) after tedious hours of packing, unpacking, arranging, sorting, and repacking glass! Some have traveled hundreds of miles to share their glass with **you**, the public. Others have spent hours discussing and recording their prices, often after already long show hours. Without these extraordinary people, this book would not exist. Here are the names of some of those special people: Earl and Beverly Hines, Dan Tucker and Lorrie Kitchen, Charles Larson, Paul and Margaret Arras, Gary and Sue Clark, John and Judy Bine, Bill and Lottie Porter, Quinten Keech, Charlie and Ruth Collins, Yvonne Heil, Kenn Whitmyer, Jim and Helen Kennon, Hank and Debbie Pugliese, Jim and Doris Wilson, Mr. and Mrs. Leroy Allen, Carrie Domitz, Debbie and Randy Coe, John and Linda Neary, Jane White, Gail Ashburn, Lisa Stroup, Tom Clouser, and numerous unnamed readers from throughout the U.S. and Canada who shared pictures and information about their heretofore unlisted pieces.

Family is the single most important aid in my work. Were it not for my mom, "Grannie Bear," listing and packing the glass after Dad cleans it for each of the photography sessions, some of it might never be seen in these books. Charles helped cart boxes from storage and Sybil spent several days with Cathy out in the cold garage sorting glass into various patterns and boxes. Chad and Marc have both helped loading and unloading van loads of glass for each photography session, not to mention seeing to the home fires when I am traveling.

Cathy, with her editing pencil, still labors to make sense out of the material that I write. I deal in ideas; she deals with subjects and verbs. My writing in Florida and her traveling back and forth to Kentucky is becoming a bigger chore than we anticipated. Express mail loves me for sending my unedited pages for her corrections. She's had twenty-one years of this glass and book business experience (research, editing, proofing, travel, packing and unpacking, both me and the glassware). We both trained to teach. I hope we have been successful in that field beyond our youthful dreams!

Thanks also to Sherry Kraus of Collector Books for translating all my Microsoft Words into Quark. Thanks to Della Maze for helping me sort through several computer program problems with my new System 7.0.

You, my readers, are the inspiration to continue. As long as you keep sending me pertinent information and listings that may have suffered omission, I'll keep trying to pass the information to the public. Your help keeps me going!

INDEX

INDEX BY COMPANY

AMERICAN, Line #2056, Fostoria Glass Company, 1915 – 1986

Colors: crystal; some amber, blue, green, yellow, pink tinting to purple in late 1920's; white, red in 1980's and currently being made in red for Lancaster Colony by Dalzell Viking

My recent mail regarding the American pattern concerns the origin of various pieces. Since the closing of the **original** Fostoria factory in 1986, Lancaster Colony has continued to market its "Whitehall" glassware line which is similar to American, and made by Indiana Glass at Dunkirk, Indiana. You will find an abundance of "Whitehall" in pink at present, although an avocado green and a smoky blue have also been made. Check the Housewares section of your local Wal-Mart or similar store for the latest colors or items being made. This pink is also often confused with Jeannette's Cube pattern from the Depression era!

Red is currently being marketed at the Fostoria "outlet" stores in an abundance of pieces. This excellent quality glassware is being made at Dalzell Viking. Any piece that is marked with an asterisk (*) in the listings below is **currently** (or has been **recently**) reissued by them. American was never made in red until the 1980's and then it was made by Viking Glass for Fostoria. Dalzell Viking has now taken over the manufacturing of red for Lancaster Colony, present owner of the Fostoria name. You can see the **original** green and blue colors in the pictures on the next few pages.

Colored pieces of older American are in demand, but know from whom you are buying if you are a novice. If the price seems too good to be true, then it probably is!

Be sure to read this about the cookie jars before buying one! I have shown one in two pictures this time. **Most** of the new issues I have seen have wavy lines in the pattern itself and crooked knobs on the top. Old cookie jars do not. A telling point that works **90%** of the time is to try to turn the lid around while it rests inside the cookie jar. The new lids seem to hang-up and stop somewhere along the inside making the whole cookie jar turn. The old jars will allow you to turn the lid completely around without catching on the sides! This one item has been a tremendous setback to longtime collectors of American; but it is not unusual for a company's monetary concerns to be placed above those of collectors.

	*Crystal		*Crystal
Appetizer, tray, 10½", w/6 inserts	235.00	Bowl, 5½", preserve, 2 hdld., w/cover.	80.00
Appetizer, insert, 3¼"	27.50	Bowl, 6", bonbon, 3 ftd.	15.00
Ash tray, 2⅞", sq.	6.50	* Bowl, 6", nappy	12.00
Ash tray, 3⅞", oval	9.00	Bowl, 6", olive, oblong	10.00
Ash tray, 5", sq.	35.00	Bowl, 6½", wedding,	
Ash tray, 5½", oval	12.00	w/cover, sq., ped.ft., 8" h.	85.00
Basket, w/reed handle, 7" x 9"	80.00	Bowl, 6½", wedding, sq., ped. ft., 5¼" h.	45.00
Basket, 10", new in 1988	30.00	Bowl, 7", bonbon, 3 ftd.	10.00
Bell	225.00	Bowl, 7", cupped, 4½" h.	40.00
Bottle, bitters, w/tube, 5¾", 4½ oz.	65.00	* Bowl, 7", nappy	22.50
Bottle, condiment or catsup w/stopper..	90.00	Bowl, 8", bonbon, 3 ftd.	17.50
Bottle, cologne, w/stopper, 6 oz., 5¾"	70.00	Bowl, 8", deep	55.00
Bottle, cologne, w/stopper, 7¼", 8 oz.	70.00	Bowl, 8", ftd.	57.50
Bottle, cordial, w/stopper, 7¼", 9 oz.	85.00	Bowl, 8", ftd., 2 hdld., "trophy" cup	80.00
Bottle, water, 44 oz., 9¼"	500.00	* Bowl, 8", nappy	12.50
Bowl, banana split, 9" x 3½"	225.00	* Bowl, 8", pickle, oblong	13.00
Bowl, finger, 4½" diam., smooth edge .	25.00	Bowl, 8½", 2 hdld.	15.00
Bowl, 3½", rose	17.50	* Bowl, 8½", boat	10.00
Bowl, 3¾", almond, oval	12.50	Bowl, 9", boat, 2 pt.	10.50
Bowl, 4¼", jelly, 4¼" h.	15.00	* Bowl, 9", oval veg.	25.00
* Bowl, 4½", 1 hdld.	8.00	Bowl, 9½", centerpiece	30.00
Bowl, 4½", 1 hdld., sq.	8.00	Bowl, 9½", 3 pt., 6" w.	37.50
Bowl, 4½", jelly, w/cover, 6¾" h.	22.00	Bowl, 10", celery, oblong	15.00
* Bowl, 4½", nappy	10.00	Bowl, 10", deep	22.00
Bowl, 4½", oval	8.00	Bowl, 10", float	35.00
Bowl, 4¾", fruit, flared	15.00	Bowl, 10", oval, float	32.50
Bowl, 5", cream soup, 2 hdld.	45.00	Bowl, 10", oval, veg., 2 pt.	25.00
Bowl, 5", 1 hdld., tri-corner	11.00	Bowl, 10½", fruit, 3 ftd.	25.00
* Bowl, 5", nappy	7.00	Bowl, 11", centerpiece	40.00
Bowl, 5", nappy, w/cover	25.00	Bowl, 11", centerpiece, tri-corner	30.00
Bowl, 5", rose	22.00	Bowl, 11", relish/celery, 3 pt.	30.00
Bowl, 5½", lemon, w/cover	40.00	Bowl, 11½", float	50.00

7

	*Crystal
Bowl, 11½", fruit, rolled edge, 2¾" h. ..	42.50
Bowl, 11½", oval, float	45.00
Bowl, 11½", rolled edge	40.00
Bowl, 11¾", oval, deep	40.00
Bowl, 12", boat...................................	17.50
Bowl, 12", fruit/sm. punch, ped. ft., (Tom & Jerry)	140.00
Bowl, 12", lily pond	55.00
Bowl, 12", relish "boat," 2 pt.	20.00
Bowl, 13", fruit, shallow	55.00
Bowl, 14", punch, w/high ft. base (2 gal.)	225.00
Bowl, 14", punch, w/low ft. base........	200.00
Bowl, 15", centerpiece, "hat" shape	155.00
Bowl, 16", flat, fruit, ped. ft.	135.00
Bowl, 18", punch, w/low ft. base (3¾ gal.)	285.00
Box, pomade, 2" square.....................	350.00
* Box, w/cover, puff, 3⅛" x 2¾"	200.00
Box, w/cover, 4½" x 4½"	200.00
Box, w/cover, handkerchief, 5⅝" x 4⅝" .	225.00
Box, w/cover, hairpin, 3½" x 1¾"	200.00
Box, w/cover, jewel, 5¼" x 2¼"	225.00
Box, w/cover, jewel, 2 drawer, 4¼" x 3¼".	1,500.00
* Box, w/cover, glove, 9½" x 3½"	225.00
* Butter, w/cover, rnd. plate, 7¼"	100.00
* Butter, w/cover, ¼ lb.	17.50
Cake stand, (see salver)	
Candelabrum, 6½", 2-lite, bell base w/bobeche & prisms	110.00
Candle lamp, 8½", w/chimney, candle part, 3½".....................................	110.00
Candlestick, twin, 4⅛" h., 8½" spread .	55.00
Candlestick, 2", chamber with fingerhold	37.50
Candlestick, 3", rnd. ft.	15.00
Candlestick, 4⅜", 2-lite, rnd. ft.	32.50
Candlestick, 6", octagon ft...................	20.00
Candlestick, 6½", 2-lite, bell base	85.00
Candlestick, 6¼", round ft...................	200.00
* Candlestick, 7", sq. column.................	95.00
Candlestick, 7¼", "Eiffel" tower	125.00
Candy box, w/cover, 3 pt., triangular ..	65.00
Candy, w/cover, ped. ft.	30.00
Cheese (5¾" compote) & cracker (11½" plate).................................	50.00
Cigarette box, w/cover, 4¾".................	37.50
Coaster, 3¾"	6.00
Comport, 4½", jelly............................	8.00
* Comport, 5", jelly, flared	12.00
* Comport, 6¾", jelly, w/cover................	30.00
Comport, 8½", 4" high	40.00
Comport, 9½", 5¼" high......................	50.00
Comport, w/cover, 5"...........................	25.00

	*Crystal
* Cookie jar, w/cover, 8⅞" h..................	300.00
Creamer, tea, 3 oz., 2⅜" (#2056½)	8.50
Creamer, individual, 4¾ oz.	8.50
Creamer, 9½ oz.	11.00
Crushed fruit, w/cover & spoon, 10" ...	1,000.00
Cup, flat	7.50
Cup, ftd., 7 oz.	9.00
Cup, punch, flared rim.........................	11.00
Cup, punch, straight edge	10.00
Decanter, w/stopper, 24 oz., 9¼" h.	90.00
Dresser set: powder boxes w/covers & tray	400.00
Flower pot, w/perforated cover, 9½" diam.; 5½" h.	1,000.00
Goblet, #2056, 2½ oz., wine, hex ft., 4⅜" h.	12.00
Goblet, #2056, 4½ oz., oyster cocktail, 3½" h.	17.50
Goblet, #2056, 4½ oz., sherbet, flared, 4⅜" h.	9.00
Goblet, #2056, 4½ oz., fruit, hex ft., 4¾" h.	9.00
Goblet, #2056, 5 oz., low ft., sherbet, flared, 3¼" h.	9.00
Goblet, #2056, 6 oz., low ft., sundae, 3⅛" h.	9.00
Goblet, #2056, 7 oz., claret, 4⅞" h.	37.50
* Goblet, #2056, 9 oz., low ft., 4⅜" h.	11.00
Goblet, #2056, 10 oz., hex ft., water, 6⅞" h.	12.00
Goblet, #2056, 12 oz., low ft., tea, 5¾" h..	14.00
Goblet, #2056½, 4½ oz., sherbet, 4½" h....	10.00
Goblet, #2056½, 5 oz., low sherbet, 3½" h.	10.00
Goblet, #5056, 1 oz., cordial, 3⅛", w/plain bowl..................................	27.50
Goblet, #5056, 3½ oz., claret, 4⅝", w/plain bowl..................................	13.50
Goblet, #5056, 3½ oz., cocktail, 4", w/plain bowl..................................	12.00
Goblet, #5056, 4 oz., oyster cocktail, 3½", w/plain bowl...........................	10.00
Goblet, #5056, 5½ oz., sherbet, 4⅛", w/plain bowl..................................	10.00
Goblet, #5056, 10 oz., water, 6⅛", w/plain bowl..................................	12.00
Hair receiver, 3" x 3"..........................	195.00
Hat, 2⅛", (sm. ash tray)	12.50
Hat, 3" tall	25.00
Hat, 4" tall	45.00
Hat, western style...............................	175.00

* See note on new American on page 12.

	*Crystal
Hurricane lamp, 12" complete	150.00
Hurricane lamp base	50.00
Ice bucket, w/tongs	60.00
Ice cream saucer (2 styles)	60.00
Ice dish for 4 oz. crab or 5 oz. tomato liner	32.50
Ice dish insert	10.00
Ice tub, w/liner, 5⅝"	60.00
Ice tub, w/liner, 6½"	75.00
Jam pot, w/cover	50.00
Jar, pickle, w/pointed cover, 6" h.	275.00
Marmalade, w/cover & chrome spoon	35.00
* Mayonnaise, div.	7.50
Mayonnaise, w/ladle, ped. ft.	35.00
Mayonnaise, w/liner & ladle	30.00
Molasses can, 11 oz., 6¾" h., 1 hdld.	325.00
* Mug, 5½ oz., "Tom & Jerry," 3¼" h.	40.00
* Mug, 12 oz., beer, 4½" h.	65.00
Mustard, w/cover	27.50
Napkin ring	12.50
Oil, 5 oz.	32.50
Oil, 7 oz.	32.50
Picture frame	15.00
Pitcher, ½ gal. w/ice lip, 8¼", flat bottom	75.00
Pitcher, ½ gal., w/o ice lip	250.00
Pitcher, ½ gal., 8", ftd.	65.00
Pitcher, 1 pt., 5⅜", flat	27.50
Pitcher, 2 pt., 7¼", ftd.	65.00
Pitcher, 3 pt., 8", ftd.	65.00
Pitcher, 3 pt., w/ice lip, 6½", ftd., "fat"	50.00
* Pitcher, 1 qt., flat	25.00
Plate, cream soup liner	12.00
Plate, 6", bread & butter	12.00
Plate, 7", salad	9.00
Plate, 7½" x 4⅜", crescent salad	42.50
Plate, 8", sauce liner, oval	22.50
Plate, 8½", salad	10.00
Plate, 9", sandwich (sm. center)	14.00
Plate, 9½", dinner	20.00
Plate, 10", cake, 2 hdld.	18.00
Plate, 10½" sandwich (sm. center)	16.00
Plate, 11½", sandwich (sm. center)	16.00
Plate, 12", cake, 3 ftd.	22.50
Plate, 13½", oval torte	45.00
Plate, 14", torte	17.50
Plate, 18", torte	100.00
Plate, 20", torte	125.00
* Platter, 10½", oval	37.50
Platter, 12", oval	55.00
Ring holder	200.00
Salad set: 10" bowl, 14" torte, wood fork & spoon	67.50
Salt, individual	6.00

	*Crystal
Salver, 10", sq., ped. ft. (cake stand)	67.50
Salver, 10", rnd., ped. ft. (cake stand)	50.00
* Salver, 11", rnd., ped. ft. (cake stand)	30.00
Sauce boat & liner	45.00
Saucer	3.00
Set: 2 jam pots w/tray	110.00
Set: decanter, 6 - 2 oz. whiskeys on 10½" tray	215.00
Set: toddler, w/baby tumbler & bowl	85.00
Set: youth, w/bowl, hdld. mug, 6" plate	85.00
Set: condiment, 2 oils, 2 shakers, mustard w/cover & spoon w/tray	275.00
Shaker, 3", ea.	9.50
* Shaker, 3½", ea.	5.50
Shaker, 3¼", ea.	9.50
Shakers w/tray, individual, 2"	15.00
Sherbet, handled, 3½" high, 4½ oz.	75.00
Shrimp bowl, 12¼"	325.00
Spooner, 3¾"	32.50
** Strawholder, 10"	250.00
Sugar, tea, 2¼" (#2056½)	8.50
Sugar, hdld., 3¼" h.	8.50
Sugar shaker	45.00
Sugar, w/o cover	10.00
Sugar, w/cover, no hdl., 6¼" (cover fits strawholder)	60.00
Sugar, w/cover, 2 hdld.	17.50
Syrup, 6½ oz., #2056½, Sani-cut server	55.00
Syrup, 6 oz., non pour screw top, 5¼" h.	200.00
Syrup, 10 oz., w/glass cover & 6" liner plate	110.00
Syrup, w/drip proof top	35.00
Toothpick	22.50
Tray, cloverleaf for condiment set	135.00
Tray, tid bit, w/question mark metal handle	27.50
Tray, 5" x 2½", rect.	65.00
Tray, 6" oval, hdld.	35.00
Tray, pin, oval, 5½" x 4½"	125.00
Tray, 6½" x 9" relish, 4 part	40.00
Tray, 9½", service, 2 hdld.	27.50
Tray, 10", muffin (2 upturned sides)	27.50
Tray, 10", square, 4 part	75.00
Tray, 10", square	110.00
Tray, 10½", cake, w/question mark metal hdl.	25.00
Tray, 10½" x 7½", rect.	70.00
Tray, 10½" x 5", oval hdld.	42.50
Tray, 10¾", square, 4 part	100.00
Tray, 12", sand. w/ctr. handle	35.00
Tray, 12", round	115.00
Tray, 13½", oval, ice cream	125.00
Tray for sugar & creamer, tab. hdld., 6¾"	9.00

* See note on new American on page 12.

** Bottom only

AMERICAN, Line #2056, Fostoria Glass Company, 1915 – 1986 (continued)

	*Crystal		*Crystal
Tumbler, hdld. iced tea	195.00	Urn, 7½", sq. ped. ft	30.00
Tumbler, #2056, 2 oz., whiskey, 2½" h.	10.00	Vase, 4½", sweet pea	80.00
Tumbler, #2056, 3 oz.,		Vase, 6", bud, ftd.	12.50
ftd. cone, cocktail, 2⅞" h.	13.50	* Vase, 6", bud, flared	12.50
Tumbler, #2056, 5 oz., ftd., juice, 4¾".	10.00	Vase, 6", straight side	35.00
Tumbler, #2056, 6 oz., flat, old-		Vase, 6½", flared rim	15.00
fashioned, 3⅜" h.	12.00	Vase, 7", flared	75.00
Tumbler, #2056, 8 oz. flat, water, flared,		* Vase, 8", straight side	40.00
4⅛" h.	13.00	* Vase, 8", flared	80.00
* Tumbler, #2056, 9 oz. ftd., water, 4⅞" h.	13.00	Vase, 8", porch, 5" diam.	325.00
Tumbler, #2056, 12 oz.,		Vase, 8½", bud, flared	20.00
flat, tea, flared, 5¼" h.	13.50	Vase, 8½", bud, cupped	20.00
Tumbler, #2056½, 5 oz.,		Vase, 9", w/sq. ped. ft.	40.00
straight side, juice	12.00	Vase, 9½", flared	110.00
Tumbler, #2056½, 8 oz.,		Vase, 10", cupped in top	165.00
straight side, water, 3⅞" h.	12.00	Vase, 10", porch, 8" diam.	300.00
Tumbler, #2056½, 12 oz.,		* Vase, 10", straight side	90.00
straight side, tea, 5" h.	16.00	Vase, 10", swung	165.00
Tumbler, #5056, 5 oz., ftd.,		Vase, 10", flared	85.00
juice, 4⅛" w/plain bowl	10.00	Vase, 12", straight side	125.00
Tumbler, #5056, 12 oz.,		Vase, 12", swung	175.00
ftd., tea, 5½" w/plain bowl	12.00	Vase, 14", swung	250.00
Urn, 6", sq., ped. ft	25.00	Vase, 20", swung	325.00

* Note: May 1992. Fostoria Outlet stores are continuing to stock American! I have placed an asterisk by all pieces that are being made. I do not know every piece that has been reissued, but I suspect all pieces with asterisks in my previous editions are being made since these moulds should be in working order. Lancaster Colony is having American remade at Dalzell Viking. They have even hired former Fostoria employees to get the color right!

If you live near a Fostoria "outlet" store, you might want to drop by every few months to see what is being dragged out of the mould "attic."

APPLE BLOSSOM, Line #3400, Cambridge Glass Company, 1930's

Colors: blue, pink, light and dark green, yellow, crystal, amber

Yellow Apple Blossom continues to be collected more than any other color of this pattern. It has to do with availability. Collectors can find pieces of yellow Apple Blossom whereas other colors are rarely seen. Don't pass by a set of blue or green, however! They are a valuable collectible, just more difficult to find in today's market! If you find a set of blue, let me know – you will notice the lack of blue in the photographs!

As in many Cambridge patterns, most stemware lines can be found with searching, but basic serving pieces and unusual items are elusive. Happy Hunting!

	Crystal	Yellow Amber	Pink *Green
Ash tray, 6", heavy..	50.00	150.00	
Bowl, #3025, ftd., finger, w/plate	20.00	32.50	37.50
Bowl, #3130, finger, w/plate	30.00	32.50	37.50
Bowl, 5¼", 2 hdld., bonbon..............................	12.00	25.00	25.00
Bowl, 5½", 2 hdld., bonbon..............................	12.00	25.00	25.00
Bowl, 5½", fruit "saucer".................................	10.00	13.50	15.00
Bowl, 6", 2 hdld., "basket" (sides up)...............	15.00	25.00	30.00
Bowl, 6", cereal..	12.00	25.00	27.50
Bowl, 9", pickle..	13.00	30.00	35.00
Bowl, 10", 2 hdld..	25.00	65.00	75.00
Bowl, 10", baker...	25.00	60.00	70.00
Bowl, 11", fruit, tab hdld.................................	25.00	70.00	75.00
Bowl, 11", low ftd...	25.00	75.00	85.00
Bowl, 12", relish, 4 pt.....................................	25.00	45.00	60.00
Bowl, 12", 4 ftd..	35.00	65.00	75.00
Bowl, 12", flat	32.50	50.00	55.00
Bowl, 12", oval, 4 ftd......................................	35.00	60.00	75.00
Bowl, 12½", console	30.00	50.00	55.00
Bowl, 13"..	30.00	55.00	60.00
Bowl, cream soup, w/liner plate........................	17.50	27.50	35.00
Butter w/cover, 5½"..	115.00	200.00	325.00
Candelabrum, 3-lite, keyhole............................	25.00	37.50	47.50
Candlestick, 1-lite, keyhole..............................	15.00	25.00	27.50
Candlestick, 2-lite, keyhole..............................	20.00	30.00	35.00
Candy box w/cover, 4 ftd. "bowl"	65.00	85.00	125.00
Cheese (compote) & cracker (11½" plate)	40.00	55.00	75.00
Comport, 4", fruit cocktail................................	12.50	20.00	25.00
Comport, 7", tall	30.00	45.00	60.00
Creamer, ftd.	12.50	17.50	22.50
Creamer, tall ftd...	12.50	20.00	25.00
Cup..	15.00	22.00	26.00
Cup, A.D.	35.00	45.00	75.00
Fruit/oyster cocktail, #3025, 4½ oz.	12.50	17.50	20.00
Mayonnaise, w/liner & ladle, (4 ftd. bowl).........	35.00	50.00	65.00
Pitcher, 50 oz., ftd., flattened sides.................	100.00	175.00	225.00
Pitcher, 64 oz., #3130	110.00	195.00	250.00
Pitcher, 64 oz., #3025	110.00	200.00	265.00
Pitcher, 67 oz., squeezed middle, loop hdld.	125.00	225.00	275.00
Pitcher, 76 oz.	125.00	200.00	265.00
Pitcher, 80 oz., ball	115.00	135.00	250.00
Pitcher w/cover, 76 oz., ftd., #3135	175.00	350.00	450.00
Plate, 6", bread/butter.....................................	5.00	7.00	8.00
Plate, 6", sq., 2 hdld.......................................	8.00	9.00	10.00
Plate, 7½", tea...	9.00	12.00	13.00
Plate, 8½"..	12.00	20.00	22.00
Plate, 9½", dinner	40.00	65.00	75.00
Plate, 10", grill	20.00	40.00	50.00
Plate, sandwich, 11½", tab hdld.......................	22.00	32.50	35.00
Plate, sandwich, 12½", 2 hdld..........................	25.00	35.00	37.50

* Blue 25% to 50% more.

APPLE BLOSSOM, Line #3400, Cambridge Glass Company, 1930's (continued)

	Crystal	Yellow Amber	Pink *Green
Plate, sq., bread/butter	4.00	7.00	8.00
Plate, sq., dinner	40.00	65.00	75.00
Plate, sq., salad	10.00	12.00	13.00
Plate, sq., service	17.50	20.00	22.00
Platter, 11½	35.00	60.00	70.00
Platter, 13½" rect., w/tab handle	40.00	85.00	95.00
Salt & pepper, pr.	37.50	75.00	90.00
Saucer	3.00	5.00	5.00
Saucer, A.D.	10.00	15.00	17.50
Stem, #1066, parfait	65.00	95.00	135.00
Stem, #3025, 7 oz., low fancy ft., sherbet	11.00	15.00	16.00
Stem, #3025, 7 oz., high sherbet	12.00	18.00	20.00
Stem, #3025, 10 oz.	18.00	22.00	25.00
Stem, #3130, 1 oz., cordial	55.00	90.00	125.00
Stem, #3130, 3 oz., cocktail	15.00	24.00	27.50
Stem, #3130, 6 oz., low sherbet	10.00	15.00	16.00
Stem, #3130, 6 oz., tall sherbet	10.00	18.00	20.00
Stem, #3130, 8 oz., water	15.00	22.00	30.00
Stem, #3135, 3 oz., cocktail	13.00	24.00	27.50
Stem, #3135, 6 oz., low sherbet	10.00	15.00	16.00 '
Stem, #3135, 6 oz., tall sherbet	10.00	18.00	20.00
Stem, #3135, 8 oz., water	14.00	22.00	30.00
Stem, #3400, 6 oz., ftd., sherbet	9.00	15.00	16.00
Stem, #3400, 9 oz., water	12.50	22.00	30.00
Sugar, ftd.	11.00	16.00	20.00
Sugar, tall ftd.	11.00	18.00	22.50
Tray, 11" ctr. hdld. sand.	25.00	37.50	45.00
Tumbler, #3025, 4 oz.	12.00	17.00	19.00
Tumbler, #3025, 10 oz.	15.00	20.00	22.00
Tumbler, #3025, 12 oz.	18.00	30.00	37.50
Tumbler, #3130, 5 oz., ftd.	11.00	20.00	25.00
Tumbler, #3130, 8 oz., ftd.	12.00	25.00	27.50
Tumbler, #3130, 10 oz., ftd.	13.00	25.00	27.50
Tumbler, #3130, 12 oz., ftd.	17.50	32.50	40.00
Tumbler, #3135, 5 oz., ftd.	10.00	20.00	25.00
Tumbler, #3135, 8 oz., ftd.	12.00	25.00	27.50
Tumbler, #3135, 10 oz., ftd.	13.00	25.00	27.50
Tumbler, #3135, 12 oz., ftd.	17.50	32.50	40.00
Tumbler, #3400, 2½ oz., ftd.	12.00	45.00	60.00
Tumbler, #3400, 9 oz., ftd.	12.00	25.00	27.50
Tumbler, #3400, 12 oz., ftd.	17.50	32.50	40.00
Tumbler, 12 oz., flat (2 styles) - 1 mid indent to match 67 oz. pitcher	20.00	32.50	40.00
Tumbler, 6"	15.00	30.00	35.00
Vase, 5"	25.00	40.00	45.00
Vase, 6", rippled sides	27.50	50.00	65.00
Vase, 8", 2 styles	35.00	65.00	85.00
Vase, 12", keyhole base w/neck indent	40.00	135.00	195.00

* Blue prices 25% to 30% more.
Note: See Pages 210-211 for stem identification.

BAROQUE, Line #2496, Fostoria Glass Company, 1936 – 1966

Colors: crystal, "Azure" blue, "Topaz" yellow, green, pink, red, cobalt blue, black amethyst

I have had several calls and many letters reporting red and green candlesticks since the last book. There have been more reports of cobalt blue and black amethyst, but no console bowls to match those candlesticks have been reported as yet! There have been no letters from owners of pink cups to go with the saucer shown on page 21. By the way, that ruffled bowl in the center (behind the pink saucer) is the mayonnaise shown without a liner.

The 9" tall covered piece in the back at the top of page 21 is the sweetmeat. This is to distinguish it from the jelly which is only 7½" tall. Note the tops on the shakers. They came with both metal and glass tops, although most collectors prefer the glass lids. Metal lids were replacements when the glass ones were broken.

Straight sided tumblers are more difficult to find than the footed ones, but many collectors seem to prefer them to the cone-shaped footed pieces. If everyone were to like the same style, the demand would exceed the supply very quickly!

The blue individual sized shakers are shown on the right. These are difficult to find in color.

Remember that crystal Baroque's blanks (#2496) were used on many of Fostoria's etched lines including Chintz and Navarre.

	Crystal	Blue	Yellow
Ash tray	7.50	15.00	13.00
Bowl, cream soup	30.00	65.00	70.00
Bowl, ftd., punch	325.00	1,250.00	
Bowl, 3¾", rose	25.00	55.00	45.00
Bowl, 4", hdld. (4 styles)	11.00	22.50	20.00
Bowl, 5", fruit	15.00	25.00	30.00
Bowl, 6", cereal	20.00	35.00	30.00
Bowl, 6", sq.	8.00	20.00	22.00
Bowl, 6½", 2 pt.	9.00	25.00	20.00
Bowl, 7", 3 ftd.	12.50	25.00	25.00
Bowl, 7½", jelly, w/cover	30.00	85.00	50.00
Bowl, 8", pickle	8.50	27.50	22.50
Bowl, 8½", hdld.	14.00	35.00	30.00
Bowl, 9½", veg., oval	25.00	60.00	45.00
Bowl, 10", hdld.	15.00	60.00	40.00
Bowl, 10½", hdld., 4 ftd.	17.50	47.50	37.50
Bowl, 10" x 7½"	25.00		
Bowl, 10", relish, 3 pt.	20.00	30.00	22.50
Bowl, 11", celery	12.00	45.00	25.00
Bowl, 11", rolled edge	20.00	50.00	37.50
Bowl, 12", flared	21.50	40.00	32.50
Candelabrum, 8¼", 2-lite, 16 lustre	85.00	95.00	75.00
Candelabrum, 9½", 3-lite, 24 lustre	100.00	115.00	85.00
Candle, 7¾", 8 lustre	50.00	85.00	75.00
Candlestick, 4"	12.50	35.00	30.00
Candlestick, 4½", 2-lite	15.00	55.00	50.00
Candlestick, 5½"	9.00	40.00	35.00
* Candlestick, 6", 3-lite	17.50	75.00	60.00
Candy, 3 part w/cover	30.00	95.00	65.00

* Red $135.00
  Green $100.00
  Black Amethyst $125.00
  Cobalt Blue $125.00

19

	Crystal	Blue	Yellow
Comport, 4¾"	15.00	30.00	25.00
Comport, 6½"	17.50	35.00	30.00
Creamer, 3¼", indiv.	9.00	30.00	25.00
Creamer, 3¾", ftd.	8.00	14.00	14.00
Cup	9.00	30.00	20.00
Cup, 6 oz., punch	12.00	30.00	
Ice bucket	30.00	95.00	60.00
Mayonnaise, 5½", w/liner	15.00	55.00	40.00
Mustard, w/cover	22.00	50.00	37.50
Oil, w/stopper, 5½"	85.00	375.00	185.00
Pitcher, 6½"	110.00	675.00	450.00
Pitcher, 7", ice lip	110.00	625.00	400.00
Plate, 6"	3.00	10.00	8.00
Plate, 7½"	4.00	12.50	10.00
Plate, 8½"	6.00	20.00	17.50
Plate, 9½"	15.00	50.00	40.00
Plate, 10", cake	20.00	35.00	30.00
Plate, 11", ctr. hdld., sand	25.00		
Plate, 14", torte	13.00	37.50	20.00
Platter, 12", oval	22.00	60.00	40.00
Salt & pepper, pr.	45.00	120.00	100.00
Salt & pepper, indiv., pr.	50.00	190.00	120.00
Saucer	2.00	5.00	4.00
Sherbet, 3¾", 5 oz.	10.00	27.50	17.50
Stem, 6¾", 9 oz., water	12.00	27.50	22.50
Sugar, 3", indiv.	5.00	27.50	22.50
Sugar, 3½", ftd.	6.00	15.00	11.00
Sweetmeat, covered, 9"	75.00	165.00	135.00
Tray, 11", oval	15.00	47.50	37.50
Tray, 6¼" for indiv. cream/sugar	15.00	25.00	20.00
Tumbler, 3½", 6½ oz., old-fashioned	20.00	75.00	45.00
Tumbler, 3", 3½ oz., ftd., cocktail	10.00	18.00	15.00
Tumbler, 6", 12 oz., ftd., tea	20.00	40.00	30.00
Tumbler, 3¾", 5 oz., juice	12.00	37.50	25.00
Tumbler, 5½", 9 oz., ftd., water	12.00	30.00	25.00
Tumbler, 4¼", 9 oz., water	25.00	50.00	25.00
Tumbler, 5¾", 14 oz., tea	20.00	65.00	45.00
Vase, 6½"	45.00	125.00	100.00
Vase, 7"	40.00	125.00	85.00

BLACK FOREST, Possibly Paden City for Van Deman & Son, Late 1920's – Early 1930's

Colors: amber, black, ice blue, crystal, green, pink, red, cobalt

Since I have slighted this elusive but increasingly popular pattern in the past, I hope you enjoy the extra effort of three pages of pictures this time! Black Forest and Deerwood patterns are often confused; so study the pattern shots of each. Black Forest depicts moose and trees; while deer and trees are the predominant pattern on Deerwood. If you have trouble telling moose from deer, then you are in big trouble with these two patterns!

The newly pictured bulbous decanter shown in pink at the top of page 23 holds 28 ozs. and is 8½" tall without the stopper while that shot glass to match it is 2½" tall and holds 2 ozs. Notice the cobalt pitcher on the top of page 25 is 8" high and holds 40 ozs. and the large, footed, covered five part relish in the center of the bottom picture on page 25. It is 10½" wide and stands 6¾" with lid. Aren't these neat pieces?

Note the night set (pitcher and tumbler) in Black Forest. The tumbler has a molded band that will not allow it to drop down into the pitcher when turned upside down on it.

I met a delightful new collector at a western glass show who said that she didn't care if this pattern were scarce. If she only ever owned the one pink bowl she just purchased, she'd be happy. Depression glass ownership definitely brings a sparkling glow to some people.

	Amber	Black	Crystal	Green	Pink	Red
Batter Jug			125.00			
Bowl, 4½", finger				15.00		
Bowl, 9¼", center hdld.				65.00	65.00	
Bowl, 11", console	50.00	50.00	35.00	30.00	30.00	
Bowl, 11", fruit		30.00		25.00	25.00	
Bowl, 13", console		65.00				
Bowl, 3 ftd.			60.00			
Cake plate, 2" pedestal	35.00	45.00		40.00	35.00	
Candlestick, mushroom style	30.00	35.00	15.00	30.00	30.00	
Candlestick double			35.00			
Candy dish, w/cover, several styles	85.00	85.00			75.00	
Creamer, 2 styles		35.00	20.00	35.00	35.00	65.00
Comport, 4", low ftd.				25.00	25.00	
Comport, 5½", high ftd.		30.00		28.00	25.00	
Cup and saucer, 3 styles		85.00		85.00	85.00	110.00
Decanter, w/stopper, 8½", 28 oz., bulbous			90.00	125.00	125.00	
Decanter w/stopper, 8¾", 24 oz., straight			75.00	110.00	110.00	
Ice bucket				75.00	75.00	
Ice pail, 6", 3" high	75.00					
Ice tub, 2 styles (Ice blue $175.00)	80.00	75.00			65.00	
Mayonnaise, with liner		60.00		60.00	60.00	
Night Set: pitcher, 6½", 42 oz. & tumbler				375.00	375.00	
Pitcher, 8", 40 oz.				350.00	350.00	
Pitcher, 8", 62 oz.			165.00	325.00	325.00	
Pitcher, 9", 80 oz.			275.00	375.00	375.00	
Pitcher, 10½", 72 oz.			300.00	400.00	400.00	
Plate, 6½", bread/butter		22.00		22.00		
Plate, 8", luncheon		25.00			25.00	30.00
Plate, 11", 2 hdld.		45.00		25.00	25.00	
Relish, 10½", 5 pt. covered				125.00	125.00	
Salt and pepper, pr.			110.00		125.00	
Server, center hdld.	50.00	40.00	35.00	35.00	35.00	
Stem, 2 oz., wine, 4¼"			17.50	50.00		
Stem, 6 oz., champagne, 4¾"			17.50		30.00	
Stem, 9 oz., water, 6"			22.50			
Sugar, 2 styles		35.00	20.00	35.00	35.00	65.00
Tumbler, 3 oz., juice, flat or footed, 3½"			25.00	20.00		
Tumbler, 8 oz., old fashioned, 3⅞"					30.00	
Tumbler, 9 oz., ftd., 5½"	30.00					
Tumbler, 12 oz., tea, 5½"				40.00	40.00	
Vase, 6½" (Cobalt $125.00)		55.00		50.00	50.00	
Vase, 10"		75.00		65.00	65.00	
Whipped cream pail	75.00					

24

CADENA, Tiffin Glass Company, Early 1930's

Colors: crystal, yellow; some pink

A Cadena yellow cup and saucer is shown here for the first time, but my purchase of a yellow cordial came too late to include. The crystal cordial will have to suffice for now. As with most Tiffin patterns, stemware can be found, but serving pieces and basic dinnerware items such as dinner plates and cups and saucers are elusive.

I have not found a pink cordial for my collection. In fact, very little pink is being found at all! Little of this pattern is seen at Depression shows and that makes for fewer collectors. You will find a piece or two in your travels, but seeing a whole set for sale is perhaps a thing of the past. However, one yellow set stayed at a large flea market in Cincinnati, Ohio, for months without anyone ever knowing what it was until a knowledgeable dealer finally purchased it for a very good price. Evidently, Tiffin did not market this pattern as extensively as they did their Cherokee Rose, Fuchsia, and Flanders patterns.

Remember that the pitcher cover is plain (no pattern is etched on it).

	Crystal	Pink/Yellow
Bowl, cream soup	20.00	30.00
Bowl, finger, ftd.	15.00	22.50
Bowl, grapefruit, ftd.	20.00	40.00
Bowl, 6", hdld.	10.00	20.00
Bowl, 10", pickle	12.50	25.00
Bowl, 12", console	22.50	45.00
Candlestick	17.50	30.00
Creamer	15.00	25.00
Cup	25.00	52.50
Goblet, 4¾", sherbet	15.00	22.00
Goblet, 5¼", cocktail	17.50	25.00
Goblet, 5¼", ¾ oz., cordial	50.00	75.00
Goblet, 6", wine	25.00	40.00
Goblet, 6½", champagne	17.00	30.00
Goblet, 7½", water	20.00	35.00
Mayonnaise, ftd., w/liner	25.00	45.00
Oyster cocktail	15.00	25.00
Pitcher, ftd., w/cover	225.00	325.00
Plate, 6"	5.00	8.00
Plate, 7¾"	7.00	12.00
Plate, 9¼"	30.00	37.50
Saucer	10.00	12.50
Sugar	15.00	23.00
Tumbler, 4¼", ftd., juice	17.50	27.50
Tumbler, 5¼", ftd., water	20.00	30.00
Vase, 9"	35.00	65.00

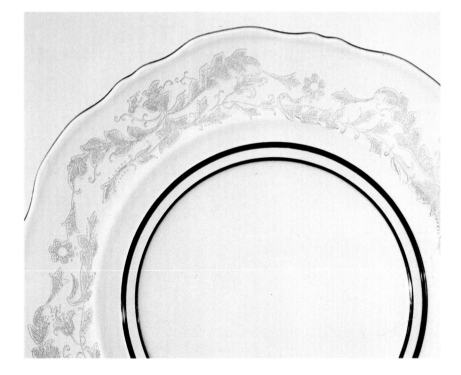

CANDLELIGHT, Cambridge Glass Company, 1940's – Early 1950's

Colors: crystal, Crown Tuscan with gold decoration

Candlelight is a Cambridge pattern that I have received many requests to include in this book! Finally, with collectors helping, I was able to acquiesce your wishes. Although Candlelight is not as widely collected as other Cambridge patterns, almost everyone recognizes the pattern. The bowl in the pattern shot has a "cut" Candlelight pattern instead of acid etched.

There are other pieces with "cut" Candlelight including candlesticks to go with the bowl pictured, cocktail icer, salad plate, vase, and water goblets. There may be additional pieces that are "cut," but I have not seen them. Price the "cut" candlelight pieces up to double the prices of the etched.

You may find other pieces of the etched Candlelight also. Let me know what you have or find, and I'll try to expand the listing in the future.

	Crystal
Bowl, 7", ftd., 2 hdld., #3900/130	30.00
Bowl, 10", 4 toed, flared, #3900/54	55.00
Bowl, 11", 2 hdld., #3900/34	60.00
Bowl, 11½", ftd., 2 hdld., #3900/28	65.00
Bowl, 12", 4 toed, flared, #3900/62	62.50
Bowl, 12", 4 toed, oval, hdld., #3900/65	85.00
Candle, 5", #3900/67	37.50
Candle, 6", 2-lite, #3900/72	37.50
Candle, 6", 3-lite, #3900/74	45.00
Candy w/lid, rnd. #3900/165	95.00
Comport, 5⅜", blown, #3121	57.50
Comport, 5½", #3900/136	50.00
Creamer, #3900/41	20.00
Creamer, indiv., #3900/40	20.00
Cruet, 6 oz., w/stopper, #3900/100	95.00
Cup, #3900/17	27.50
Ice bucket, #3900/671	100.00
Icer, 2 pc., cocktail, #968	65.00
Lamp, hurricane, #1617	120.00
Lamp, hurricane, keyhole, w/bobeche,#1603	150.00
Lamp, hurricane, w/bobeche, #1613	250.00
Mayonnaise, 3 pc., #3900/129	57.50
Mayonnaise, div., 4 pc., #3900/111	65.00
Mayonnaise, ftd., 2 pc., #3900/19	47.50
Pitcher, Doulton, #3400/141	275.00
Plate, 6½", #3900/20	12.50
Plate, 8", 2 hdld., #3900/131	25.00
Plate, 8", salad, #3900/22	15.00
Plate, 10½", dinner, #3900/24	65.00
Plate, 12", 4 toed, #3900/26	55.00
Plate, 13", torte, 4 toed, #3900/33	55.00
Plate, 13½", cake, 2 hdld., #3900/35	55.00
Plate, 14", rolled edge, #3900/166	60.00
Relish, 7", 2 hdld., #3900/123	32.50
Relish, 7", div., 2 hdld., #3900/124	35.00
Relish, 9", 3 pt., #3900/125	42.50

	Crystal
Relish, 12", 3 pt., #3900/126	52.50
Relish, 12", 5 pt., #3900/120	57.50
Salt & pepper, pr., #3900/1177	45.00
Saucer, #3900/17	5.00
Stem, 1 oz., cordial, #3776	65.00
Stem, 2½ oz., wine, #3776	30.00
Stem, 2½ oz., wine, #3111	35.00
Stem, 3 oz., cocktail, #3111	27.50
Stem, 3 oz., cocktail, #3776	25.00
Stem, 4½ oz., claret, #3776	32.50
Stem, 4½ oz., oyster cocktail, #3111	27.50
Stem, 4½ oz., oyster cocktail, #3776	22.50
Stem, 7 oz., low sherbet, #3111	17.50
Stem, 7 oz., low sherbet, #3776	16.50
Stem, 7 oz., tall sherbet, #3111	22.50
Stem, 7 oz., tall sherbet, #3776	20.00
Stem, 9 oz., water, #3776	30.00
Stem, 10 oz., water, #3111	30.00
Sugar, #3900/41	17.50
Sugar, indiv., #3900/40	17.50
Tumbler, 5 oz., ftd., juice, #3111	20.00
Tumbler, 5 oz., juice, #3776	18.00
Tumbler, 12 oz., ftd., iced tea., #3111	25.00
Tumbler, 12 oz., iced tea, #3776	22.50
Tumbler, 13 oz., #3900/115	35.00
Vase, 5", ftd., bud, #6004	
Vase, 5", globe, #1309	52.50
Vase, 6", ftd., #6004	35.00
Vase, 8", ftd., #6004	45.00
Vase, 9", ftd., keyhole, #1237	
Vase, 10", bud, #274	42.50
Vase, 11", ftd. pedestal, #1299	100.00
Vase, 11", ftd., #278	65.00
Vase, 12", ftd., keyhole, #1238	87.50
Vase, 13", ftd, #279	97.50

CANDLEWICK, Line #400, Imperial Glass Company, 1936 – 1984

Colors: crystal, blue, pink, yellow, black, red, cobalt blue, green, carmel slag

Prices on colored (red, black, and light blue) Candlewick escalated very fast; but lately, prices of colored Candlewick have slowed considerably which is usually the fate of a too rapid rise. Most of the Ruby Red and black fancy bowls have steadied in price around $200.00 with the Viennese Blue (light blue) bringing about half of that. Ruby Red stems abound in the 3400 and 3800 lines with most of these except the cordial selling in the $40.00 to $60.00 range. Cordials are selling in Ruby Red and Ritz Blue (cobalt) from $100.00 to $125.00. Other Ritz Blue stems are fetching $60.00 to $80.00.

I should point out a few hard-to-find items shown on the following pages. I might also remind you that there are several unusual Candlewick items shown in my three volumes of *Very Rare Glassware of the Depression Years.*

In the top photograph on page 31 are etched floral designed pieces. Many of these were gold decorated over the flowers. The flat, old-fashioned tumbler on the right (in front of the high sherbet) is the only one of those I have owned. Maybe you see them, but I haven't run into them before now!

On the bottom of page 31 is a setting of cut Candlewick purchased in late 1939 or 1940. Unfortunately, the owner sold all the dinner plates, cups, and saucers before I had a chance to buy the set. The 7½" lily bowl shown on the right was only made in 1939 and is quite hard to find.

The bottom photo on page 33 shows just about any kind of candlestick you could want in Candlewick. Note the green and silver decorated one as well as several different hurricane lamps. Also shown are several lamp globes. The oval one in the center has an original Candlewick sticker. The one shown on the right with the yellowish cast is of questionable origin, but the others are most likely the "real" thing. Original lamp shades are selling for $100.00 to $125.00 when you can find one.

The top of page 35 (left rear) shows the 400/18, hard-to-find line of tumblers. The bottom photo shows the family punch bowl, some DeVilbis perfumes and a dresser set.

Page 37 shows some of the late Candlewick colors along with the Viennese Blue. All the Viennese Blue pieces were made before 1940 as were the Ruby Red and Ritz Blue.

I have included several advertisements from 1940's magazines with the ad on page 38 being from December 1943. Let me know if you like this idea for the future!

	Crystal
Ash tray, eagle, 6½", 1776/1	50.00
Ash tray, heart, 4½", 400/172	9.00
Ash tray, heart, 5½", 400/173	11.00
Ash tray, heart, 6½", 400/174	15.00
Ash tray, indiv 400/64.	6.00
Ash tray, oblong, 4½", 400/134/1	6.00
Ash tray, round, 2¾", 400/19	8.00
Ash tray, round, 4", 400/33	10.00
Ash tray, round, 5", 400/133	8.00
Ash tray, square, 3¼", 400/651	30.00
Ash tray, square, 4½", 400/652	30.00
Ash tray, square, 5¾", 400/653	35.00
Ash tray, 6", matchbook holder center, 400/60	90.00
Ash tray set, 3 pc. rnd. nest. (crys. or colors), 400/550	20.00
Ash tray set, 3 pc. sq. nesting, 400/650	95.00
Ash tray set, 4 pc. bridge (cig. hold at side), 400/118	35.00
Basket, 5", beaded hdld., 400/273	185.00
Basket, 6½", hdld., 400/40/0	27.50
Basket, 11", hdld., 400/73/0	200.00
Bell, 4", 400/179	75.00
Bell, 5", 400/108	75.00
Bottle, bitters, w/tube, 4 oz., 400/117	55.00
Bowl, bouillon, 2 hdld., 400/126	40.00
Bowl, #3400, finger, ftd.	25.00
Bowl, #3800, finger	25.00
Bowl, 4½", nappy, 3 ftd., 400/206	65.00
Bowl, 4¾", round, 2 hdld., 400/42B	10.00
Bowl, 5", cream soup, 400/50	40.00
Bowl, 5", fruit, 400/1F	12.00
Bowl, 5", heart w/hand., 400/49H	17.50
Bowl, 5", square, 400/231	80.00
Bowl, 5½", heart, 400/53H	17.50
Bowl, 5½", jelly, w/cover, 400/59	55.00
Bowl, 5½", sauce, deep, 400/243	35.00
Bowl, 6", baked apple, rolled edge, 400/53X	27.50
Bowl, 6", cottage cheese, 400/85	25.00
Bowl, 6", fruit, 400/3F	11.00
Bowl, 6", heart w/hand., 400/51H	22.50
Bowl, 6", mint w/hand., 400/51F	18.00
Bowl, 6", round, div., 2 hdld., 400/52	22.00
Bowl, 6", 2 hdld., 400/52B	15.00
Bowl, 6", 3 ftd., 400/183	57.50
Bowl, 6", sq., 400/232	110.00
Bowl, 6½", relish, 2 pt., 400/84	22.00
Bowl, 6½", 2 hdld., 400/181	30.00
Bowl, 7", round, 400/5F	20.00
Bowl, 7", round, 2 hdld., 400/62B	15.00
Bowl, 7", relish, sq., div., 400/234	100.00
Bowl, 7", ivy, high, bead ft., 400/188	150.00
Bowl, 7", lily, 4 ft., 400/74J	60.00
Bowl, 7", relish, 400/60	25.00
Bowl, 7", sq., 400/233	125.00
Bowl, 7¼", rose, ftd. w/crimp edge, 400/132C	225.00
Bowl, 7½", pickle/celery 400/57	25.00
Bowl, 7½", lily, bead rim, ftd., 400/75N	125.00
Bowl, 7½", belled, (console base), 400/127B	45.00

	Crystal
Bowl, 8", round, 400/7F	35.00
Bowl, 8", relish, 2 pt., 400/268	20.00
Bowl, 8", cov. veg., 400/65/1	250.00
Bowl, 8½", rnd., 400/69	32.50
Bowl, 8½", nappy, 4 ftd., 400/74B	45.00
Bowl, 8½", 3 ftd., 400/182	110.00
Bowl, 8½", 2 hdld., 400/72B	22.00
Bowl, 8½", pickle/celery, 400/58	20.00
Bowl, 8½", relish, 4 pt., 400/55	20.00
Bowl, 9", round, 400/10F	40.00
Bowl, 9", crimp, ftd., 400/67C	125.00
Bowl, 9", sq., fancy crimp edge, 4 ft., 400/74SC	60.00
Bowl, 9", heart, 400/49H	85.00
Bowl, 9", heart w/hand., 400/73H	110.00
Bowl, 10", 400/13F	40.00
Bowl, 10", banana, 400/103E	1,250.00
Bowl, 10", 3 toed, 400/205	125.00
Bowl, 10", belled, (punch base), 400/128B	50.00
Bowl, 10", cupped edge, 400/75F	40.00
Bowl, 10", deep, 2 hdld., 400/113A	110.00
Bowl, 10", divided, deep, 2 hdld., 400/114A	125.00
Bowl, 10", fruit, bead stem (like compote), 400/103F	135.00
Bowl, 10", relish, oval, 2 hdld., 400/217	40.00
Bowl, 10", relish, 3 pt., 3 ft., 400/208	80.00
Bowl, 10", 3 pt., w/cover, 400/216	275.00
Bowl, 10½", belled, 400/63B	60.00
Bowl, 10½", butter/jam, 3 pt., 400/262	70.00
Bowl, 10½", salad, 400/75B	40.00
Bowl, 10½", relish, 3 section, 400/256	30.00
Bowl, 11", celery boat, oval, 400/46	55.00
Bowl, 11", centerpiece, flared, 400/13B	40.00
Bowl, 11", float, inward rim, ftd., 400/75F	40.00
Bowl, 11", oval, 400/124A	235.00
Bowl, 11", oval w/partition, 400/125A	250.00
Bowl, 12", round, 400/92B	40.00
Bowl, 12", belled, 400/106B	85.00
Bowl, 12", float, 400/92F	40.00
Bowl, 12", hdld., 400/113B	65.00
Bowl, 12", shallow, 400/17F	45.00
Bowl, 12", relish, oblong, 4 sect., 400/215	110.00
Bowl, 13", centerpiece, mushroom, 400/92L	47.50
Bowl, 13", float, 1½" deep, 400/101	55.00
Bowl, 13½", relish, 5 pt., 400/209	75.00
Bowl, 14", belled, 400/104B	85.00
Bowl, 14", oval, flared, 400/131B	165.00
Butter and jam set, 5 piece, 400/204	225.00
Butter, w/ cover, rnd., 5½", 400/144	30.00
Butter, w/ cover, no beads, California, 400/276	110.00
Butter, w/ bead top, ¼ lb., 400/161	30.00
Cake stand, 10", low foot, 400/67D	50.00
Cake stand, 11", high foot, 400/103D	65.00
Calendar, 1947, desk	150.00
Candleholder, 3 way, beaded base, 400/115	100.00
Candleholder, 2-lite, 400/100	20.00
Candleholder, flat, 3½", 400/280	20.00
Candleholder, 3½", rolled edge, 400/79R	10.50
Candleholder, 3½", w/fingerhold, 400/81	40.00
Candleholder, flower, 4", 2 bead stem, 400/66F	40.00
Candleholder, flower, 4½", 2 bead stem, 400/66C	55.00

	Crystal
Candleholder, 4½", 3 toed, 400/207	37.50
Candleholder, 3-lite on cir. bead. ctr., 400/147	25.00
Candleholder, 5", hdld./bowled up base, 400/90	40.00
Candleholder, 5" heart shape, 400/40HC	40.00
Candleholder, 5½", 3 bead stems, 400/224	80.00
Candleholder, flower, 5", (epergne inset), 400/40CV	85.00
Candleholder, 5", flower, 400/40C	27.50
Candleholder, 6½", tall, 3 bead stems, 400/175	70.00
Candleholder, flower, 6", round, 400/40F	17.50
Candleholder, urn, 6", holders on cir. ctr. bead, 400/129R	100.00
Candleholder, flower, 6½", square, 400/40S	25.00
Candleholder, mushroom, 400/86	22.00
Candleholder, flower 9" centerpiece, 400/196FC	125.00
Candy box, round, 5½", 400/59	42.50
Candy box, sq., 6½", rnd. lid, 400/245	135.00
Candy box, w/ cover, 7", 400/259	125.00
Candy box, w/ cover, 7" partitioned, 400/110	60.00
Candy box, w/ cover, round, 7", 3 sect., 400/158	150.00
Candy box, w/ cover, beaded, ft., 400/140	200.00
Cigarette box w/cover, 400/134	30.00
Cigarette holder, 3", bead ft., 400/44	40.00
Cigarette set: 6 pc., (cigarette box & 4 rect. ash trays), 400/134/6	67.50
Clock, 4", round	250.00
Coaster, 4", 400/78	6.00
Coaster, w/spoon rest, 400/226	13.00
Cocktail, seafood w/bead ft., 400/190	50.00
Cocktail set: 2 pc., plate w/indent; cocktail, 400/97	35.00
Compote, 4½", 400/63B	25.00
Compote, 5", 3 bead stems, 400/220	50.00
Compote, 5½", 4 bead stem, 400/45	22.00
Compote, 5½, low, plain stem, 400/66B	18.00
Compote, 5½", 2 bead stem, 400/66B	18.00
Compote, 8", bead stem, 400/48F	70.00
Compote, 10", ftd. fruit, crimped, 40/103C	110.00
Compote, ft. oval, 400/137	750.00
Condiment set: 4 pc., (2 squat bead ft. shakers, marmalade), 400/1786	67.50
Console sets: 3 pc. (14" oval bowl, two 3-lite candles), 400/1531B	275.00
3 pc. (mushroom bowl, w/mushroom candles), 400/8692L	105.00
Creamer, domed foot, 400/18	110.00
Creamer, 6 oz., bead handle, 400/30	7.50
Creamer, indiv. bridge, 400/122	7.50
Creamer, plain ft., 400/31	9.00
Creamer, flat, bead handle, 400/126	30.00
Cup, after dinner, 400/77	17.50
Cup, coffee, 400/37	7.50
Cup, punch, 400/211	7.50
Cup, tea, 400/35	8.00
Decanter, w/stopper, 15 oz. cordial, 400/82/2	275.00
Decanter w/stopper, 18 oz., 400/18	350.00
Decanter, w/stopper, 26 oz., 400/163	275.00
Deviled egg server, 12", ctr. hdld., 400/154	95.00
Egg cup, bead. ft., 400/19	45.00

	Crystal
Fork & spoon, set, 400/75	35.00
Hurricane lamp, 2 pc. candle base, 400/79	110.00
Hurricane lamp, 2 pc., hdld. candle base, 400/76	135.00
Hurricane lamp, 3 pc. flared & crimped edge globe, 400/152	140.00
Ice tub, 5½" deep, 8" diam., 400/63	80.00
Ice tub, 7", 2 hdld., 400/168	185.00
Icer, 2 pc., seafood/fruit cocktail, 400/53/3	95.00
Icer, 2 pc., seafood/fruit cocktail #3800 line, one bead stem	60.00
Jam set, 5 pc., oval tray w/2 marmalade jars w/ladles, 400/1589	100.00
Jar tower, 3 sect., 400/655	250.00
Knife, butter, 4000	200.00
Ladle, marmalade, 3 bead stem, 400/130	10.00
Ladle, mayonnaise, 6¼", 400/135	10.00
Marmalade set, 3 pc., beaded ft. w/cover & spoon, 400/1989	40.00
Marmalade set, 3 pc. tall jar, domed bead ft., lid, spoon, 400/8918	65.00
Marmalade set, 4 pc., liner saucer, jar, lid, spoon, 400/89	42.50
Mayonnaise set, 2 pc. scoop side bowl, spoon, 400/23	35.00
Mayonnaise set, 3 pc. hdld. tray/hdld. bowl/ladle, 400/52/3	45.00
Mayonnaise set, 3 pc. plate, heart bowl, spoon, 400/49	33.00
Mayonnaise set, 3 pc. scoop side bowl, spoon, tray, 400/496	40.00
Mayonnaise 4 pc., plate, divided bowl, 2 ladles, 400/84	40.00
Mirror, 4½", rnd., standing	85.00
Mustard jar, w/spoon, 400/156	30.00
Oil, 4 oz., bead base, 400/164	55.00
Oil, 6 oz., bead base, 400/166	65.00
Oil, 4 oz., bulbous bottom, 400/274	45.00
Oil, 4 oz., hdld., bulbous bottom, 400/278	65.00
Oil, 6 oz., hdld., bulbous bottom, 400/279	75.00
Oil, 6 oz., bulbous bottom, 400/275	55.00
Oil, w/stopper, etched "Oil," 400/121	65.00
Oil, w/stopper, etched "Vinegar," 400/121	65.00
Party set, 2 pc., oval plate w/indent for cup, 400/98	30.00
Pitcher, 14 oz., short rnd., 400/330	100.00
Pitcher, 16 oz., low ft., 400/19	200.00
Pitcher, 16 oz., no ft., 400/16	165.00
Pitcher, 20 oz., plain, 400/416	40.00
Pitcher, 40 oz., juice/cocktail, 400/19	165.00
Pitcher, 40 oz., manhattan, 400/18	210.00
Pitcher, 40 oz., plain, 400/419	40.00
Pitcher, 64 oz., plain, 400/424	50.00
Pitcher, 80 oz., plain, 400/424	55.00
Pitcher, 80 oz., 400/24	125.00
Pitcher, 80 oz., beaded ft., 400/18	200.00
Plate, 4½", 400/34	6.00
Plate, 5½", 2 hdld., 400/42D	10.00
Plate, 6", bread/butter, 400/1D	8.00
Plate, 6", canape w/off ctr. indent, 400/36	10.00
Plate, 6¾", 2 hdld. crimped, 400/52C	25.00
Plate, 7", salad, 400/3D	8.00

	Crystal
Plate, 7½", 2 hdld., 400/52D	10.00
Plate, 7½", triangular, 400/266	75.00
Plate, 8", oval, 400/169	22.50
Plate, 8", salad, 400/5D	9.00
Plate, 8", w/indent, 400/50	11.00
Plate, 8¼", crescent salad, 400/120	42.50
Plate, 8½", 2 hdld., crimped, 400/62C	20.00
Plate, 8½", 2 hdld., 400/62D	12.00
Plate, 8½", salad, 400/5D	10.00
Plate, 8½", 2 hdld. (sides upturned), 400/62E	25.00
Plate, 9", luncheon, 400/7D	12.50
Plate, 9", oval, salad, 400/38	35.00
Plate, 9", w/indent, oval, 400/98	15.00
Plate, 10", 2 hdld., sides upturned, 400/72E	22.50
Plate, 10", 2 hdld. crimped, 400/72C	30.00
Plate, 10", dinner, 400/10D	35.00
Plate, 10", 2 hdld., 400/72D	17.50
Plate, 12", 2 hdld., 400/145D	27.50
Plate, 12", 2 hdld. crimp., 400/145C	32.50
Plate, 12", service, 400/13D	27.50
Plate, 12½", cupped edge, torte, 400/75V	27.50
Plate, 12½", oval, 400/124	65.00
Plate, 13½", cupped edge, serving, 400/92V	37.50
Plate, 14" birthday cake (holes for 72 candles), 400/160	335.00
Plate, 14", 2 hdld., sides upturned, 400/113E	35.00
Plate, 14", 2 hdld., torte, 400/113D	30.00
Plate, 14", service, 400/92D	30.00
Plate, 14", torte, 400/17D	40.00
Plate, 17", cupped edge, 400/20V	42.50
Plate, 17", torte, 400/20D	42.50
Platter, 13", 400/124D	90.00
Platter, 16", 400/131D	165.00
Punch ladle, 400/91	22.50
Punch set, family, 8 demi cups, ladle, lid, 400/139/77	400.00
Punch set, 15 pc. bowl on base, 12 cups, ladle, 400/20	225.00
Relish & dressing set, 4 pc. (10½" 4 pt. relish w/marmalade), 400/1112	90.00
Salad set, 4 pc., buffet; lg. rnd. tray, div. bowl, 2 spoons, 400/17	100.00
Salad set, 4 pc. (rnd. plate, flared bowl, fork, spoon), 400/75B	85.00
Salt & pepper pr., bead ft., straight side, chrome top, 400/247	16.00
Salt & pepper pr., bead ft., bulbous, chrome top, 400/96	15.00
Salt & pepper pr., bulbous w/bead stem, plastic top, 400/116	40.00
Salt & pepper, pr., indiv., 400/109	10.00
Salt & pepper, pr., ftd. bead base, 400/190	45.00
Salt dip, 2", 400/61	9.00
Salt dip, 2¼", 400/19	9.00
Salt spoon, 3, 400/616	9.00
Salt spoon, w/ribbed bowl, 4000	9.00
Sauce boat, 400/169	95.00
Sauce boat liner, 400/169	35.00
Saucer, after dinner, 400/77AD	5.00
Saucer, tea or coffee, 400/35 or 400/37	2.50

	Crystal
Set: 2 pc. hdld. cracker w/cheese compote, 400/88	37.50
Set: 2 pc. rnd. cracker plate w/indent; cheese compote, 400/145	45.00
Snack jar w/cover, bead ft., 400/139/1	400.00
Stem, 1 oz., cordial, 400/190	65.00
Stem, 4 oz., cocktail, 400/190	18.00
Stem, 5 oz., tall sherbet, 400/190	15.00
Stem, 5 oz., wine, 400/190	22.50
Stem, 6 oz., sherbet, 400/190	14.00
Stem, 10 oz., water 400/190	18.00
Stem, #3400, 1 oz., cordial	35.00
Stem, #3400, 4 oz., cocktail	14.00
Stem, #3400, 4 oz. oyster cocktail	14.00
Stem, #3400, 4 oz., wine	24.00
Stem, #3400, 5 oz., claret	40.00
Stem, #3400, 5 oz., low sherbet	10.00
Stem, #3400, 6 oz., parfait	45.00
Stem, #3400, 6 oz., sherbet/saucer champagne	17.50
Stem, #3400, 9 oz., goblet, water	15.00
Stem, #3800, low sherbet	25.00
Stem, #3800, brandy	25.00
Stem, #3800, 1 oz. cordial	40.00
Stem, #3800, 4 oz., cocktail	25.00
Stem, #3800, 4 oz. wine	27.50
Stem, #3800, 6 oz., champagne/sherbet	25.00
Stem, #3800, 9 oz. water goblet	25.00
Stem, #3800, claret	30.00
Stem, #4000, 1¼ oz., cordial	30.00
Stem, #4000, cocktail	22.00
Stem, #4000, 5 oz., wine	25.00
Stem, #4000, 6 oz., tall sherbet	14.00
Stem, #4000, 11 oz., goblet	18.00
Stem, #4000, 12 oz., tea	20.00
Strawberry set, 2 pc. (7" plate/sugar dip bowl), 400/83	50.00
Sugar, domed foot, 400/18	110.00
Sugar, 6 oz., bead hdld., 400/30	6.50
Sugar, flat, bead handle, 400/126	27.50
Sugar, indiv. bridge, 400/122	6.00
Sugar, plain ft., 400/31	6.50
Tete-a-tete 3 pc. brandy, a.d. cup, 6½" oval tray, 400/111	55.00
Tid bit server, 2 tier, cupped, 400/2701	45.00
Tid bit set, 3 pc., 400/18TB	150.00
Toast, w/cover, set, 7¾", 400/123	225.00
Tray, 5½", hdld., upturned handles, 400/42E	18.00
Tray, 5½", lemon, ctr. hdld., 400/221	30.00
Tray, 5¼" x 9¼", condiment, 400/148	40.00
Tray, 6½", 400/29	15.00
Tray, 6", wafer, handle bent to ctr. of dish, 400/51T	22.00
Tray, 10½", ctr. hdld. fruit, 400/68F	50.00
Tray, 11½", ctr. hdld. party, 400/68D	30.00
Tray, 13½", 2 hdld. celery, oval, 400/105	30.00
Tray, 13", relish, 5 sections, 400/102	60.00
Tray, 14", hdld., 400/113E	40.00
Tumbler, 3½ oz., cocktail, 400/18	38.00
Tumbler, 5 oz., juice, 400/18	35.00
Tumbler, 6 oz., sherbet, 400/18	37.00

	Crystal
Tumbler, 7 oz., old-fashioned 400/18	30.00
Tumbler, 7 oz., parfait, 400/18	40.00
Tumbler, 9 oz., water, 400/18	35.00
Tumbler, 12 oz., tea, 400/18	40.00
Tumbler, 3 oz., ftd., cocktail, 400/19	15.00
Tumbler, 3 oz., ftd., wine, 400/19	16.00
Tumbler, 5 oz., low sherbet, 400/19	14.00
Tumbler, 5 oz., juice, 400/19	10.00
Tumbler, 7 oz., old-fashioned, 400/19	30.00
Tumbler, 10 oz., 400/19	11.00
Tumbler, 12 oz., 400/19	18.00
Tumbler, 14 oz., 400/19, tea	20.00
Tumbler, #3400, 5 oz., ft., juice	15.00
Tumbler, #3400, 9 oz., ftd.	14.00
Tumbler, #3400, 10 oz., ftd.	14.00
Tumbler, #3400, 12 oz., ftd.	16.00
Tumbler, #3800, 5 oz., juice	25.00
Tumbler, #3800, 9 oz.	25.00
Tumbler, #3800, 12 oz.	25.00
Vase, 4", bead ft., sm. neck, ball, 400/25	40.00
Vase, 5¾", bead ft., bud, 400/107	45.00
Vase, 5¾", bead ft., mini bud, 400/107	40.00
Vase, 6", flat, crimped edge, 400/287C	20.00
Vase, 6", ftd., flared rim, 400/138B	80.00
Vase, 6" diam., 400/198	175.00
Vase, 6" fan, 400/287 F	27.50
Vase, 7", ftd., bud, 400/186	200.00
Vase, 7", ftd., bud, 400/187	175.00
Vase, 7", ivy bowl, 400/74J	50.00
Vase, 7", rolled rim w/bead hdld., 400/87 R	35.00
Vase, 7", rose bowl, 400/142 K	110.00
Vase, 7¼", ftd., rose bowl, crimped top, 400/132C	225.00
Vase, 7½", ftd., rose bowl, 400/132	150.00
Vase, 8", fan, w/bead hdld., 400/87F	35.00
Vase, 8", flat, crimped edge, 400/143C	60.00
Vase, 8", fluted rim w/bead hdlds., 400/87C	27.50
Vase, 8½", bead ft., bud, 400/28C	70.00
Vase, 8½", bead ft., flared rim, 400/21	100.00
Vase, 8½", bead ft., inward rim, 400/27	100.00
Vase, 8½", hdld. (pitcher shape), 400/227	300.00
Vase, 10", bead ft., straight side, 400/22	140.00
Vase, 10", ftd., 400/193	150.00

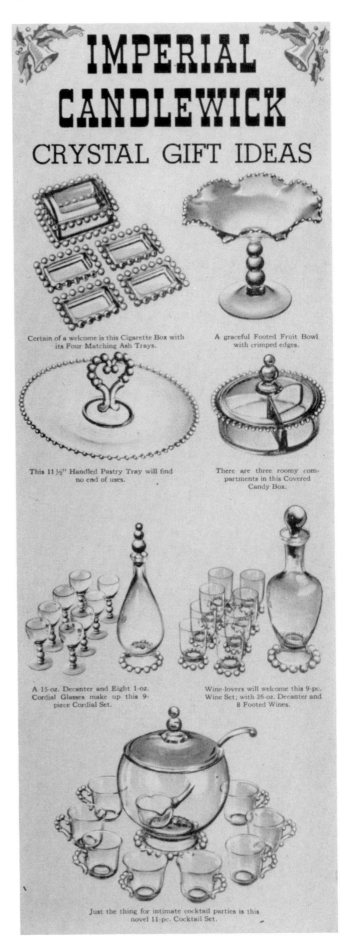

IMPERIAL CANDLEWICK
CRYSTAL GIFT IDEAS

Certain of a welcome is this Cigarette Box with its Four Matching Ash Trays.

A graceful Footed Fruit Bowl with crimped edges.

This 11½" Handled Pastry Tray will find no end of uses.

There are three roomy compartments in this Covered Candy Box.

A 15-oz. Decanter and Eight 1-oz. Cordial Glasses make up this 9-piece Cordial Set.

Wine-lovers will welcome this 9-pc. Wine Set; with 26-oz. Decanter and 8 Footed Wines.

Just the thing for intimate cocktail parties is this novel 11-pc. Cocktail Set.

IMPERIAL GLASS CORPORATION
BELLAIRE, OHIO

Easter Dinner
IMPERIAL CANDLEWICK
Family Style

A beautiful table crystal to express your joy in living—and dining . . . to reflect the rich colors of the awakening season and help you make your table an invitation to good company as well as to complement your Easter cuisine. Each piece of this extensive and varied service is designed for functional use . . . superbly hand-crafted crystal for daily family appreciation as well as for your most memorable occasions.

Imperial Candlewick is an open stock pattern. Add to your collection as your need and budget permits, for a perfect, scintillating table service.

HAND-CRAFTED AT IMPERIAL GLASS CORPORATION, BELLAIRE, OHIO

CAPE COD, Imperial Glass Company, 1932 – 1984

MARTIN BRUEHL

Mission Accomplished

Farewell to the old order, hail to the new standard of fine things and a manner of joyous living! Captured prize for this, as for *every* happy occasion, is the diamond-like brilliance of our Cape Cod Crystal table service. There is a tradition in this design; it delighted your Grandmother and your great Grandmother when it graced proud tables of yesterdays. For *your* table today Imperial craftsmen have given the Cape Cod pattern a new grace, balance and sparkling fire as they blow, mould and finish each piece by hand. Cape Cod is crystal tableware to be proudly possessed, used every day, cherished always. Available in fine stores everywhere; crafted by THE IMPERIAL GLASS CORPORATION, BELLAIRE, OHIO.

CAPE COD, Imperial Glass Company, 1932 – 1984 (continued)

Colors: crystal, cobalt blue, red, green, black, milk glass, pink

The advertisement shown on page 41 was taken from a 1948 magazine. Although Imperial seemed to push Cape Cod through national advertising campaigns as it did Candlewick, there was never the demand generated for Cape Cod as there was for Candlewick. This is also true with collectors today! Rarely found pieces of Cape Cod sell for one-third to one-half the prices of rare Candlewick. I have no idea why, but I have seen it occur over and over! There is generally not quite the present devotion to collecting Cape Cod as there is with Candlewick.

I had nineteen pieces omitted from the price list last time between the two pages of prices. If you are familiar with windows on a Macintosh computer, I can only say that someone was transferring my Microsoft Word files into Quark and forgot to unroll the shade. In any case, two months after the book was out, I received a letter asking how much a Cape Cod cup was worth? I looked to see why the question was asked and that is when the missing pieces were discovered. I printed up fifty "omissions" lists for the rush. **Today, some nineteen months later, we have only had a dozen or so requests for price lists for pieces missing. Maybe that helps explain why rarely found Cape Cod items do not yet sell well!**

Colored Cape Cod has its devotees, but it is Ritz Blue (cobalt blue) and Ruby Red that are most in demand. These two colors are selling 50% to 100% more than crystal. Prices for other colors are not that much more than crystal with most of them selling at reasonable prices – if at all!

	Crystal
Ash tray, 4", 160/134/1	12.00
Ash tray, 5½", 160/150	15.00
Basket, 9", handled, crimped, 160/221/0	160.00
Basket, 11" tall, handled, 160/40	100.00
Bottle, bitters, 4 oz., 160/235	55.00
Bottle, cologne, w/stopper, 1601	55.00
Bottle, condiment, 6 oz., 160/224	65.00
Bottle, cordial, 18 oz., 160/256	100.00
Bottle, decanter, 26 oz., 160/244	95.00
Bottle, ketchup, 14 oz., 160/237	125.00
Bowl, 3", handled mint, 160/183	15.00
Bowl, 3", jelly, 160/33	10.00
Bowl, 4" finger, 1602	10.00
Bowl, 4½", finger, 1604½A	10.00
Bowl, 4½", handled spider, 160/180	17.50
Bowl, 4½", dessert, tab handled, 160/197	18.00
Bowl, 5", dessert, heart shape, 160/49H	15.00
Bowl, 5", flower, 1605N	15.00
Bowl, 5½", fruit, 160/23B	10.00
Bowl, 5½", handled spider, 160/181	17.50
Bowl, 5½", tab handled, soup, 160/198	15.00
Bowl, 6", fruit, 160/3F	10.00
Bowl, 6", baked apple, 160/53X	9.00
Bowl, 6", handled, round mint, 160/51F	18.00
Bowl, 6", handled heart, 160/40H	18.00
Bowl, 6", handled mint, 160/51H	22.00
Bowl, 6", handled tray, 160/51T	18.00
Bowl, 6½", handled portioned spider, 160/187	27.50
Bowl, 6½", handled spider, 160/182	25.00
Bowl, 6½", tab handled, 160/199	20.00
Bowl, 7", nappy, 160/5F	20.00
Bowl, 7½", 160/7F	20.00
Bowl, 7½", 2-handled, 160/62B	25.00
Bowl, 8¾", 160/10F	25.00
Bowl, 9", footed fruit, 160/67F	55.00
Bowl, 9½", 2-handled, 160/145B	35.00
Bowl, 9½", crimped, 160/221C	60.00
Bowl, 9½", float, 160/221F	55.00
Bowl, 10", footed, 160/137B	60.00
Bowl, 10", oval, 160/221	60.00
Bowl, 10", round, 160/8A	35.00
Bowl, 11", flanged edge, 1608X	75.00
Bowl, 11", oval, 160/124	60.00
Bowl, 11", oval divided, 160/125	62.50
Bowl, 11", salad, 160/8B	37.50
Bowl, 11¼", oval, 1602	60.00
Bowl, 12", 160/75B	37.50

	Crystal
Bowl, 12", oval, 160/131B	60.00
Bowl, 12", oval crimped, 160/131C	70.00
Bowl, 12", punch, 160/20B	55.00
Bowl, 13", console, 160/75L	40.00
Bowl, 15", console, 16010L	60.00
Butter, 5", w/cover, handled, 160/144	25.00
Butter, w/cover, ¼ lb., 160/161	42.50
Cake plate, 10", 4 toed, 160/220	85.00
Cake stand, 10½", footed, 160/67D	37.50
Cake stand, 11", 160/103D	65.00
Candleholder, twin, 160/100	45.00
Candleholder, 3", single, 160/170	15.00
Candleholder, 4", 160/81	18.00
Candleholder, 4", Aladdin style, 160/90	110.00
Candleholder, 4½", saucer, 160/175	18.00
Candleholder, 5", 160/80	17.50
Candleholder, 5", flower, 160/45B	50.00
Candleholder, 5½", flower, 160/45N	45.00
Candleholder, 6", centerpiece, 160/48BC	65.00
Candy, w/cover, 160/110	60.00
Carafe, wine, 26 oz., 160/185	135.00
Celery, 8", 160/105	25.00
Celery, 10½", 160/189	35.00
Cigarette box, 4½", 160/134	35.00
Cigarette holder, ftd., 1602	12.50
Cigarette holder, Tom & Jerry mug, 160/200	30.00
Cigarette lighter, 1602	22.00
Coaster, w/spoon rest, 160/76	9.50
Coaster, 3", square, 160/85	10.00
Coaster, 4", round, 160/78	10.00
Coaster, 4½", flat, 160/1R	8.00
Comport, 5¼", 160F	22.00
Comport, 5¾", 160X	25.00
Comport, 6", 160/45	20.00
Comport, 6", w/cover, ftd., 160/140	55.00
Comport, 7", 160/48B	30.00
Comport, 11¼", oval, 1602, 6½" tall	95.00
Creamer, 160/190	15.00
Creamer, 160/30	8.00
Creamer, ftd., 160/31	12.00
Cruet, w/stopper, 4 oz., 160/119	20.00
Cruet, w/stopper, 5 oz., 160/70	22.00
Cruet, w/stopper, 6 oz., 160/241	35.00
Cup, tea, 160/35	7.00
Cup, coffee, 160/37	7.00
Cup, bouillon, 160/250	25.00
Decanter, bourbon, 160/260	65.00

	Crystal
Decanter, rye, 160/260	65.00
Decanter w/stopper, 30 oz., 160/163	52.50
Decanter w/stopper, 24 oz., 160/212	60.00
Egg cup, 160/225	32.50
Epergne, 2 pc., plain center, 160/196	180.00
Fork, 160/701	10.00
Gravy bowl, 18 oz., 160/202	55.00
Horseradish, 5 oz. jar, 160/226	65.00
Ice bucket, 6½", 160/63	100.00
Icer, 3 pc., bowl, 2 inserts, 160/53/3	40.00
Jar, 12 oz., hdld. peanut w/lid, 160/210	50.00
Jar, 10", "Pokal," 160/133	65.00
Jar, 11", "Pokal," 160/128	65.00
Jar, 15", "Pokal," 160/132	100.00
Jar, candy w/lid, wicker hand., 5" h., 160/194	70.00
Jar, cookie, w/lid, wicker hand., 6½" h., 160/195	85.00
Jar, peanut butter w/lid, wicker hand., 4" h., 160/193	60.00
Ladle, marmalade, 160/130	8.00
Ladle, mayonnaise, 160/165	8.00
Ladle, punch	20.00
Lamp, hurricane, 2 pc., 5" base, 160/79	70.00
Lamp, hurricane, 2 pc., bowl-like base, 1604	45.00
Marmalade, 3 pc. set, 160/89/3	30.00
Marmalade, 4 pc. set, 160/89	35.00
Mayonnaise, 3 pc. set, 160/52H	35.00
Mayonnaise, 3 pc., 160/23	25.00
Mayonnaise, 12 oz., hdld., spouted, 160/205	45.00
Mug, 12 oz., handled, 160/188	40.00
Mustard, w/cover & spoon, 160/156	20.00
Nut dish, 3", hdld., 160/183	12.50
Nut dish, 4", hdld., 160/184	15.00
Pepper mill, 160/236	20.00
Pitcher, milk, 1 pt., 160/240	40.00
Pitcher, ice lipped, 40 oz., 160/19	70.00
Pitcher, martini, blown, 40 oz., 160/178	150.00
Pitcher, ice lipped, 2 qt., 160/239	85.00
Pitcher, 2 qt., 160/24	75.00
Pitcher, blown, 5 pt., 160/176	135.00
Plate, 4½" butter, 160/34	7.00
Plate, 6", cupped, (liner for 160/208 salad dressing), 160/209	20.00
Plate, 6½", bread & butter, 160/1D	4.00
Plate, 7", 160/3D	6.00
Plate, 7", cupped (liner for 160/205 Mayo), 160/206	20.00
Plate, 8", center handled tray, 160/149D	30.00
Plate, 8", crescent salad, 160/12	42.50
Plate, 8", cupped, (liner for gravy), 160/203	25.00
Plate, 8", salad, 160/5D	8.00
Plate, 8½", 2-handled, 160/62D	25.00
Plate, 9", 160/7D	17.50
Plate, 9½", 2 hdld., 160/62D	35.00
Plate, 10", dinner, 160/10D	32.50
Plate, 11½", 2-handled, 160/145D	32.00
Plate, 12½" bread, 160/222	60.00
Plate, 13", birthday, 72 candle holes, 160/72	300.00
Plate, 13", cupped torte, 1608V	32.00
Plate, 13", torte, 1608F	35.00
Plate, 14", cupped, 160/75V	33.00
Plate, 14", flat, 160/75D	33.00
Plate, 16", cupped, 160/20V	50.00
Plate, 17", 2 styles, 160/10D or 20D	40.00

	Crystal
Platter, 13½", oval, 160/124D	45.00
Puff Box, w/cover, 1601	35.00
Relish, 8", hdld., 2 part. 160/223	35.00
Relish, 9½", 4 pt., 160/56	32.50
Relish, 9½", oval, 3 part, 160/55	32.50
Relish, 11", 5 part, 160/102	50.00
Relish, 11¼", 3 part, oval, 1602	50.00
Salad dressing, 6 oz., hdld., spouted, 160/208	40.00
Salad set, 14" plate, 12" bowl, fork & spoon, 160/75	90.00
Salt & pepper, individual, 160/251	14.00
Salt & pepper, pr., ftd., 160/116	16.00
Salt & pepper, pr., ftd., stemmed, 160/243	27.50
Salt & pepper, pr., 160/96	12.00
Salt & pepper, pr. square, 160/109	18.00
Salt dip, 160/61	12.00
Salt spoon, 1600	6.00
Saucer, tea, 160/35	2.00
Saucer, coffee, 160/37	2.00
Server, 12", ftd. or turned over, 160/93	75.00
Spoon, 160/701	7.50
Stem, 1½ oz., cordial, 1602	10.00
Stem, 3 oz., wine, 1602	7.00
Stem, 3½ oz., cocktail, 1602	7.00
Stem, 5 oz., claret, 1602	12.00
Stem, 6 oz., low sundae, 1602	7.00
Stem, 6 oz., parfait, 1602	12.00
Stem, 6 oz., sherbet, 1600	7.50
Stem, 6 oz., tall sherbet, 1602	8.50
Stem, 9 oz., water, 1602	9.50
Stem, 10 oz., water, 1600	10.00
Stem, 11 oz., dinner goblet, 1602	10.00
Stem, 14 oz., goblet, magnum, 160	22.50
Stem, oyster cocktail, 1602	8.00
Sugar, 160/190	15.00
Sugar, 160/30	7.00
Sugar, ftd., 160/31	12.00
Toast, w/cover, 160/123	95.00
Tom & Jerry footed punch bowl, 160/200	250.00
Tray, square covered sugar & creamer, 160/25/26	135.00
Tray, 7", for creamer/sugar, 160/29	12.00
Tray, 11", pastry, center handle, 160/68D	50.00
Tumbler, 2½ oz., whiskey, 160	10.00
Tumbler, 6 oz., ftd., juice, 1602	8.00
Tumbler, 6 oz., juice, 1600	7.00
Tumbler, 7 oz., old-fashioned, 160	9.00
Tumbler, 10 oz., ftd., water, 1602	9.00
Tumbler, 10 oz., water, 160	9.00
Tumbler, 12 oz., ftd., ice tea, 1602	12.00
Tumbler, 12 oz., ftd., tea, 1600	11.00
Tumbler, 12 oz., ice tea, 160	12.50
Tumbler, 14 oz., double old-fashioned, 160	20.00
Tumbler, 16 oz., 160	25.00
Vase, 6¼", ftd., 160/22	30.00
Vase, 6½", ftd., 160/110B	55.00
Vase, 7½", ftd., 160/22	35.00
Vase, 8", fan, 160/87F	75.00
Vase, 8½", flip, 160/143	45.00
Vase, 8½", ftd., 160/28	40.00
Vase, 10", cylinder, 160/192	65.00
Vase, 10½", hdld., urn, 160/186	100.00
Vase, 11", ftd., 160/21	55.00

CAPRICE, Cambridge Glass Company, 1940's – 1957

Colors: crystal, Moonlight Blue, white, amber, amethyst, pink, emerald green, pink, cobalt blue, milk glass

There has been a surge of collectors turning to pink Caprice of late. Prices are approaching those of blue in basic pieces and are selling a little above in harder to find pieces. I have now included the pink prices with the blue below. Realize that not all pieces made in blue were made in pink. There were enough items made in pink to assemble a set, but the set will be lacking many pieces found in blue and crystal!

There have been five blue Doulton pitchers sold in the last two years. All have been purchased for collections! One collector bought three! He said that they got cheaper as they were offered to him, and buying three helped even out the cost of each!

Many Caprice items are not being found on the market at any price including 2½ oz. footed whiskies, 5 oz. moulded sherbets (both shown in blue in the middle of the top photo on page 47), clarets (both blown and moulded), finger bowls, and the moulded straight sided 9 and 12 oz. tumblers.

There are other hard-to-find items, but those items are on most collectors want lists. There are many collectors of crystal also, but they are helped by more reasonable prices. Crystal candle reflectors and punch bowls are rarely found and there is a strong demand for them when they do turn up! Most of the other colors of Caprice are purchased by collectors looking for additions to their Caprice. As far as I know, all of the other colors can not be collected into completed sets as can be crystal and blue Caprice.

	Crystal	Blue, Pink		Crystal	Blue, Pink
Ash tray, 2¾", 3 ftd., shell, #213 ...	6.00	10.00	Candlestick, 2½", ea., #67	13.00	35.00
* Ash tray, 3", #214	6.00	12.00	Candlestick, 2-lite, keyhole, 5",		
* Ash tray, 4", #215	7.00		#646	16.00	50.00
* Ash tray, 5", #216		25.00	Candlestick, 3-lite, #74.................	30.00	65.00
Bonbon, 6", oval, ftd., #155..........	20.00	40.00	Candlestick, 5", ea. keyhole, #647	20.00	55.00
Bonbon, 6", sq., 2 hdld., #154.......	12.00	32.50	Candlestick, 7", ea. w/prism, #70 .	17.50	50.00
Bonbon, 6", sq., ftd., #133	14.00	35.00	Candy, 6", 3 ftd. w/cover, #165	42.50	100.00
Bottle, 7 oz., bitters, #186	175.00		Candy, 6", w/cover (divided),		
Bowl, 2", 4 ftd., almond #95	15.00	40.00	#168	55.00	110.00
* Bowl, 5", 2 hdld., jelly, #151	15.00	30.00	Celery & relish, 8½", 3 pt., #124....	20.00	40.00
Bowl, 8", 4 ftd., #49......................	30.00	60.00	Cigarette box, w/cover, 3½" x 2¼",		
* Bowl, 8", 3 pt., relish, #124...........	17.50	32.50	#207	17.50	45.00
Bowl, 9½", crimped, 4 ftd., #52	30.00	67.50	Cigarette box, w/cover, 4½" x 3½",		
Bowl, 9", pickle, #102	20.00	50.00	#208	22.00	85.00
Bowl, 10", salad, 4 ftd., #57	32.50	100.00	Cigarette holder, 2" x 2¼",		
Bowl, 10", sq., 4 ftd., #58	30.00	95.00	triangular, #205	13.00	50.00
Bowl, 10½", crimped, 4 ftd.,			Cigarette holder, 3" x 3",		
#53	30.00	100.00	triangular, #204	20.00	40.00
Bowl, 11", crimped, 4 ftd., #60	32.00	100.00	Coaster, 3½", #13	13.00	25.00
* Bowl, 11", 2 hdld., oval, 4 ftd.,			Comport, 6", #130.......................	22.00	60.00
#65	30.00	85.00	Comport, 7", low ftd., #130..........	20.00	65.00
* Bowl, 12", 4 pt. relish, oval, #126.	60.00	135.00	Comport, 7", #136.......................	35.00	85.00
* Bowl, 12", relish, 3 pt.,			Cracker jar & cover, #202	195.00	600.00
rectangular, #125	40.00	125.00	* Creamer, large, #41......................	10.00	17.50
Bowl, 12½", belled, 4 ftd., #62	30.00	70.00	* Creamer, medium, #38	8.00	15.00
Bowl, 12½", crimped, 4 ftd., #61 ..	32.50	75.00	* Creamer, ind., #40	10.00	20.00
Bowl, 13", crimped, 4 ftd., #66	32.50	75.00	Cup, #17.................................	13.00	32.00
Bowl, 13½", 4 ftd., shallow			Decanter, w/stopper, 35 oz., #187.	125.00	400.00
cupped #82	35.00	77.50	Finger bowl & liner, #16...............	30.00	85.00
Bridge set:			Ice bucket, #201...........................	45.00	150.00
*Cloverleaf, 6½", #173...............	25.00	75.00	Marmalade, w/cover, 6 oz., #89....	45.00	185.00
*Club, 6½", #170....................	25.00	75.00	* Mayonnaise, 6½", 3 pc. set, #129..	25.00	100.00
Diamond, 6½", #171	25.00	75.00	* Mayonnaise, 8", 3 pc. set, #106.....	40.00	110.00
*Heart, 6½", #169	30.00	95.00	Mustard, w/cover, 2 oz., #87........	35.00	135.00
*Spade, 6½", #172	25.00	70.00	* Oil, 3 oz., w/stopper #101	22.00	85.00
* Butterdish, ¼ lb., #52	209.00		* Oil, 5 oz., w/stopper #100............	65.00	175.00
Cake plate, 13", ftd., #36	150.00	300.00	Pitcher, 32 oz., ball shape, #179 ...	75.00	300.00
Candle reflector	200.00		Pitcher, 80 oz., ball shape, #183 ...	90.00	295.00

*Moulds owned by Summit Art Glass and many of these pieces have been reproduced.

CAPRICE, Cambridge Glass Company, 1940's – 1957 (continued)

	Crystal	Blue, Pink
Pitcher, 90 oz., tall Doulton style, #178	700.00	4,250.00
Plate, 6½", bread & butter, #21	10.00	20.00
Plate, 6½", hdld., lemon, #152	11.00	20.00
Plate, 7½", salad, #23....................	12.50	22.00
Plate, 8½", #22	14.00	32.50
* Plate, 9½", dinner, #24	40.00	125.00
Plate, 11", cabaret, 4 ftd., #32........	22.00	55.00
Plate, 11½", cabaret, #26	25.00	55.00
Plate, 14", cabaret, 4 ftd., #33........	27.50	80.00
Plate, 14", 4 ftd., #28	27.50	80.00
Plate, 16", #30..............................	35.00	90.00
Punch bowl, ftd.	2,000.00	
* Salad dressing, 3 pc., ftd. & hdld., 2 spoons, #112	165.00	400.00
Saucer, #17	2.50	5.50
Salt & pepper, pr., ball, #91..........	37.50	100.00
* Salt & pepper, pr., flat, #96...........	22.00	75.00
Salt & pepper, indiv., ball, pr., #90	30.00	100.00
Salt & pepper, indiv., flat, pr., #92	30.00	125.00
Salver, 13", 2 pc. (cake atop pedestal), #31	140.00	300.00
Stem, #300, blown, 1 oz., cordial...	40.00	125.00
Stem, #300, blown, 2½ oz., wine ..	27.50	60.00
Stem, #300, blown, 3 oz., cocktail	22.00	42.50
Stem, #300, blown, 4½ oz., claret ...	50.00	175.00
Stem, #300, blown, 4½ oz., low oyster cocktail	20.00	50.00
Stem, #300, blown, 5 oz., parfait ..	75.00	235.00
Stem, #300, blown, 6 oz., low sherbet	10.00	15.00
Stem, #300, blown, 6 oz., tall sherbet	12.00	22.50
Stem, #300, blown, 9 oz. water.....	16.00	37.50
Stem, #301, blown, 1 oz., cordial .	35.00	
Stem, #301, blown, 2½ oz., wine ..	27.50	
Stem, #301, blown, 3 oz., cocktail	20.00	
Stem, #301, blown, 4½ oz., claret .	40.00	
Stem, #301, blown, 6 oz., sherbet .	13.00	
Stem, #301, blown, 9 oz., water....	17.50	
* Stem, 3 oz., wine, #6	27.50	100.00
* Stem, 3½ oz., cocktail, #3.............	24.00	50.00
* Stem, 4½ oz., claret, #5	35.00	175.00
Stem, 4½ oz., fruit cocktail, #7	27.50	75.00

	Crystal	Blue, Pink
Stem, 5 oz., low sherbet, #4	20.00	85.00
* Stem, 7 oz., tall sherbet, #2...........	17.50	32.50
Stem, 10 oz., water, #1	26.00	42.50
* Sugar, large, #41	10.00	15.00
* Sugar, medium, #38	8.00	15.00
* Sugar, indiv., #40.........................	10.00	20.00
* Tray, for sugar & creamer, #37.......	12.50	30.00
Tray, 9" oval, #42	18.00	40.00
* Tumbler, 2 oz., flat, #188...............	20.00	50.00
Tumbler, 3 oz., ftd., #12	20.00	45.00
Tumbler, 5 oz., ftd., #11	20.00	45.00
Tumbler, 5 oz., flat, #180..............	20.00	45.00
Tumbler, #300, 2½ oz., whiskey....	40.00	200.00
Tumbler, #300, 5 oz., ftd., juice	18.00	32.50
Tumbler, #300, 10 oz.	20.00	40.00
Tumbler, #300, 12 oz.	20.00	40.00
Tumbler, #301, blown, 4½ oz., low oyster cocktail	15.00	
Tumbler, #301, blown, 5 oz., juice	13.00	
Tumbler, #301, blown, 12 oz., tea.	17.00	
* Tumbler, 9 oz., straight side, #14..	30.00	85.00
* Tumbler, 10 oz., ftd., #10	18.00	40.00
Tumbler, 12 oz., ftd., #9	22.00	45.00
* Tumbler, 12 oz., straight side, #15	35.00	85.00
Tumbler, #310, 5 oz., flat, juice.....	15.00	40.00
Tumbler, #310, 7 oz., flat, old-fashioned	30.00	100.00
Tumbler, #310, 10 oz., flat, table...	15.00	35.00
Tumbler, #310, 11 oz., flat, tall, 4¹³⁄₁₆"	20.00	75.00
Tumbler, #310, 12 oz., flat, tea	30.00	125.00
Vase, 3½", #249............................	45.00	130.00
Vase, 4", #252...............................	45.00	135.00
Vase, 4½", #344, crimped	80.00	165.00
Vase, 5", ivy bowl, #232	40.00	150.00
Vase, 5½", #345............................	40.00	150.00
Vase, 6", #254..............................	55.00	175.00
Vase, 6", #342..............................	45.00	150.00
Vase, 6½", #338, crimped	90.00	175.00
Vase, 7½", #346, crimped	100.00	200.00
Vase, 8½", #339............................	50.00	175.00
Vase, 8½", #343, crimped	135.00	295.00
Vase, 9½" #340, crimped	150.00	350.00

*Moulds owned by Summit Art Glass and many of these pieces have been reproduced.

CARIBBEAN, Line #112, Duncan Miller Glass Company, 1936 – 1955

Colors: blue, crystal, amber, red

Caribbean blue dinnerware pieces such as cups, saucers, and plates have become almost nonexistent. Already many collectors have begun to buy the crystal out of frustration in finding blue. One collector in Florida recently confided that his wife's collecting Caribbean was the best thing that had happened to him since she started several patterns ten years ago. All her other patterns were completed, and she had spent less money in the last year collecting Caribbean simply because she was not finding any new pieces to buy!

Caribbean is one of the most difficult patterns to price in this book as there is never enough seen at shows to ascertain a fairly representative price!

	Crystal	Blue
Ash tray, 6", 4 indent	15.00	32.50
Bowl, 3¾" x 5", folded side, hdld.	15.00	32.50
Bowl, 4½", finger	15.00	30.00
Bowl, 5", fruit nappy (takes liner), hdld.	10.00	22.50
Bowl, 5" x 7", folded side, hdld.	15.00	35.00
Bowl, 6½", soup (takes liner)	15.00	35.00
Bowl, 7", hdld.	20.00	40.00
Bowl, 7¼", ftd., hdld., grapefruit	15.00	35.00
Bowl, 8½"	22.50	60.00
Bowl, 9", salad	25.00	65.00
Bowl, 9¼", veg., flared edge	25.00	60.00
Bowl, 9¼", veg., hdld.	25.00	60.00
Bowl, 9½", epergne, flared edge	35.00	75.00
Bowl, 10", 6¼ qt., punch	85.00	400.00
Bowl, 10", 6¼ qt. punch, flared top	85.00	450.00
Bowl, 10¾", oval, flower, hdld.	30.00	75.00
Bowl, 12", console, flared edge	35.00	85.00
Candelabrum, 4¾", 2-lite	30.00	70.00
Candlestick, 7¼", 1-lite, w/bl. prisms	40.00	150.00
Candy dish w/cover, 4" x 7"	35.00	85.00
Cheese/cracker crumbs, 3½" h., plate 11", hdld.	32.50	75.00
Cigarette holder, (stack ash tray top)	30.00	75.00
Cocktail shaker, 9", 33 oz.	60.00	165.00
Creamer	12.00	25.00
Cruet	35.00	75.00
Cup, tea	15.00	55.00
Cup, punch	7.50	20.00
Epergne, 4 pt., flower (12" bowl; 9½" bowl; 7¾" vase; 14" plate)	165.00	350.00
Ice bucket, 6½", hdld.	50.00	125.00
Ladle, punch	30.00	90.00
Mayonnaise, w/liner, 5¾", 2 pt., 2 spoons, hdld.	40.00	90.00
Mayonnaise, w/liner, 5¾", hdld., 1 spoon	35.00	80.00
Mustard, 4", w/slotted cover	30.00	60.00
Pitcher, 4¼", 9 oz., syrup	50.00	125.00
Pitcher, 4¾" 16 oz., milk	80.00	200.00
Pitcher, w/ice lip, 9", 72 oz., water	175.00	425.00
Plate, 6", hdld., fruit nappy liner	4.00	12.00
Plate 6¼", bread/butter	5.00	12.00
Plate, 7¼", rolled edge, soup liner	5.00	12.50
Plate, 7½", salad	10.00	20.00
Plate, 8", hdld., mayonnaise liner	5.00	13.00
Plate, 8½", luncheon	12.00	30.00
Plate, 10½", dinner	45.00	110.00
Plate, 11", hdld., cheese/cracker liner	15.00	40.00
Plate, 12", salad liner, rolled edge	20.00	45.00
Plate, 14"	20.00	50.00

	Crystal	Blue
Plate, 16", torte	30.00	70.00
Plate, 18", punch underliner	35.00	80.00
Relish, 6", round, 2 pt.	10.00	22.50
Relish, 9½", 4 pt., oblong	25.00	60.00
Relish, 9½", oblong	22.00	55.00
Relish, 12¾", 5 pt., rnd.	35.00	80.00
Relish, 12¾", 7 pt., rnd.	35.00	80.00
Salt dip, 2½"	8.00	17.50
Salt & pepper, 3", metal tops	30.00	70.00
Salt & pepper, 5", metal tops	35.00	85.00
Saucer	3.00	7.50
Server, 5¾", ctr. hdld.	11.50	40.00
Server, 6½", ctr. hdld.	20.00	45.00
Stem, 3", 1 oz., cordial	60.00	135.00
Stem, 3½", 3½ oz., ftd., ball stem, wine	20.00	35.00
Stem, 3⅝", 2½ oz., wine (egg cup shape)	22.50	32.50
Stem, 4", 6 oz., ftd., ball stem, champagne	12.00	25.00
Stem, 4¼", ftd., sherbet	6.00	15.00
Stem, 4¾", 3 oz., ftd., ball stem, wine	17.50	45.00
Stem, 5¾", 8 oz., ftd., ball stem	14.00	35.00
Sugar	9.00	20.00
Syrup, metal cutoff top	65.00	145.00
Tray, 6¼", hand., mint, div.	12.00	28.00
Tray, 12¾", rnd.	20.00	45.00
Tumbler, 2¼", 2 oz., shot glass	22.00	50.00
Tumbler, 3½", 5 oz., flat	17.50	35.00
Tumbler, 5¼" 11½ oz., flat	17.50	35.00
Tumbler, 5½", 8½ oz., ftd.	20.00	40.00
Tumbler, 6½", 11 oz., ftd., ice tea	25.00	50.00
Vase, 5¾", ftd., ruffled edge	20.00	40.00
Vase, 7¼", ftd., flared edge, ball	25.00	50.00
Vase, 7½", ftd., flared edge, bulbous	30.00	60.00
Vase, 7¾", flared edge, epergne	30.00	65.00
Vase, 8", ftd., straight side	35.00	75.00
Vase, 9", ftd., ruffled top	45.00	150.00
Vase, 10", ftd.	45.00	125.00

53

CENTURY, Line #2630, Fostoria Glass Company

Colors: crystal

Prices for wines and footed iced teas continue to climb. This pattern was added to my *Collectible Glassware from the 40's, 50's, 60's...* because it actually falls within that time frame. However, on a whole, collectors expect this #2630 line to be in the Elegant book and so it will also continue here for a while.

Note that I have used some etched Fostoria patterns that are on the #2630 Century line in the pictures. Many of these patterns are beginning to attract some collectors, so if you run into a set priced reasonably, you might consider purchasing it for when there is more demand!

There are two sized dinner plates as is the case in most of Fostoria's patterns. The larger plate (usually listed as a service plate) is the harder to find. They were priced higher originally, and many people did without the larger plates.

There is some confusion between the candy and the covered preserve. The candy w/cover stands 7" tall, but the preserve w/cover only stands 6" tall. The taller candy is more in demand.

Be sure to avoid heavily scratched plates unless they are very reasonably priced and you intend to use them. Future sale of worn plates will be "iffy" at best!

	Crystal		Crystal
Ash tray, 2¾"	9.00	Pitcher, 7⅛", 48 oz.	95.00
Basket, 10¼" x 6½", wicker hdld.	65.00	Plate, 6", bread/butter	5.00
Bowl, 4½", hdld.	12.00	Plate, 7½", salad	7.50
Bowl, 5", fruit	13.00	Plate, 7½", crescent salad	32.50
Bowl, 6", cereal	22.00	Plate, 8", party, w/indent for cup	20.00
Bowl, 6¼", snack, ftd.	12.50	Plate, 8½", luncheon	12.50
Bowl, 7⅛", 3 ftd., triangular	14.00	Plate, 9½", small dinner	20.00
Bowl, 7¼", bonbon, 3 ftd.	15.00	Plate, 10", hdld., cake	20.00
Bowl, 8", flared	22.50	Plate, 10½", dinner	27.50
Bowl, 8½", salad	22.50	Plate, 14", torte	30.00
Bowl, 9", lily pond	25.00	Platter, 12"	47.50
Bowl, 9½", hdld., serving bowl	25.00	Preserve, w/cover, 6"	30.00
Bowl, 9½", oval, serving bowl	30.00	Relish, 7⅜", 2 part	15.00
Bowl, 10", oval, hdld.	30.00	Relish, 11⅛", 3 part	21.50
Bowl, 10½", salad	30.00	Salt and pepper, 2⅜", individual, pr.	12.50
Bowl, 10¾", ftd., flared	32.50	Salt and pepper, 3⅛", pr.	17.50
Bowl, 11, ftd., rolled edge	37.50	Salver, 12¼", ftd. (like cake stand)	47.50
Bowl, 11¼", lily pond	32.50	Saucer	3.50
Bowl, 12", flared	35.00	Stem, 3½ oz., cocktail, 4⅛"	18.00
Butter, w/cover, ¼ lb.	30.00	Stem, 3½ oz., wine, 4½"	27.50
Candy, w/cover, 7"	32.50	Stem, 4½ oz., oyster cocktail, 3¾"	19.00
Candlestick, 4½"	15.00	Stem, 5½ oz., sherbet, 4½"	11.00
Candlestick, 7", double	27.50	Stem, 10 oz., goblet, 5¾"	22.00
Candlestick, 7¾", triple	35.00	Sugar, 4", ftd.	8.00
Comport, 2¾", cheese	15.00	Sugar, individual	8.00
Comport, 4⅜"	17.50	Tid bit, 8⅛", 3 ftd., upturned edge	17.50
Cracker plate, 10¾"	30.00	Tid bit, 10¼", 2 tier, metal hdld.	25.00
Creamer, 4¼"	8.00	Tray, 4¼", for ind. salt/pepper	12.50
Creamer, individual	8.00	Tray, 7⅛", for ind. sug/cr	12.00
Cup, 6 oz., ftd.	15.00	Tray, 9⅛", hdld., utility	25.00
Ice Bucket	65.00	Tray, 9½", hdld., muffin	25.00
Mayonnaise, 3 pc.	27.50	Tray, 11½", center hdld.	27.50
Mayonnaise, 4 pc., div. w/2 ladles	32.50	Tumbler, 5 oz., ftd., juice, 4¾"	20.00
Mustard, w/spoon, cover	27.50	Tumbler, 12 oz., ftd., tea, 5⅞"	25.00
Oil, w/stopper, 5 oz.	40.00	Vase, 6", bud	17.50
Pickle, 8¾"	15.00	Vase, 7½", hdld.	65.00
Pitcher, 6⅛", 16 oz.	50.00	Vase, 8½", oval	62.00

CHANTILLY, Cambridge Glass Company, Late 1940's – Early 1950's

Colors: crystal

Although I received many letters regarding sterling silver based Cambridge items, the pieces shown with sterling bases in the fourth edition seem to be more of a novelty than they are collectible. I have had trouble selling them at the shows I display glass, including the National Cambridge convention. Frankly, every **owner** thinks sterling items should be worth more than their plain counterparts. **Buyers** do not tend to share this view! By the way, the little ruffled vase-like item with sterling base in the fourth edition was a cigarette urn.

The stemware line most often collected in Chantilly is #3625. As with other Cambridge patterns, there are several blanks and hundreds of items that can be collected in this pattern.

Most of the pieces found with etched Chantilly can also be found with etched Rose Point. There is a more complete listing for Rose Point in this book since there are so many collectors of that pattern. Rare Chantilly items pictured include the crescent salad plate, quarter pound butter, and pitcher in the top photograph.

	Crystal		Crystal
Bowl, 7", bonbon, 2 hdld., ftd.	16.00	Saucer	2.50
Bowl, 7", relish/pickle, 2 pt.	18.00	Stem, #3600, 1 oz., cordial	45.00
Bowl, 7", relish/pickle	20.00	Stem, #3600, 2½ oz., cocktail	24.00
Bowl, 9", celery/relish, 3 pt.	25.00	Stem #3600, 2½ oz., wine	30.00
Bowl, 10", 4 ftd., flared	35.00	Stem, #3600, 4½ oz., claret	35.00
Bowl, 11", tab hdld.	30.00	Stem, #3600, 4½ oz., low oyster cocktail	15.00
Bowl, 11½", tab hdld. ftd.	32.50	Stem, #3600, 7 oz., tall sherbet	17.50
Bowl, 12", celery/relish, 3 pt.	32.50	Stem, #3600, 7 oz., low sherbet	15.00
Bowl, 12", 4 ftd., flared	32.50	Stem, #3600, 10 oz., water	20.00
Bowl, 12", 4 ftd., oval	35.00	Stem, #3625, 1 oz., cordial	50.00
Bowl, 12", celery/relish, 5 pt.	35.00	Stem, #3625, 3 oz., cocktail	27.50
Butter, w/cover, round	125.00	Stem, #3625, 4½ oz., claret	35.00
Butter, ¼ lb.	200.00	Stem, #3625, 4½ oz., low oyster cocktail	16.00
Candlestick, 5"	17.50	Stem, #3625, 7 oz., low sherbet	16.00
Candlestick, 6", 2-lite, "fleur-de-lis"	32.50	Stem, #3625, 7 oz., tall sherbet	18.00
Candlestick, 6", 3-lite	37.50	Stem, #3625, 10 oz., water	25.00
Candy box, w/cover, ftd.	125.00	Stem, #3775, 1 oz., cordial	45.00
Candy box, w/cover, rnd.	55.00	Stem, #3775, 2½ oz., wine	30.00
Cocktail icer, 2 pc.	55.00	Stem, #3775, 3 oz., cocktail	25.00
Comport, 5½"	30.00	Stem, #3775, 4½ oz., claret	35.00
Comport, 5⅜", blown	37.50	Stem, #3775, 4½ oz., oyster cocktail	15.00
Creamer	14.50	Stem, #3775, 6 oz., low sherbet	15.00
Creamer, indiv., #3900, scalloped edge	12.50	Stem, #3775, 6 oz., tall sherbet	17.50
Cup	17.50	Stem, #3779, 1 oz., cordial	55.00
Decanter, ftd.	150.00	Stem, #3779, 2½ oz., wine	30.00
Decanter, ball	175.00	Stem, #3779, 3 oz., cocktail	25.00
Hat, small	150.00	Stem, #3779, 4½ oz., claret	35.00
Hat, large	200.00	Stem, #3779, 4½ oz., low oyster cocktail	15.00
Hurricane lamp, candlestick base	110.00	Stem, #3779, 6 oz., tall sherbet	17.50
Hurricane lamp, keyhole base w/prisms	150.00	Stem, #3779, 6 oz., low sherbet	15.00
Ice bucket, w/chrome handle	65.00	Stem, #3779, 9 oz., water	20.00
Marmalade & cover	55.00	Sugar	13.50
Mayonnaise, (sherbet type bowl w/ladle)	25.00	Sugar, indiv., #3900, scalloped edge	11.00
Mayonnaise, div. w/liner & 2 ladles	40.00	Tumbler, #3600, 5 oz., ftd., juice	15.00
Mayonnaise, w/liner & ladle	37.50	Tumbler, #3600, 12 oz., ftd., tea	20.00
Mustard & cover	45.00	Tumbler, #3625, 5 oz., ftd., juice	15.00
Oil, 6 oz., hdld., w/stopper	55.00	Tumbler, #3625, 10 oz., ftd., water	17.50
Pitcher, ball	120.00	Tumbler, #3625, 12 oz., ftd., tea	22.00
Pitcher, Doulton	250.00	Tumbler, #3775, 5 oz., ftd., juice	14.00
Pitcher, upright	175.00	Tumbler, #3775, 10 oz., ftd., water	15.00
Plate, crescent, salad	75.00	Tumbler, #3775, 12 oz., ftd., tea	20.00
Plate, 6½", bread/butter	6.50	Tumbler, #3779, 5 oz., ftd., juice	15.00
Plate, 8", salad	12.50	Tumbler, #3779, 12 oz., ftd., tea	20.00
Plate, 8", tab hdld., ftd., bonbon	15.00	Tumbler, 13 oz.	22.00
Plate, 10½", dinner	55.00	Vase, 5", globe	30.00
Plate, 12", 4 ftd., service	30.00	Vase, 6", high ftd., flower	22.00
Plate, 13", 4 ftd.	30.00	Vase, 8", high ftd., flower	30.00
Plate 13½", tab hdld., cake	32.50	Vase, 9", keyhole base	35.00
Plate, 14", torte	35.00	Vase, 10", bud	30.00
Salad dressing bottle	75.00	Vase, 11", ftd., flower	40.00
Salt & pepper, pr., flat	27.50	Vase, 11", ped. ftd., flower	45.00
Salt & pepper, footed	30.00	Vase, 12", keyhole base	50.00
Salt & pepper, handled	30.00	Vase, 13", ftd., flower	65.00

Note: See Pages 210-211 for stem identification.

CHARTER OAK, #3362 A.H. Heisey Co., 1926 – 1935

Colors: crystal, Flamingo, Moongleam, Hawthorne, Marigold

Charter Oak is a new Heisey entry for this book. Although I have only shown Flamingo, there are several other colors that can be collected in sets. Some collectors use Yeoman cup and saucers to go with this set since there were no Charter Oak cup and saucers made.

The #4262 Charter Oak lamp was produced from 1928-1931. This lamp looks like a blown comport with an acorn in the stem. It has a diamond optic font and was filled with water to magnify the design and to stabilize the lamp.

The #130 one lite candleholder base is an oak leaf with stem curled up and acorn for the candle cup! Maybe I can show you one next time!

	Crystal	Flamingo	Moongleam	Hawthorne	Marigold
Bowl, 11" floral #116 (oak leaf)	30.00	45.00	47.50	75.00	
Bowl, finger #3362	10.00	17.50	20.00		
Candleholder, 1-lite, #130 "Acorn"	100.00	125.00	135.00		
Candlestick, 3",#116 (oak leaf)	25.00	30.00	35.00	125.00	
Candlestick, 5", 3-lite, #129 "Tricorn"		65.00	85.00	125.00	150.00
Comport, 6" low ft., #3362	45.00	50.00	55.00	70.00	100.00
Comport, 7" ftd., #3362	50.00	55.00	60.00	75.00	150.00
Lamp #4262 (blown comport/water filled to magnify design & stabilize lamp)	400.00	700.00	850.00		
Pitcher, flat #3362		85.00	95.00		
Plate, 6" salad #1246 (Acorn & Leaves)	5.00	10.00	12.50	20.00	
Plate, 7" luncheon/salad #1246 (Acorn & Leaves)	8.00	12.00	17.50	22.50	
Plate, 8" luncheon #1246 (Acorn & Leaves)	10.00	15.00	20.00	25.00	
Plate, 10½" dinner #1246 (Acorn & Leaves)	27.50	35.00	45.00	65.00	
Stem, 3 oz. cocktail #3362	10.00	15.00	20.00	45.00	40.00
Stem, 3½ oz. low ft., oyster cocktail #3362	8.00	10.00	15.00	40.00	35.00
Stem, 4½ oz parfait #3362	15.00	25.00	30.00	60.00	50.00
Stem, 6 oz. saucer champagne #3362	10.00	15.00	20.00	50.00	40.00
Stem, 6 oz. sherbet, low ft. #3362	10.00	15.00	20.00	50.00	40.00
Stem, 8 oz. goblet, high ft. #3362	15.00	30.00	35.00	95.00	60.00
Stem, 8 oz. luncheon goblet, low ft. #3362	15.00	30.00	35.00	95.00	60.00
Tumbler, 10 oz. flat #3362	10.00	15.00	20.00	35.00	30.00
Tumbler, 12 oz. flat #3362	12.50	17.50	22.50	40.00	35.00

59

CHEROKEE ROSE, Tiffin Glass Company, 1940's – 1950's

Colors: crystal

At this point in writing I can not remember whether I used a black and white or a colored photograph for this pattern. I work with a black and white photograph when I write and color has never been a problem in the past. However, now it matters in the bottom photograph with a gold trimmed goblet on the left which would not look gold trimmed if I used the black and white! Pattern has been difficult to see on many of the etched patterns in this book where I did not have room for a pattern shot, so we tried to pick up pattern better by using some black and white photos for crystal patterns. Let me know what you think about this idea.

I find mostly stemware in this pattern. What I usually find is #17399 or the tear drop style which is shown on most of the stemware in the picture. The other stem #17403 is represented by the cordial on the far right in the top photograph. Both stemware lines sell for the same price.

There are still no reports of cups and saucers; so I doubt that they do exist at this point. It's a shame that a pattern which was made to compete with Cambridge's Rose Point (that had three styles of cups and saucers) has none! Cherokee Rose is often asked for at shows I attend, so people are looking for it.

	Crystal		Crystal
Bowl, 5", finger.	17.50	Stem, 2 oz., sherry	30.00
Bowl, 6", fruit or nut	17.50	Stem, 3½ oz., cocktail	20.00
Bowl, 7", salad	27.50	Stem, 3½ oz., wine	35.00
Bowl, 10", deep salad	40.00	Stem, 4 oz., claret	40.00
Bowl, 10½", celery, oblong	30.00	Stem, 4½ oz., parfait	40.00
Bowl, 12", crimped	40.00	Stem, 5½ oz., sherbet/champagne	20.00
Bowl, 12½" centerpiece, flared	40.00	Stem, 9 oz., water	25.00
Bowl, 13", centerpiece	45.00	Sugar	20.00
Cake plate, 12½", center hdld.	35.00	Table bell	50.00
Candlesticks, pr., double branch	75.00	Tumbler, 4½ oz., oyster cocktail	20.00
Comport, 6"	30.00	Tumbler, 5 oz., ftd., juice	20.00
Creamer	20.00	Tumbler, 8 oz., ftd., water	22.50
Mayonnaise, liner and ladle	45.00	Tumbler, 10½ oz., ftd., ice tea	30.00
Pitcher	295.00	Vase, 6", bud	25.00
Plate, 6", sherbet	5.00	Vase, 8", bud	35.00
Plate, 8", luncheon	12.00	Vase, 8½", tear drop	50.00
Plate, 13½", turned-up edge, lily	35.00	Vase, 9¼", tub	60.00
Plate, 14", sandwich	30.00	Vase, 10", bud	35.00
Relish, 6½", 3 pt.	25.00	Vase, 11", bud	40.00
Relish, 12½", 3 pt.	35.00	Vase, 11", urn	75.00
Stem, 1 oz., cordial	55.00	Vase, 12", flared	75.00

CHINTZ, (Plate Etching #338), Fostoria Glass Company

Colors: crystal

Fostoria's Chintz was added to my *Collectible Glassware from the 40's, 50's, 60's...* because it fit the parameters of that book. I have been told by several dealers that Fostoria Chintz sells as well as Rose Point, but I have not found enough of it in my area to be sure. Stemware abounds as it does for many patterns of this time period. Evidently, people purchased stemware whether they purchased the serving pieces or not.

That oval divided bowl on the right in the top photograph is the divided sauce boat. Note that many Chintz pieces are found on the #2496 blank (known as Baroque).

Harder to find pieces include the bell, salad dressing bottle, and the Sani-cut syrup pitcher; vases are also few and far between!

	Crystal
Bell, dinner	100.00
Bowl, #869, 4½", finger	40.00
Bowl, #2496, 4⅝", tri-cornered	20.00
Bowl, #2496, cream soup	37.50
Bowl, #2496, 5", fruit	25.00
Bowl, #2496, 5", hdld.	22.50
Bowl, #2496, 7⅝", bonbon	30.00
Bowl, #2496, 8½", hdld.	47.50
Bowl, #2496, 9½", vegetable	65.00
Bowl, #2484, 10", hdld.	55.00
Bowl, #2496, 10½" hdld.	60.00
Bowl, #2496, 11½", flared	55.00
Bowl, #6023, ftd	35.00
Candlestick, #2496, 3½", double	27.50
Candlestick, #2496, 4"	15.00
Candlestick, #2496, 5½"	27.50
Candlestick, #2496, 6", triple	39.50
Candlestick, #6023, double	35.00
Candy, w/cover, #2496, 3 part	100.00
Celery, #2496, 11"	32.50
Comport, #2496, 3¼", cheese	22.50
Comport, #2496, 4¾"	30.00
Comport, #2496, 5½"	35.00
Cracker, #2496, 11", plate	37.50
Creamer, #2496, 3¾", ftd.	16.00
Creamer, #2496½, individual	20.00
Cup, #2496, ftd.	20.00
Ice bucket, #2496	125.00
Jelly, w/cover, #2496, 7½"	80.00
Mayonnaise, #2496½, 3 piece	55.00
Oil, w/stopper, #2496, 3½ oz.	95.00
Pickle, #2496, 8"	30.00
Pitcher, #5000, 48 oz., ftd.	325.00
Plate, #2496, 6", bread/butter	9.00
Plate, #2496, 7½", salad	14.00
Plate, #2496, 8½", luncheon	20.00

	Crystal
Plate, #2496, 9½", dinner	45.00
Plate, #2496, 10", hdld., cake	40.00
Plate, #2496, 11", cracker	40.00
Plate, #2496, 14", upturned edge	47.50
Plate, #2496, 16", torte, plain edge	100.00
Platter, #2496, 12"	85.00
Relish, #2496, 6", 2 part, square	30.00
Relish, #2496, 10" x 7½", 3 part	37.50
Relish, #2419, 5 part	37.50
Salad dressing bottle, #2083, 6½"	275.00
Salt and pepper, #2496, 2¾", flat, pr.	85.00
Sauce boat, #2496, oval	67.50
Sauce boat, #2496, oval, divided	65.00
Sauce boat liner, #2496, oval	27.50
Saucer, #2496	5.00
Stem, #6026, 1 oz., cordial, 3⅞"	45.00
Stem, #6026, 4 oz., cocktail, 5"	25.00
Stem, #6026, 4 oz., oyster cocktail, 3⅝"	25.00
Stem, #6026, 4½ oz., claret-wine, 5⅜"	37.50
Stem, #6026, 6 oz., low sherbet, 4⅜"	20.00
Stem, #6026, 6 oz., saucer champagne, 5½"	20.00
Stem, #6026, 9 oz., water goblet, 7⅝"	30.00
Sugar, #2496, 3½", ftd.	15.00
Sugar, #2496½, individual	20.00
Syrup, #2586, sani-cut	300.00
Tid bit, #2496, 8¼", 3 ftd., upturned edge.	25.00
Tray, #2496½, 6½", for ind. sugar/creamer.	20.00
Tray, #2375, 11", center hdld.	37.50
Tumbler, #6026, 5 oz., juice, ftd.	25.00
Tumbler, #6026, 9 oz., water or low goblet	25.00
Tumbler, #6026, 13 oz., tea, ftd.	30.00
Vase, #4108, 5"	75.00
Vase, #4143, 6", ftd.	95.00
Vase, #4143, 7½", ftd.	125.00
Vase, #4128, 5"	75.00

CHINTZ, #1401 (Empress Blank) and CHINTZ #3389 (Duquesne Blank) A.H. Heisey Co., 1931 – 1938

Colors: crystal, "Sahara" yellow, "Moongleam" green, "Flamingo" pink, and "Alexandrite" orchid

I found a crystal ice bucket in this pattern to add to the photograph, but it disappeared among the Sahara pieces and I had to scrap the photo! Finding additional Chintz pieces to photograph has proved difficult. Pieces with the encircled flowers are known as "formal" Chintz. Don't confuse this pattern with Fostoria's Chintz, and learn to specify the company name when you ask for a pattern named Chintz. It was a popular name used by several companies!

	Crystal	Sahara
Bowl, finger, #4107	8.00	15.00
Bowl, 5½", ftd., preserve, hdld	15.00	27.00
Bowl, 6", ftd., mint	18.00	30.00
Bowl, 6", ftd., 2 hdld., jelly	15.00	30.00
Bowl, 7", triplex relish	16.00	35.00
Bowl, 7½", Nasturtium	16.00	30.00
Bowl, 8½", ftd., 2 hdld., floral	32.00	65.00
Bowl, 11", dolp. ft., floral	40.00	100.00
Bowl, 13", 2 pt., pickle & olive	15.00	35.00
Comport, 7", oval	40.00	85.00
Creamer, 3 dolp. ft.	20.00	45.00
Creamer, individual	12.00	25.00
Grapefruit, ftd., #3389, Duquesne	30.00	60.00
Ice bucket, ftd.	75.00	125.00
Mayonnaise, 5½", dolp. ft.	35.00	65.00
Oil, 4 oz.	60.00	125.00
Pitcher, 3 pint, dolp. ft.	115.00	220.00
Plate, 6", square, bread	6.00	15.00
Plate, 7", square, salad	8.00	18.00
Plate, 8", square, luncheon	10.00	22.00
Plate, 10½", square, dinner	40.00	85.00
Plate, 12", two hdld.,	25.00	45.00
Plate, 13", hors d' oeuvre, two hdld.	20.00	37.50
Platter, 14", oval	30.00	65.00
Stem, #3389, Duquesne, 1 oz., cordial	110.00	225.00
Stem, #3389, 2½ oz., wine	17.50	45.00
Stem, #3389, 3 oz., cocktail	15.00	35.00
Stem, #3389, 4 oz., claret	20.00	45.00
Stem, #3389, 4 oz., oyster cocktail	10.00	20.00
Stem, #3389, 5 oz., parfait	14.00	35.00
Stem, #3389, 5 oz., saucer champagne	11.00	22.50
Stem, #3389, 5 oz., sherbet	8.00	17.50
Stem, #3389, 9 oz., water	15.00	30.00
Sugar, 3 dolp. ft.	20.00	42.50
Sugar, individual	12.00	28.00
Tray, 10", celery	14.00	27.50
Tray, 12", sq., ctr. hdld., sandwich	35.00	65.00
Tray, 13", celery	18.00	26.00
Tumbler, #3389, 5 oz., ftd., juice	11.00	22.00
Tumbler, #3389, 8 oz., soda	12.00	24.00
Tumbler, #3389, 10 oz., ftd., water	13.00	25.00
Tumbler, #3389, 12 oz., iced tea	14.00	30.00
Vase, 9", dolp. ft.	85.00	175.00

65

CLEO, Cambridge Glass Company, Introduced 1930

Colors: amber, blue, crystal, green, pink, yellow

It amazes me how many different pieces were made in Cleo. However, it seems that all the unusual items always turn up in amber or crystal instead of blue, pink, or green. There are avid Cleo collectors searching for pink, green, or blue, but fewer for amber colored pieces.

The crystal syrup pitcher shown on the right on the bottom of page 67 would be a "find" in a color. The footed blue Cleo mayonnaise with an Aero Optic design (shown on the right in the top photograph) is unusual as is an amber sweet pea vase found at the bottom of page 68. Notice the little 1½" salt, 2½" individual almond, and the wafer tray in pink on the top of page 69. I wonder if they have ever been found in blue! Let me know your new discoveries.

Item	Blue	Pink/Green/Yellow/Amber
Almond, 2½", individual		65.00
Basket, 7", 2 hdld. (upturned sides) DECAGON	35.00	22.00
Basket, 11", 2 hdld. (upturned sides) DECAGON	50.00	30.00
Bouillon cup, w/saucer, 2 hdld., DECAGON	40.00	27.50
Bowl, 2 pt., relish	40.00	22.00
Bowl, 5½", fruit	25.00	15.00
Bowl, 5½" 2 hdld., bonbon, DECAGON	30.00	20.00
Bowl, 6", 4 ft., comport	50.00	35.00
Bowl, 6", cereal, DECAGON	32.00	20.00
Bowl, 6½", 2 hdld., bonbon DECAGON	35.00	22.00
Bowl, 6½", cranberry	37.50	25.00
Bowl, 7½", tab hdld., soup	40.00	30.00
Bowl, 8", miniature console		125.00
Bowl, 8½"	60.00	40.00
Bowl, 8½" 2 hdld., DECAGON	65.00	40.00
Bowl, 9", covered vegetable		125.00
Bowl, 9½", oval veg., DECAGON	75.00	40.00
Bowl, 9", pickle, DECAGON	60.00	25.00
Bowl, 10", 2 hdld., DECAGON	65.00	35.00
Bowl, 11", oval	75.00	35.00
Bowl, 11½", oval	75.00	35.00
Bowl, 12", console	65.00	35.00
Bowl, cream soup w/saucer, 2 hdld., DECAGON	50.00	30.00
Bowl, finger w/liner, #3077	40.00	25.00
Bowl, finger w/liner, #3115	40.00	25.00
Candlestick, 1-lite, 2 styles	35.00	22.00
Candlestick, 2-lite	75.00	35.00
Candy box		75.00
Candy & cover, tall		145.00
Comport, 7", tall, #3115	75.00	40.00
Creamer, DECAGON	27.50	17.50
Creamer, ewer style, 6"		75.00
Creamer, ftd.	30.00	20.00
Cup, DECAGON	25.00	15.00
Decanter, w/stopper		225.00
Gravy boat, w/liner plate, DECAGON	250.00	150.00
Ice pail	95.00	60.00
Ice tub	85.00	45.00
Mayonnaise, w/liner and ladle, DECAGON	95.00	45.00
Mayonnaise, ftd.	45.00	30.00
Oil, 6 oz., w/stopper, DECAGON		125.00
Pitcher, 3½ pt., #38		175.00
Pitcher, w/cover, 22 oz.		150.00
Pitcher, w/cover, 60 oz., #804		225.00
Pitcher, w/cover, 62 oz., #955		225.00
Pitcher, w/cover, 63 oz., #3077		250.00
Pitcher, w/cover, 68 oz., #937		275.00
Plate, 7"	15.00	12.00
Plate, 7", 2 hdld., DECAGON	20.00	14.00
Plate, 9½", dinner, DECAGON	85.00	60.00
Plate, 11", 2 hdld., DECAGON	110.00	30.00
Platter, 12"	150.00	100.00
Platter, 15"	275.00	175.00
Platter, w/cover, oval (toast)		300.00
Platter, asparagus, indented, w/sauce & spoon		300.00
Salt dip, 1½"		65.00
Saucer, DECAGON	5.00	3.00
Server, 12", ctr. hand.	65.00	35.00
Stem, #3077, 1 oz., cordial	150.00	125.00
Stem, #3077, 2½ oz., cocktail	42.50	27.50
Stem, #3077, 3½ oz., wine	85.00	60.00
Stem, #3077, 6 oz., low sherbet	25.00	15.00
Stem, #3077, 6 oz., tall sherbet	32.50	17.50
Stem, #3115, 9 oz.		30.00
Stem, #3115, 3½ oz., cocktail		25.00
Stem, #3115, 6 oz., fruit		15.00
Stem, #3115, 6 oz., low sherbet		13.00
Stem, #3115, 6 oz., tall sherbet		15.00
Stem, #3115, 9 oz.		25.00
Sugar cube tray		145.00
Sugar, DECAGON	25.00	17.50
Sugar, ftd.	30.00	20.00
Sugar sifter, ftd., 6¾"		250.00
Syrup pitcher, drip cut		150.00
Syrup pitcher, glass lid		165.00
Toast & cover, round		350.00
Tobacco humidor		325.00

CLEO, Cambridge Glass Company, Introduced 1930

	Blue	Pink/Green/Yellow/Amber		Blue	Pink/Green/Yellow/Amber
Tray, 12", handled serving...........		150.00	Tumbler, #3115, 5 oz., ftd.		25.00
Tray, 12", oval service DECAGON	150.00	100.00	Tumbler, #3115, 8 oz., ftd.		25.00
Tray, creamer & sugar, oval		50.00	Tumbler, #3115, 10 oz., ftd.		37.50
Tumbler, #3077, 2½ oz., ftd.........	85.00	55.00	Tumbler, #3115, 12 oz., ftd.		35.00
Tumbler, #3077, 5 oz., ftd.	40.00	20.00	Tumbler, 12 oz., flat....................		35.00
Tumbler, #3077, 8 oz., ftd.	40.00	25.00	Vase, 5½".....................................		65.00
Tumbler, #3077, 10 oz., ftd.	45.00	27.50	Vase, 9½".....................................		100.00
Tumbler, #3022, 12 oz., ftd.	65.00	35.00	Vase, 11"......................................		125.00
Tumbler, #3115, 2½ oz., ftd.........		45.00	Wafer tray		195.00

COLONY, Line #2412, Fostoria Glass Company, 1920's – 1970's

Colors: crystal; some yellow, blue, green, white amber, red in 1980's

Colony evolved from an earlier Fostoria pattern called Queen Ann, represented by the amber flat bowl shown in the middle of the bottom photograph. The candlesticks and oval bowl shown in the rear were made in the early 1980's.

Cream soups, 48 oz., ice lipped, pitcher, flat teas, and the 12" vase all remain scarce. Dinner plates without scratched centers also plague collectors who want mint condition pieces. Otherwise this pattern was very durable and more of it seems to be surfacing of late, an encouraging sign for collectors.

The red vases, creamer, and sugars being seen were a product of Viking made for Fostoria in the early 1980's. Do not be too surprised to see these again as Dalzell Viking is currently making red for Lancaster Colony who now owns the Fostoria name.

	Crystal
Ash tray, 3", round	7.00
Ash tray, 3½"	10.00
Ash tray, 4½", round	12.50
Ash tray, 6", round	17.50
Bowl, 2¾" ftd., almond	15.00
Bowl, 4½", rnd.	7.00
Bowl, 4¾", finger	12.00
Bowl, 4¾", hdld.	8.00
Bowl, 5", bonbon	9.00
Bowl, 5", cream soup	40.00
Bowl, 5", hdld.	7.50
Bowl, 5½", sq.	10.00
Bowl, 5¾", high ft.	15.00
Bowl, 5", rnd.	12.00
Bowl, 6", rose	25.00
Bowl, 7", bonbon, 3 ftd.	10.00
Bowl, 7", olive, oblong	10.00
Bowl, 7¾", salad	22.50
Bowl, 8", cupped	32.50
Bowl, 8", hdld.	32.50
Bowl, 9", rolled console	32.50
Bowl, 9½", pickle	12.50
Bowl, 9¾", salad	35.00
Bowl, 10", fruit	32.50
Bowl, 10½", low ft.	65.00
Bowl, 10½", high ft.	85.00
Bowl, 10½", oval	30.00
Bowl, 10½", oval, 2 part	32.50
Bowl, 11", oval, ftd.	37.50
Bowl, 11", flared	35.00
Bowl, 11½", celery	30.00
Bowl, 13", console	35.00
Bowl, 13¼", punch, ftd.	300.00
Bowl, 14", fruit	40.00
Butter dish, ¼ lb.	32.50
Candlestick, 3½"	11.00
Candlestick, 6½", double	22.50
Candlestick, 7"	20.00
Candlestick, 7½", w/8 prisms	55.00
Candlestick, 9"	30.00
Candlestick, 9¾", w/prisms	75.00
Candlestick, 14½", w/10 prisms	125.00
Candy w/cover, 6½"	35.00
Candy, w/cover, ftd., ½ lb.	60.00
Cheese & cracker	50.00
Cigarette box	35.00
Comport, 4"	15.00
Comport, cover, 6½"	35.00
Creamer, 3¼" indiv.	6.50
Creamer, 3¾"	6.00
Cup, 6 oz., ftd.	7.50
Cup, punch	12.00
Ice bucket	60.00
Ice bucket, plain edge	95.00
Lamp, electric	125.00
Mayonnaise, 3 pc.	35.00
Oil w/stopper, 4½ oz.	37.50
Pitcher, 16 oz., milk	65.00
Pitcher, 48 oz., ice lip	185.00
Pitcher, 2 qt., ice lip	95.00
Plate, ctr. hdld., sandwich	27.50
Plate, 6", bread & butter	4.00
Plate, 6½", lemon, hdld.	12.00
Plate, 7", salad	8.00
Plate, 8", luncheon	10.00
Plate, 9", dinner	22.50
Plate, 10", hdld., cake	22.00
Plate, 12", ftd., salver	55.00
Plate, 13", torte	27.50
Plate, 15", torte	45.00
Plate, 18", torte	65.00
Platter, 12"	45.00
Relish, 10½", hdld., 3 part	20.00
Salt, 2½" indiv.	12.00
Salt & pepper, pr., 3⅝"	12.50
Saucer	2.00
Stem, 3⅜", 4 oz., oyster cocktail	11.00
Stem, 3⅝", 5 oz., sherbet	8.00
Stem, 4", 3½ oz., cocktail	11.00
Stem, 4¼", 3¼ oz., wine	22.00
Stem, 5¼", 9 oz., goblet	14.00
Sugar, 2¾", indiv.	6.00
Sugar, 3½"	5.00
Tray for indiv. sugar/cream	10.00
Tumbler, 3⅝", 5 oz., juice	16.00
Tumbler, 3⅞", 9 oz., water	14.00
Tumbler, 4⅞", 12 oz., tea	22.50
Tumbler, 4½", 5 oz., ftd.	12.50
Tumbler, 5¾", 12 oz., ftd.	16.00
Vase, 6", bud, flared	14.00
Vase, 7", cupped	35.00
Vase, 7½", flared	40.00
Vase, 9", cornucopia	55.00
Vase, 12", straight	150.00

CRYSTOLITE, Blank #1503, A.H. Heisey & Co.

Colors: crystal, Zircon/Limelight, Sahara and rare in amber

The 11", footed cake salver (cake stand) has once again disappeared from view. I have always wondered why glass "finds" run in cycles. Years go by without a piece being seen, and suddenly, there are a half dozen that appear. A year or so later and you do not see the piece again. In the twenty-three years I have been in this glass business, I have seen it happen over and over again!

The swan handled pitcher, 6" basket, rye bottle, and iced tea tumblers remain elusive, but other items are also beginning to disappear. Cocktail shakers, syrup pitchers, and cordials are part of this disappearing group. Don't hesitate on buying any of these pieces!

	Crystal
Ash tray, 3½", square	4.00
Ash tray, 4½", square	4.50
Ash tray, 5", w/book match holder	25.00
Ash tray (coaster), 4", rnd.	6.00
Basket, 6", hdld.	350.00
Bonbon, 7", shell	17.00
Bonbon, 7½", 2 hdld.	15.00
Bottle, 1 qt., rye, #107 stopper	250.00
Bottle, 4 oz., bitters, w/short tube	175.00
Bottle, 4 oz., cologne w/#108 stopper	65.00
w/drip stop	135.00
Bottle, syrup w/drip & cut top	85.00
Bowl, 7½ quart, punch	120.00
Bowl, 2", indiv. swan nut (or ash tray)	18.00
Bowl, 3", indiv. nut, hdld.	15.00
Bowl, 4½", dessert (or nappy)	8.00
Bowl, 5", preserve	12.00
Bowl, 5", 1000 island dressing, ruffled top	18.00
Bowl, 5½", dessert	12.00
Bowl, 6", oval jelly, 4 ft.	16.00
Bowl, 6", preserve, 2 hdld.	13.00
Bowl, 7", shell praline	35.00
Bowl, 8", dessert (sauce)	30.00
Bowl, 8", 2 pt. conserve, hdld.	16.00
Bowl, 9", leaf pickle	20.00
Bowl, 10", salad, rnd.	47.50
Bowl, 11", w/attached mayonnaise (chip 'n dip)	150.00
Bowl, 12", gardenia, shallow	30.00
Bowl, 13", oval floral, deep	30.00
Candle block, 1-lite, sq.	15.00
Candle block, 1-lite, swirl	15.00
Candlestick, 1-lite, ftd.	15.00
Candlestick, 1-lite, w/#4233, 5", vase	25.00
Candlestick, 2-lite	25.00
Candlestick, 2-lite, bobeche & 10 "D" prisms	50.00
Candlestick sans vase, 3-lite	20.00
Candlestick w/#4233, 5", vase, 3-lite	45.00
Candy, 6½", swan	35.00
Candy box, w/cover, 5½"	50.00
Candy box, w/cover, 7"	55.00
Cheese, 5½", ftd.	20.00
Cigarette box, w/cover, 4"	17.00
Cigarette box, w/cover, 4½"	20.00
Cigarette holder, ftd.	17.50
Cigarette holder, oval	17.50
Cigarette holder, rnd.	17.50
Cigarette lighter	30.00
Coaster, 4"	6.00
Cocktail shaker, 1 qt. w/#1 strainer; #86 stopper	250.00
Comport, 5", fed., deep, #5003, blown rare	275.00
Creamer, indiv.	17.00
Cup	20.00
Cup, punch or custard	7.00
Hurricane block, 1-lite, sq.	17.50
Hurricane block, w/#4061, 10" plain globe, 1-lite, sq.	90.00

	Crystal
Ice tub, w/silver plate handle	75.00
Jam jar, w/cover	50.00
Ladle, glass, punch	25.00
Ladle, plastic	7.50
Mayonnaise, 5½", shell, 3 ft.	32.00
Mayonnaise, 6", oval, hdld.	26.00
Mayonnaise ladle	9.00
Mustard & cover	37.00
Oil bottle, 3 oz.	40.00
Oil bottle, w/stopper, 2 oz.	30.00
Oval creamer, sugar, w/tray, set	47.50
Pitcher, ½ gallon, ice, blown	100.00
Pitcher, 2 quart swan, ice lip	800.00
Plate, 7", salad	9.00
Plate, 7", shell	24.00
Plate, 7", underliner for 1000 island dressing bowl	10.00
Plate, 7½", coupe	20.00
Plate, 8", oval, mayonnaise liner	14.00
Plate, 8½", salad	15.00
Plate, 10½", dinner	60.00
Plate, 11", ftd., cake salver	250.00
Plate, 11", torte	24.00
Plate, 12", sand.	35.00
Plate, 14", sand.	40.00
Plate, 14", torte	35.00
Plate, 20", buffet or punch liner	90.00
Puff box, w/cover, 4¾"	50.00
Salad dressing set, 3 pc.	38.00
Salt & pepper, pr.	30.00
Saucer	5.00
Stem, 1 oz., cordial, wide optic, blown, #5003	110.00
Stem, 3½ oz., cocktail, w.o., blown, #5003	20.00
Stem, 3½ oz., claret, w.o., blown, #5003	25.00
Stem, 3½ oz., oyster cocktail, w.o. blown, #5003	18.00
Stem, 6 oz., sherbet/saucer champagne, #5003	14.00
Stem, 10 oz., water, #1503, pressed	480.00
Stem, 10 oz., w.o., blown, #5003	24.00
Sugar, indiv.	15.00
Syrup pitcher, drip cut	100.00
Tray, 5½", oval, liner indiv. creamer/sugar set	40.00
Tray, 9", 4 pt., leaf relish	25.00
Tray, 10", 5 pt., rnd. relish	35.00
Tray, 12", 3 pt., relish	25.00
Tray, 12", rect., celery	35.00
Tray, 12", rect., celery/olive	35.00
Tumbler, 5 oz., ftd., juice, w.o., blown, #5003	24.00
Tumbler, 8 oz., pressed, #5003	60.00
Tumbler, 10 oz., pressed	70.00
Tumbler, 10 oz., iced tea, w.o., blown, #5003	30.00
Tumbler, 12 oz., ftd., iced tea, w.o., blown #5003	24.00
Urn, 7", flower	75.00
Vase, 3", short stem	20.00
Vase, 6", ftd.	22.50
Vase, 12"	225.00

"DANCING GIRL," Sunrise Medallion #758, Morgantown Glass Works, Late 1920's – Early 1930's

Colors: pink, green, blue, crystal

The Morgantown Collectors of America have been at pains to broadcast the actual name of this pattern, Sunrise Medallion (etching #758). In the next book I will list this pattern under its proper name. It takes a while for collectors to catch up to changes!

The green sugar bowl is shown for the first time; find me a creamer please!

The crystal cordial I saw had a twisted stem which is stemware line #7642½. I just purchased six blue cordials at the Houston Depression Glass show, but they are from the plain stemware line #7630. You will have to wait until the next book to see one of these. At the price I paid to get one for my collection, the other five will have new homes in the near future!

Measurements in most glassware catalogues were in ounces only. The twisted stem items are slightly taller than their plain stem varieties. Measurements given below are from the #7630 line. I will endeavor to list measurements for both stemware lines in the next book.

The Morgantown Collectors of America's address is listed in the back of the book. If you would like more information about Morgantown Glass, please contact them!

	Crystal	Blue	Pink/ Green
Bowl, finger, ftd.		60.00	
Creamer		250.00	175.00
Cup	35.00	85.00	75.00
Parfait, 5 oz.	55.00	95.00	75.00
Pitcher		400.00	
Plate, 5⅞", sherbet	6.00	12.00	10.00
Plate, 7½", salad	10.00	22.00	17.50
Saucer	10.00	20.00	15.00
Stem, 1½ oz., cordial	90.00	250.00	
Stem, 2½ oz., wine	35.00	65.00	55.00
Stem, 2½", 3½ oz., oyster cocktail	22.50	40.00	35.00
Stem, 4¾", 7 oz., sherbet or champagne	25.00	40.00	30.00
Stem, 6⅛", cocktail	30.00	60.00	40.00
Stem, 7¾", 9 oz., water	35.00	65.00	45.00
Sugar		250.00	175.00
Tumbler, 2½ oz., ftd.	25.00		
Tumbler, 4¼", 5 oz., ftd.	15.00	55.00	35.00
Tumbler, 4¾", 9 oz., ftd.	20.00	60.00	40.00
Tumbler, 5½", 11 oz., ftd.	25.00	75.00	45.00
Vase, 10", slender, bud	45.00		90.00
Vase, 10", bulbous bottom			125.00

DECAGON, Cambridge Glass Company, 1930's – 1940's

Colors: green, pink, red, cobalt blue, amber, Moonlight blue, black

The Decagon blank is more noted for its major etchings than for itself. Cleo, Rosalie, and Imperial Hunt Scene are better known than this Decagon blank on which they are etched! Some of the stems pictured are etched, but Decagon pattern itself actually has no etching at all. The Royal Blue (cobalt) and Moonlight blue are the most collected colors although there are devotees of green. One couple has been after me for years to find green dinner plates. So far, all I have found have had an etching! I still need one blue relish insert to replace the one broken during photography years ago if anybody comes across one!

	Pastel Colors	Red Blue		Pastel Colors	Red Blue
Basket, 7", 2 hdld. (upturned sides)	12.00	20.00	Mayonnaise, w/liner & ladle	18.00	30.00
Bowl, bouillon, w/liner	7.50	12.50	Oil, 6 oz., tall, w/hdld. & stopper	45.00	75.00
Bowl, cream soup, w/liner	10.00	22.00	Plate, 6¼", bread/butter	3.00	5.00
Bowl, 2½", indiv., almond	17.50	30.00	Plate, 7", 2 hdld.	9.00	15.00
Bowl, 3¾", flat rim, cranberry	12.00	17.50	Plate, 7½"	4.00	10.00
Bowl, 3½" belled, cranberry	12.00	17.50	Plate, 8½", salad	6.00	10.00
Bowl, 5½", 2 hdld., bonbon	10.00	17.00	Plate, 9½", dinner	20.00	30.00
Bowl, 5½", belled, fruit	5.50	10.00	Plate, 10", grill	8.00	14.00
Bowl, 5¾", flat rim, fruit	6.00	11.00	Plate, 10", service	20.00	25.00
Bowl, 6", belled, cereal	10.00	15.00	Plate, 12½", service	9.00	17.50
Bowl, 6", flat rim, cereal	10.00	15.00	Relish, 6 inserts	70.00	100.00
Bowl, 6", ftd., almond	20.00	35.00	Salt dip, 1½", ftd.	11.00	20.00
Bowl, 6¼", 2 hdld., bonbon	10.00	17.00	Sauce boat & plate	45.00	75.00
Bowl, 8½", flat rim, soup "plate"	12.50	25.00	Saucer	1.00	2.50
Bowl, 9", rnd., veg.	14.00	24.00	Server, center hdld.	12.00	20.00
Bowl, 9", 2 pt., relish	9.00	15.00	Stem, 1 oz., cordial	40.00	60.00
Bowl, 9½", oval, veg.	12.00	27.50	Stem, 3½ oz., cocktail	12.00	20.00
Bowl, 10", berry	12.00	20.00	Stem, 6 oz., low sherbet	9.00	15.00
Bowl, 10½", oval, veg.	16.00	27.50	Stem, 6 oz., high sherbet	10.00	20.00
Bowl, 11", rnd. veg.	17.00	30.00	Stem, 9 oz., water	15.00	30.00
Bowl, 11", 2 pt., relish	10.00	17.50	Sugar, lightning bolt handles	7.00	12.00
Comport, 5¾"	12.50	20.00	Sugar, ftd.	9.00	20.00
Comport, 6½", low ft.	15.00	25.00	Sugar, scalloped edge	9.00	20.00
Comport, 7", tall	20.00	30.00	Sugar, tall, lg. ft.	8.00	18.00
Creamer, ftd.	9.00	20.00	Tray, 8", 2 hdld., flat pickle	10.00	17.00
Creamer, scalloped edge	8.00	18.00	Tray, 9", pickle	10.00	17.50
Creamer, lightning bolt handles	7.00	12.00	Tray, 11", oval, service	8.00	15.00
Creamer, tall, lg. ft.	10.00	22.00	Tray, 11", celery	10.00	20.00
Cup	6.00	10.00	Tray, 12", center handled	15.00	25.00
French dressing bottle, "Oil/Vinegar"	60.00	90.00	Tray, 12", oval, service	10.00	20.00
Gravy boat, w/2 hdld. liner (like spouted cream soup)	65.00	95.00	Tray, 13", 2 hdld., service	20.00	30.00
Ice bucket	35.00	60.00	Tray, 15", oval, service	20.00	40.00
Ice tub	30.00	45.00	Tumbler, 2½ oz., ftd.	12.00	22.00
Mayonnaise, 2 hdld., w/2 hdld. liner and ladle	25.00	40.00	Tumbler, 5 oz., ftd.	10.00	18.00
			Tumbler, 8 oz., ftd.	12.00	22.00
			Tumbler, 10 oz., ftd.	15.00	25.00
			Tumbler, 12 oz., ftd.	20.00	35.00

77

"DEERWOOD" or "BIRCH TREE," U.S. Glass Company, Late 1920's – Early 1930's

Colors: light amber, green, pink, black, crystal

See the Black Forest pattern shot if you confuse these two patterns. Deer and trees are the dominant theme of Deerwood, whereas Black Forest pictures moose and trees.

In Deerwood, note the crystal goblet with green stem. This is the only piece of this pattern I have seen like that. I suspect there are other pieces besides the water goblet!

U.S. Glass listed a whipped cream pail instead of a mayonnaise for those who wrote that I left out the mayonnaise pictured in the fourth edition. Terminology of the differing glass companies can give you a gigantic headache!

At least there is catalogue documentation for Deerwood which is not the case with Black Forest. All the information for Black Forest is from actual pieces!

	Amber	Green	Pink
Bowl, 10", straight edge			35.00
Bowl, 12", console		55.00	55.00
Cake plate, low pedestal			55.00
Candlestick, 2½"		35.00	
Candlestick, 4"			45.00
Candy dish, w/cover, 3 part, flat			85.00
Candy jar, w/cover, ftd. cone			90.00
Celery, 12"		50.00	
Cheese and cracker		75.00	
Comport, 10", low, ftd., flared			45.00
Creamer, 2 styles		40.00	40.00
Cup		60.00	60.00
Plate, 5½"		12.00	12.00
Plate, 7½", salad			22.00
Plate, 9½", dinner			50.00
Saucer		15.00	15.00
Server, center hdld.		40.00	40.00
Stem, 6 oz., sherbet, 4¾"		27.50	
Stem, 6 oz., cocktail, 5"		32.50	
Stem, 9 oz., water, 7"		40.00	
Sugar, 2 styles		40.00	40.00
Tumbler, 9 oz.	32.00	35.00	35.00
Tumbler, 12 oz., tea, 5½"	40.00		
Vase, 7", sweet pea, rolled edge			75.00
Vase, 10", ruffled top		90.00	80.00
Whipped cream pail, w/ladle		45.00	45.00

DIANE, Cambridge Glass Company, 1934 – Early 1950's

Colors: crystal; some pink, yellow, blue, Heatherbloom, Emerald green, amber, Crown Tuscan

Diane is one Cambridge pattern that we have had difficulty capturing on film. I hope the pictures turn out as well in the book as the four I am viewing to write this page. I hauled this pattern to Paducah three times in order to get these photographs; admittedly, I had a lot of choices to pick from this time! A set of Diane can be collected in crystal, but collecting any set in color will be nearly impossible unless you get lucky enough to find a set all in one place. Many collectors of crystal accent their sets with an occasional colored piece. The gold decorated Crown Tuscan pieces shown atop the next page are sought both by Diane collectors and by connoisseurs of the Crown Tuscan color. A few pieces of dark Emerald green, blue, and Heatherbloom have surfaced; but I have been unable to find a saucer in Heatherbloom for my lonely cup or a bottom for my dark Emerald green candy lid.

Note the martini pitcher or cocktail beverage mixer in the top photo of page 83. One of these sold on the West Coast a few years ago for an exorbitant price ($2000+). The decanter set on the tray in the Faberware holders is an unusual find!

The stemware shown on the right in the bottom picture on page 83 is known as Stradivari or Regency. Both names were used for this particular stem and the only other etching found on this line is Portia.

	Crystal		Crystal
Basket, 6", 2 hdld., ftd.	16.00	Creamer, indiv. #3500 (pie crust edge)	15.00
Bottle, bitters	125.00	Creamer, indiv. #3900, scalloped edge	15.00
Bowl, #3106, finger, w/liner	30.00	Creamer, scroll handle, #3400	15.00
Bowl, #3122	25.00	Cup	20.00
Bowl, #3400, cream soup, w/liner	27.50	Decanter, ball	175.00
Bowl, 5", berry	20.00	Decanter, lg. ftd.	150.00
Bowl, 5¼" 2 hdld., bonbon	18.00	Decanter, short ft., cordial	175.00
Bowl, 6", 2 hdld., ftd., bonbon	17.00	Hurricane lamp, candlestick base	110.00
Bowl, 6", 2 pt., relish	18.00	Hurricane lamp, keyhole base w/prisms	175.00
Bowl, 6", cereal	25.00	Ice bucket, w/chrome hand	65.00
Bowl, 6½", 3 pt. relish	20.00	Mayonnaise, div., w/liner & ladles	40.00
Bowl, 7", 2 hdld., ftd., bonbon	22.00	Mayonnaise (sherbet type w/ladle)	32.50
Bowl, 7", 2 pt., relish	20.00	Mayonnaise, w/liner, ladle	35.00
Bowl, 7", relish or pickle	22.00	Oil, 6 oz., w/stopper	110.00
Bowl, 9", 3 pt., celery or relish	30.00	Pitcher, ball	125.00
Bowl, 9½", pickle (like corn)	22.00	Pitcher, Doulton	275.00
Bowl, 10", 4 ft., flared	40.00	Pitcher, martini	750.00
Bowl, 10", baker	40.00	Pitcher, upright	150.00
Bowl, 11", 2 hdld.	35.00	Plate, 6", 2 hdld., plate.	7.00
Bowl, 11", 4 ftd.	40.00	Plate, 6", sq., bread/butter	5.00
Bowl, 11½" tab hdld., ftd.	40.00	Plate, 6½", bread/butter	5.00
Bowl, 12", 3 pt., celery & relish	32.50	Plate, 8", 2 hdld., ftd., bonbon	11.00
Bowl, 12", 4 ft.	40.00	Plate, 8", salad	10.00
Bowl, 12", 4 ft., flared	40.00	Plate, 8½"	11.00
Bowl, 12", 4 ft., oval	42.00	Plate, 10½", dinner	60.00
Bowl, 12", 4 ft., oval, w/"ears" hdld.	50.00	Plate, 12", 4 ft., service	35.00
Bowl, 12", 5 pt., celery & relish	32.50	Plate, 13", 4 ft., torte	35.00
Butter, rnd.	115.00	Plate, 13½", 2 hdld.	30.00
Cabinet flask	185.00	Plate, 14", torte	40.00
Candelabrum, 2-lite, keyhole	22.50	Platter, 13½"	65.00
Candelabrum, 3-lite, keyhole	32.50	Salt & pepper, ftd., w/glass tops, pr.	32.00
Candlestick, 1-lite, keyhole	17.50	Salt & pepper, pr., flat	28.00
Candlestick, 5"	17.50	Saucer	5.00
Candlestick, 6", 2-lite, "fleur-de-lis"	30.00	Stem, #1066, 1 oz., cordial	55.00
Candlestick, 6", 3-lite	35.00	Stem, #1066, 3 oz., cocktail	16.00
Candy box, w/cover, rnd.	75.00	Stem, #1066, 3 oz., wine	25.00
Cigarette urn	42.50	Stem, #1066, 3½ oz., tall cocktail	17.50
Cocktail shaker, glass top	125.00	Stem, #1066, 4½ oz., claret	25.00
Cocktail shaker, metal top	90.00	Stem, #1066, 5 oz., oyster/cocktail	12.00
Cocktail icer, 2 pc.	55.00	Stem, #1066, 7 oz., low sherbet	11.50
Comport, 5½"	25.00	Stem, #1066, 7 oz., tall sherbet	13.50
Comport, 5⅜", blown	35.00	Stem, #1066, 11 oz., water	20.00
Creamer	14.00	Stem, #3122, 1 oz., cordial	55.00

DIANE, Cambridge Glass Company, 1934 – Early 1950's (continued)

	Crystal
Stem, #3122, 2½ oz., wine	22.00
Stem, #3122, 3 oz., cocktail	14.00
Stem, #3122, 4½ oz., claret	30.00
Stem, #3122, 4½ oz., oyster/cocktail	15.00
Stem, #3122, 7 oz., low sherbet	11.00
Stem, #3122, 7 oz., tall sherbet	15.00
Stem, #3122, 9 oz., water goblet	20.00
Sugar, indiv., #3500 (pie crust edge)	13.00
Sugar, indiv., #3900, scalloped edge	13.00
Sugar, scroll handle, #3400	14.00
Tumbler, 2½ oz., sham bottom	35.00
Tumbler, 5 oz., ft., juice	27.00
Tumbler, 5 oz., sham bottom	30.00
Tumbler, 7 oz., old-fashioned, w/sham bottom	35.00
Tumbler, 8 oz., ft.	22.00
Tumbler, 10 oz., sham bottom	30.00
Tumbler, 12 oz., sham bottom	32.00
Tumbler, 13 oz.	30.00
Tumbler, 14 oz., sham bottom	37.50
Tumbler, #1066, 3 oz.	18.00
Tumbler, #1066, 5 oz., juice	12.50

	Crystal
Tumbler, #1066, 9 oz., water	12.00
Tumbler, #1066, 12 oz., tea	20.00
Tumbler, #3106, 3 oz., ftd.	15.00
Tumbler, #3106, 5 oz., ftd., juice	13.00
Tumbler, #3106, 9 oz., ftd., water	11.00
Tumbler, #3106, 12 oz., ftd., tea	20.00
Tumbler, #3122, 2½ oz.	25.00
Tumbler, #3122, 5 oz., juice	13.00
Tumbler, #3122, 9 oz., water	15.00
Tumbler, #3122, 12 oz., tea	17.00
Tumbler, #3135, 2½ oz., ftd., bar	25.00
Tumbler, #3135, 10 oz., ftd., tumbler	14.00
Tumbler, #3135, 12 oz., ftd., tea	25.00
Vase, 5", globe	27.50
Vase, 6", high ft., flower	32.50
Vase, 8", high ft., flower	40.00
Vase, 9", keyhole base	45.00
Vase, 10", bud	35.00
Vase, 11", flower	55.00
Vase, 11", ped. ft., flower	60.00
Vase, 12", keyhole base	65.00
Vase, 13", flower	85.00

Note: See Page 210-211 for stem identification.

ELAINE, Cambridge Glass Company, 1934 – 1950's

Colors: crystal

Hopefully, the Elaine pattern shows up better in these new pictures. New collectors often confuse this with Chantilly, so look closely at that pattern so you can tell these apart. (Chantilly has a thick scroll, whereas Elaine's is thin and delicate.) There are still few collectors of Elaine, so this might be an elegant pattern to start accumulating!

	Crystal
Basket, 6", 2 hdld. (upturned sides)	15.00
Bowl, #3104, finger, w/liner	25.00
Bowl, 5¼", 2 hdld., bonbon	13.00
Bowl, 6", 2 hdld., ftd., bonbon	16.00
Bowl, 6", 2 pt., relish	16.00
Bowl, 6½", 3 pt., relish	15.00
Bowl, 7", 2 pt., pickle or relish	16.00
Bowl, 7", ftd., tab hdld. bonbon	27.00
Bowl, 7", pickle or relish	20.00
Bowl, 9", 3 pt., celery & relish	25.00
Bowl, 9½", pickle (like corn dish)	22.00
Bowl, 10", 3 ftd., flared	30.00
Bowl, 11", tab hdld.	30.00
Bowl, 11½", ftd., tab hdld.	30.00
Bowl, 12", 3 pt., celery & relish	30.00
Bowl, 12", 4 ftd., flared	35.00
Bowl, 12", 4 ftd., oval, "ear" hdld.	40.00
Bowl, 12", 5 pt. celery & relish	37.50
Candlestick, 5"	17.50
Candlestick, 6", 2-lite	27.50
Candlestick, 6", 3-lite	35.00
Candy box, w/cover, rnd.	70.00
Cocktail icer, 2 pc.	50.00
Comport, 5½"	30.00
Comport, 5⅜", #3500 stem	39.00
Comport, 5⅜", blown	40.00
Creamer (several styles)	11.00
Creamer, indiv.	12.00
Cup	20.00
Decanter, lg., ftd.	165.00
Hat, 9"	250.00
Hurricane lamp, candlestick base	110.00
Hurricane lamp, keyhole ft., w/prisms	175.00
Ice bucket, w/chrome handle	60.00
Mayonnaise (cupped "sherbet" w/ladle)	25.00
Mayonnaise (div. bowl, liner, 2 ladles)	37.50
Mayonnaise, w/liner & ladle	30.00
Oil, 6 oz., hdld., w/stopper	60.00
Pitcher, ball	125.00
Pitcher, Doulton	275.00
Pitcher, upright	175.00
Plate, 6", 2 hdld.	10.00
Plate, 6½", bread/butter	7.00
Plate, 8", 2 hdld., ftd.	15.00
Plate, 8", salad	15.00
Plate, 8", tab hdld., bonbon	15.00
Plate, 10½", dinner	60.00
Plate, 11½" 2 hdld., ringed "Tally Ho" sand.	25.00
Plate, 12", 4 ftd., service	25.00
Plate, 13", 4 ftd., torte	30.00
Plate, 13½", tab hdld., cake	30.00
Plate, 14", torte	30.00
Salt & pepper, flat, pr.	27.50

	Crystal
Salt & pepper, ftd., pr	30.00
Salt & pepper, hdld., pr	35.00
Saucer	3.00
Stem, #1402, 1 oz., cordial	55.00
Stem, #1402, 3 oz., wine	25.00
Stem, #1402, 3½ oz., cocktail	20.00
Stem, #1402, 5 oz., claret	27.50
Stem, #1402, low sherbet	14.00
Stem, #1402, tall sherbet	15.00
Stem, #1402, goblet	20.00
Stem, #3104, (very tall stems), ¾ oz., brandy	120.00
Stem, #3104, 1 oz., cordial	120.00
Stem, #3104, 1 oz., pousse-cafe	120.00
Stem, #3104, 2 oz., sherry	90.00
Stem, #3104, 2½ oz., creme de menthe	90.00
Stem, #3104, 3 oz., wine	85.00
Stem, #3104, 3½ oz., cocktail	50.00
Stem, #3104, 4½ oz., claret	65.00
Stem, #3104, 5 oz., roemer	65.00
Stem, #3104, 5 oz., tall hock	60.00
Stem, #3104, 7 oz., tall sherbet	50.00
Stem, #3104, 9 oz., goblet	75.00
Stem, #3121, 1 oz., cordial	55.00
Stem, #3121, 3 oz., cocktail	22.00
Stem, #3121, 3½ oz., wine	30.00
Stem, #3121, 4½ oz., claret	30.00
Stem, #3121, 4½ oz., oyster cocktail	15.00
Stem, #3121, 5 oz., parfait, low stem	25.00
Stem, #3121, 6 oz., low sherbet	15.00
Stem, #3121, 6 oz., tall sherbet	17.50
Stem, #3121, 10 oz., water	21.00
Stem, #3500, 1 oz., cordial	55.00
Stem, #3500, 2½ oz., wine	27.50
Stem, #3500, 3 oz., cocktail	20.00
Stem, #3500, 4½ oz., claret	30.00
Stem, #3500, 4½ oz., oyster cocktail	14.00
Stem, #3500, 5 oz., parfait, low stem	23.00
Stem, #3500, 7 oz., low sherbet	13.00
Stem, #3500, 7 oz., tall sherbet	15.00
Stem, #3500, 10 oz., water	20.00
Sugar (several styles)	10.00
Sugar, indiv.	12.00
Tumbler, #1402, 9 oz., ftd., water	17.00
Tumbler, #1402, 12 oz., tea	25.00
Tumbler, #1402, 12 oz., tall ftd., tea	27.50
Tumbler, #3121, 5 oz., ftd., juice	19.00
Tumbler, #3121, 10 oz., ftd., water	20.00
Tumbler, #3121, 12 oz., ftd., tea	25.00
Tumbler, #3500, 5 oz., ftd., juice	17.00
Tumbler, #3500, 10 oz., ftd., water	18.00
Tumbler, #3500, 12 oz., ftd., tea	27.50
Vase, 6", ftd.	30.00
Vase, 8", ftd.	40.00
Vase, 9", keyhole, ftd.	45.00

Note: see Pages 210-211 for stem identification.

EMPRESS, Blank #1401, A.H. Heisey & Co.

Colors: "Flamingo" pink, "Sahara" yellow, "Moongleam" green, cobalt and "Alexandrite"; some Tangerine

Notice that crystal is no longer priced here. You will find crystal prices listed under the name Queen Ann. When the colors were made this pattern was called Empress; but when crystal was added later, the name was changed to Queen Ann.

Collectors of Moongleam Empress are having a difficult time acquiring additional pieces. Money may be a stumbling block for some, but **finding** pieces is an even bigger problem.

	Flam.	Sahara	Moon.	Cobalt	Alexan.
Ash tray.	85.00	90.00	190.00	220.00	210.00
Bonbon, 6"	20.00	25.00	30.00		
Bowl, cream soup	26.00	27.00	35.00		65.00
Bowl, cream soup, w/sq. liner	25.00	30.00	45.00		165.00
Bowl, frappe, w/center	45.00	60.00	75.00		
Bowl, nut, dolphin ftd., indiv.	22.00	26.00	32.00		125.00
Bowl, 4½", nappy	8.00	10.00	12.50		
Bowl, 5", preserve, 2 hdld.	18.00	22.00	27.50		
Bowl, 6", ftd., jelly, 2 hdld.	17.00	23.00	27.50		
Bowl, 6", dolp. ftd., mint	20.00	25.00	30.00		165.00
Bowl, 6", grapefruit, sq. top, grnd. bottom	12.50	15.00	22.50		
Bowl, 6½", oval, lemon, w/cover	65.00	75.00	90.00		
Bowl, 7", 3 pt., relish, triplex	40.00	30.00	45.00		200.00
Bowl, 7", 3 pt., relish, ctr. hand.	45.00	50.00	75.00		
Bowl, 7½", dolp. ftd., nappy	60.00	65.00	75.00	275.00	325.00
Bowl, 7½", dolp. ftd., nasturtium	100.00	110.00	125.00	325.00	400.00
Bowl, 8", nappy	30.00	35.00	40.00		
Bowl, 8½", ftd., floral, 2 hdld	40.00	50.00	65.00		
Bowl, 9", floral, rolled edge	32.00	38.00	42.00		
Bowl, 9", floral, flared	70.00	75.00	90.00		
Bowl, 10", 2 hdld., oval dessert	45.00	60.00	65.00		
Bowl, 10", lion head, floral	550.00	550.00	700.00		
Bowl, 10", oval, veg.	35.00	45.00	55.00		
Bowl, 10", square, salad, 2 hdld.	40.00	55.00	65.00		
Bowl, 10", triplex, relish	45.00	55.00	65.00		
Bowl, 11", dolphin ftd., floral	65.00	75.00	90.00	400.00	450.00
Bowl, 13", pickle/olive, 2 pt.	18.00	30.00	32.00		
Bowl, 15", dolp. ftd., punch	700.00	800.00	900.00		
Candlestick, low, 4 ftd., w/2 hdld.	35.00	40.00	45.00		
Candlestick, 6", dolphin ftd.	95.00	90.00	125.00	250.00	250.00
Candy, w/cover, 6", dolphin ftd.	120.00	150.00	200.00	360.00	
Comport, 6", ftd.	50.00	55.00	65.00		
Comport, 6", square	70.00	75.00	85.00		
Comport, 7", oval	60.00	66.00	75.00		
Compotier, 6", dolphin ftd.	130.00	170.00	195.00		
Creamer, dolphin ftd.	35.00	30.00	42.50		215.00
Creamer, indiv.	30.00	35.00	40.00		210.00
Cup	27.00	31.00	36.00		100.00
Cup, after dinner	40.00	50.00	60.00		
Cup, bouillon, 2 hdld.	28.00	30.00	33.00		
Cup, 4 oz., custard or punch	25.00	28.00	30.00		
Cup, #1401½, has rim as demi-cup	28.00	32.00	40.00		
Grapefruit, w/square liner	25.00	30.00	35.00		
Ice tub, w/metal handles	95.00	100.00	135.00		
Jug, 3 pint, ftd.	175.00	200.00	225.00		
Jug, flat			165.00		
Marmalade, w/cover, dolp. ftd.	70.00	80.00	95.00		
Mayonnaise, 5½", ftd. with ladle	35.00	45.00	55.00		300.00
Mustard, w/cover	60.00	65.00	75.00		
Oil bottle, 4 oz.	80.00	110.00	125.00		

	Flam.	Sahara	Moon.	Cobalt	Alexan.
Plate..	7.00	10.00	12.00		
Plate, bouillon liner	9.00	13.00	15.00		20.00
Plate, 4½"..	6.00	6.00	8.00		
Plate, 6"...	11.00	14.00	16.00		35.00
Plate, 6", square.....................................	10.00	13.00	15.00		30.00
Plate, 7"...	12.00	15.00	17.00		40.00
Plate, 7", square.....................................	12.00	15.00	17.00	55.00	45.00
Plate, 8", square.....................................	18.00	22.00	35.00	70.00	65.00
Plate, 8"...	16.00	20.00	24.00	70.00	65.00
Plate, 9"...	25.00	35.00	40.00		
Plate, 10½"...	100.00	100.00	125.00		
Plate, 10½", square	100.00	100.00	125.00		175.00
Plate, 12"..	45.00	55.00	65.00		
Plate, 12", muffin, sides upturned.................	50.00	60.00	70.00		
Plate, 12", sandwich, 2 hdld...........................	35.00	40.00	50.00		165.00
Plate, 13", hors d'oeuvre, 2 hdld.	40.00	45.00	55.00		
Plate, 13", square, 2 hdld..........................	40.00	45.00	55.00		
Platter, 14"..	35.00	40.00	47.50		
Salt & pepper, pr.	100.00	110.00	135.00		350.00
Saucer, square	8.00	14.00	16.00		25.00
Saucer, after dinner.................................	7.00	10.00	10.00		
Saucer...	8.00	14.00	16.00		25.00
Stem, 2½ oz., oyster cocktail	20.00	25.00	30.00		
Stem, 4 oz., saucer champagne	35.00	40.00	60.00		
Stem, 4 oz., sherbet.................................	22.00	28.00	35.00		
Stem, 9 oz., Empress stemware, unusual........	55.00	65.00	75.00		
Sugar, indiv.	30.00	35.00	40.00		210.00
Sugar, dolphin ftd., 3 hdld.	35.00	30.00	27.00		210.00
Tray, condiment & liner for indiv. sugar/creamer...........................	25.00	30.00	35.00		
Tray, 10", 3 pt., relish..............................	25.00	30.00	35.00		
Tray, 10", 7 pt., hors d'oeuvre.....................	160.00	150.00	200.00		
Tray, 10", celery.....................................	16.00	22.00	26.00		150.00
Tray, 12", ctr. hdld., sand.	48.00	57.00	65.00		
Tray, 12", sq. ctr. hdld., sand.	52.00	60.00	67.50		
Tray, 13", celery.....................................	20.00	24.00	30.00		
Tray, 16", 4 pt., buffet relish	50.00	75.00	86.00		
Tumbler, 8 oz., dolp. ftd., unusual.................	125.00	150.00	195.00		
Tumbler, 8 oz., grnd. bottom	130.00	35.00	39.50		
Tumbler, 12 oz., tea, grnd. bottom..................	32.00	40.00	45.00		
Vase, 8", flared.......................................	80.00	90.00	105.00		
Vase, 9", ftd...	100.00	110.00	150.00		625.00

FAIRFAX NO. 2375, Fostoria Glass Company, 1927 – 1944

Colors: blue, orchid, amber, rose, green, topaz; some ruby and black

Fairfax is the Fostoria blank on which many of the most popular Fostoria etchings are found, notably June, Versailles, and Trojan. Most collectors do not get as excited about this No. 2375 line without an etching. Azure blue and Orchid are the most collected colors.

You might notice the covered candy behind the butter dish in the bottom photograph on page 92. There is a cutting on this piece which technically makes it not Fairfax. I point that out to save a few letters over the next two years from readers with magnifiers looking for errors. Believe me, that's true!

The blue pitchers show the differences in Fostoria's blue. The light blue was called Azure; the more vivid color was called Blue. This Blue was an early color and used in only the first dinnerware lines and the popular American pattern.

Note the Azure flower vase with frog in front of the pitcher. This piece is found rarely and the frog even less often than its holder.

Fairfax collectors have a choice of stems. In the photo of blues at the top is stem and tumbler line #2375 which is usually used for Versailles and June etchings. The other stem line #5299 is shown in the bottom picture; this is more commonly found in yellow with the Trojan etch. Some collectors are mixing the stem lines; but tumblers are difficult to mix because of their different shapes. The #5299 tumblers are more cone-shaped; the #2375 tumblers are rounded.

Due to confusion among collectors and dealers alike, I have shown the various Fostoria stems on page 83 so that differences in shapes can be seen. The claret and high sherbets are major concerns. Each is 6" high. Note the claret is shaped like the wine; and the parfait is taller than the juice!

	Rose, Blue, Orchid	Amber	Green, Topaz		Rose, Blue, Orchid	Amber	Green, Topaz
Ash tray, 2½"	15.00	7.50	10.00	Pickle, 8½"	18.00	7.00	9.00
Ash tray, 4"	17.50	10.00	12.50	Pitcher, #5000	195.00	110.00	130.00
Ash tray, 5½"	20.00	13.00	17.50	Plate, canape	15.00	10.00	10.00
Baker, 9", oval	25.00	15.00	20.00	Plate, whipped cream	11.00	8.00	9.00
Baker, 10½", oval	35.00	20.00	22.50	Plate, 6", bread/butter	3.00	2.00	2.50
Bonbon	12.50	9.00	10.00	Plate, 7½", salad	5.00	3.00	3.50
Bottle, salad dressing	150.00	60.00	70.00	Plate, 7½", cream soup or mayonnaise liner	5.00	3.00	3.50
Bouillon, ftd.	11.00	7.00	8.00	Plate, 8¾", salad	10.00	4.50	5.00
Bowl, 9", lemon, 2 hdld.	12.00	6.00	7.00	Plate, 9½", luncheon	15.00	6.00	7.00
Bowl, sweetmeat	15.00	10.00	12.00	Plate, 10¼", dinner	40.00	17.00	25.00
Bowl, 5", fruit	12.00	5.00	6.00	Plate, 10¼", grill	30.00	12.00	20.00
Bowl, 6", cereal	20.00	9.00	11.00	Plate, 10", cake	17.50	13.00	15.00
Bowl, 7", soup	25.00	12.00	14.00	Plate, 12", bread, oval	40.00	25.00	27.50
Bowl, 8", rnd., nappy	27.50	13.00	14.00	Plate, 13", chop	17.50	14.00	15.00
Bowl, lg., hdld., dessert	22.00	10.00	12.00	Platter, 10½", oval	30.00	17.00	19.00
Bowl, 12"	22.00	15.00	18.00	Platter, 12", oval	35.00	20.00	22.50
Bowl, 12", centerpiece	25.00	17.50	20.00	Platter, 15", oval	60.00	27.00	32.00
Bowl, 13", oval, centerpiece	30.00	20.00	22.50	Relish, 3 part, 8½"	10.00	7.00	8.00
Bowl, 15", centerpiece	35.00	20.00	24.00	Relish, 11½"	15.00	10.00	12.00
Butter dish, w/cover	135.00	80.00	90.00	Sauce boat	40.00	20.00	25.00
Candlestick, flattened top	15.00	10.00	10.00	Sauce boat liner	15.00	9.00	10.00
Candlestick, 3"	12.50	9.00	10.00	Saucer, after dinner	6.00	4.00	5.00
Celery, 11½"	20.00	12.00	14.00	Saucer	4.00	2.50	3.00
Cheese & cracker set (2 styles)	35.00	20.00	22.50	Shaker, ftd., pr.	55.00	30.00	35.00
Comport, 5"	15.00	15.00	17.00	Shaker, indiv., ftd., pr.		20.00	25.00
Comport, 7"	25.00	10.00	12.00	Stem, 4", ¾ oz., cordial	60.00	25.00	35.00
Cream soup, ftd.	20.00	9.00	8.00	Stem, 4¼", 6 oz., low sherbet	18.00	9.00	11.00
Creamer, flat		10.00	12.00	Stem, 5¼", 3 oz., cocktail	24.00	12.00	18.00
Creamer, ftd.	11.00	7.00	9.00	Stem, 5½", 3 oz., wine	30.00	18.00	22.50
Creamer, tea	17.50	7.00	9.00	Stem, 6", 4 oz., claret	35.00	25.00	25.00
Cup, after dinner	22.00	10.00	12.50	Stem, 6", 6 oz., high sherbet	20.00	10.00	12.50
Cup, flat		4.00	6.00	Stem, 8¼", 10 oz., water	30.00	16.00	20.00
Cup, ftd.	8.00	6.00	7.00	Sugar, flat	27.50	10.00	12.00
Flower holder, oval, window box	60.00	20.00	30.00	Sugar, ftd.	10.00	6.00	8.00
Grapefruit	30.00	15.00	20.00	Sugar cover	30.00	20.00	22.50
Grapefruit liner	25.00	12.00	15.00	Sugar pail	40.00	25.00	28.00
Ice bucket	50.00	30.00	35.00	Sugar, tea	17.50	6.00	8.00
Ice bowl	15.00	12.00	10.00	Tray, 11", ctr. hdld.	20.00	12.00	15.00
Ice bowl liner	20.00	12.00	* 10.00	Tumbler, 2½ oz., ftd.	22.00	10.00	12.00
Mayonnaise	15.00	9.00	10.00	Tumbler, 4½", 5 oz., ftd.	18.00	10.00	11.00
Mayonnaise ladle	35.00	20.00	25.00	Tumbler, 5¼", 9 oz., ftd.	20.00	12.00	13.00
Mayonnaise liner, 7"	5.00	3.00	3.50	Tumbler, 6", 12 oz., ftd.	25.00	13.50	18.00
Nut cup, blown	25.00	15.00	20.00	Vase, 8" (2 styles)	60.00	35.00	45.00
Oil, ftd.	125.00	80.00	90.00	Whipped cream pail	40.00	25.00	28.00

* Green $20.00

See page 93 for stem identification.

FOSTORIA STEMS AND SHAPES

Top Row: Left to Right
1. Water, 10 oz., 8¼"
2. Claret, 4 oz., 6"
3. Wine, 3 oz., 5½"
4. Cordial, ¾ oz., 4"
5. Sherbet, low, 6 oz., 4¼"
6. Cocktail, 3 oz., 5¼"
7. Sherbet, high, 6 oz., 6"

Bottom Row: Left to Right
1. Grapefruit and liner
2. Ice tea tumbler, 12 oz., 6"
3. Water tumbler, 9 oz., 5¼"
4. Parfait, 6 oz., 5¼"
5. Juice tumbler, 5 oz., 4½"
6. Oyster Cocktail, 5½ oz.
7. Bar tumbler, 2½ oz.

FIRST LOVE, Duncan & Miller Glass Company, 1937

Color: crystal

This extensive pattern by Duncan & Miller is their best known etching! There were several mould lines incorporated into making First Love. They include #30 (Pall Mall), #111 (Terrace), #115 (Canterbury), #117 (Three Feathers), #126 (Venetian), #5111½ (Terrace blown stemware).

I would like to thank the First Love collectors and dealers in Duncan glass who helped me compile and price this list. Any additional pieces or pricing contributions that you have, please let me know!

	Crystal		Crystal
Ash tray, 3½" sq., #111	17.50	Candy, 6½", w/5" lid, #115	65.00
Ash tray, 3½" x 2½", #30	16.50	Carafe, w/stopper, water, #5200	110.00
Ash tray, 5" x 3", #12, club	35.00	Cheese stand, 3" x 5¼", #111	25.00
Ash tray, 5" x 3¼", #30	24.00	Cheese stand, 5¾" x 3½", #115	25.00
Ash tray, 6½" x 4¼", #30	35.00	Cigarette box w/lid, 4" x 4¼"	32.00
Basket, 9¼" x 10" x 7¼", #115	122.50	Cigarette box w/lid, 4½" x 3½", #30	35.00
Basket,10" x 4¼" x 7", oval hdld., #115	135.00	Cigarette box w/lid, 4¾" x 3¾"	35.00
Bottle, oil w/stopper, 8", #5200	55.00	Cocktail shaker, 14 oz., #5200	100.00
Bowl, 3" x 5", rose, #115	40.00	Cocktail shaker, 16 oz., #5200	100.00
Bowl, 4" x 1½" finger, #30	32.00	Cocktail shaker, 32 oz., #5200	125.00
Bowl, 4¼", finger, #5111½	32.00	Comport w/lid, 8¾" x 5½", #111	100.00
Bowl, 6" x 2½", oval, olive, #115	25.00	Comport, 3½"x 4¾"W, #111	30.00
Bowl, 6¾" x 4¼", ftd., flared rim, #111	30.00	Comport, 5" x 5½", flared rim, #115	32.00
Bowl, 7½" x 3", 3 pt., ftd., #117	35.00	Comport, 5¼" x 6¾", flat top, #115	32.00
Bowl, 8" sq. x 2½", hdld., #111	55.00	Comport, 6" x 4¾", low #115	35.00
Bowl, 8½" x 4", #115	37.50	Creamer, 2½", individual, #115	18.00
Bowl, 9" x 4½", ftd., #111	42.00	Creamer, 3", 10 oz., #111	18.00
Bowl, 9½" x 2½", hdld., #111	45.00	Creamer, 3¾", 7 oz., #115	15.00
Bowl, 10" x 3¾", ftd., flared rim, #111	55.00	Creamer, sugar w/butter pat lid,	
Bowl, 10" x 4½", #115	45.00	breakfast set, #28	55.00
Bowl, 10½" x 5", crimped, #115	44.00	Cruet, #25	85.00
Bowl, 10½" x 7" x 7", #126	58.00	Cruet, #30	85.00
Bowl, 10¾" x 4¾" #115	42.50	Cup, #115	18.00
Bowl, 11" x 1 ¾", #30	55.00	Decanter w/stopper, 16 oz., #5200	110.00
Bowl, 11" x 3¼", flared rim, #111	60.00	Decanter w/stopper, 32 oz., #30	125.00
Bowl, 11" x 5¼", flared rim, #6	65.00	Decanter w/stopper, 32 oz., #5200	125.00
Bowl, 11½" x 8¼", oval, #115	45.00	Hat, 4½", #30	300.00
Bowl, 12" x 3½", #6	65.00	Hat, 5½" x 8½" x 6¼", #30	300.00
Bowl, 12" x 3¼", flared, #115	60.00	Honey dish, 5" x 3", #91	25.00
Bowl, 12" x 4" x 7½", oval, #117	65.00	Ice bucket, 6", #30	85.00
Bowl, 12½", flat, ftd., #126	68.00	Lamp, hurricane, w/prisms, 15", #115	125.00
Bowl, 13" x 3¼" x 8¾", oval, flared,		Lamp shade only, #115	100.00
#115	55.00	Lid for candy urn, #111	35.00
Bowl, 13" x 7" x 9¼", #126	65.00	Mayonnaise, 4¾" x 4½", div. w/7½"	
Bowl, 13" x 7", #117	60.00	underplate	35.00
Bowl, 14" x 7½" x 6", oval, #126	65.00	Mayonnaise, 5¼" x 3", div. w/6½" plate,	
Box, candy w/lid, 4¾" x 6¼"	55.00	#115	35.00
Butter or cheese, 7" sq. x 1¼", #111	110.00	Mayonnaise, 5½" x 2½", ftd., hdld.,	
Candelabra, 2-lite, #41	35.00	#111	35.00
Candelabrum, 6", 2-lite w/prisms, #30	50.00	Mayonnaise, 5½" x 2¾", #115	35.00
Candle, 3", 1-lite, #111	25.00	Mayonnaise, 5½" x 3½", crimped, #11	32.00
Candle, 3", low, #115	25.00	Mayonnaise, 5¾" x 3", w/dish hdld.	
Candle, 3½", #115	25.00	tray, #111	35.00
Candle, 4", cornucopia, #117	25.00	Mayonnaise, w/7" tray hdld., #111	35.00
Candle, 4", low, #111	25.00	Mustard w/lid & underplate	55.00
Candle, 5¼", 2-lite, globe, #30	30.00	Nappy, 5" x 1", w/bottom star, #25	20.00
Candle, 6", 2-lite, #30	30.00	Nappy, 5" x 1¾", one hdld., #115	18.00
Candy box, 6" x 3½", 3 hdld., 3 pt.,		Nappy, 5½" x 2", div., hdld., #111	18.00
w/lid, #115	55.00	Nappy, 5½" x 2", one hdld., heart, #115	28.00
Candy box, 6" x 3½", 3 pt., w/lid,		Nappy, 6" x 1¾", hdld., #111	22.00
crown finial, #106	65.00	Perfume tray, 8" x 5", #5200	25.00
Candy jar, 5" x 7¼", w/lid, ftd., #25	65.00	Perfume, 5", #5200	65.00

A PAIR OF

Duncan

HURRICANES

*... a gift that looks like
a million dollars*

HURRICANE CANDELABRA with hand-cut and polished imported prisms are breathtaking . . . but with the lacy First Love etching on the hurricane shade they are irresistible.

These Hurricane Candelabra are made by the makers of "the loveliest glassware in America." Many pieces of Duncan glass are now collector's items and are in antique shows.

If your department store or jewelry or gift shops do not have the Duncan First Love Hurricane Candelabra, they will be glad to order them for you. There is also a full line of stemware and flatware and decorative pieces with the same etching. Write for the First Love folder.

HAND-MADE
Duncan

The loveliest glassware in America

THE DUNCAN & MILLER GLASS COMPANY

WASHINGTON, PA.

	Crystal
Pitcher, #5200	125.00
Pitcher, 9", 80 oz., ice lip, #5202	135.00
Plate, 6", #111	12.00
Plate, 6", #115	12.00
Plate, 6", hdld. lemon, #111	14.00
Plate, 6", sq., #111	14.00
Plate, 7", #111	17.50
Plate, 7½", #111	18.00
Plate, 7½", #115	18.00
Plate, 7½", mayonnaise liner, hdld. #115	15.00
Plate, 7½", sq., #111	19.00
Plate, 7½", 2 hdld., #115	19.00
Plate, 8½", #30	20.00
Plate, 8½", #111	20.00
Plate, 8½", #115	20.00
Plate, 11", #111	45.00
Plate, 11", 2 hdld., sandwich #115	30.00
Plate, 11", hdld., #111	40.00
Plate, 11", hdld., cracker w/ring #115	40.00
Plate, 11", hdld., cracker w/ring, #111	40.00
Plate, 11", hdld., sandwich, #111	40.00
Plate, 11¼", dinner, #115	55.00
Plate, 12", egg, #30	110.00
Plate, 12", torte, rolled edge, #111	40.00
Plate, 13", torte, flat edge, #111	50.00
Plate, 13", torte, rolled edge, #111	55.00
Plate, 13¼", torte, #111	55.00
Plate, 13½", cake, hdld., #115	50.00
Plate, 14", #115	50.00
Plate, 14", cake, #115	50.00
Plate, 14½", cake, lg. base, #30	50.00
Plate, 14½", cake, sm. base, #30	50.00
Relish, 6" x 1¾", hdld., 2 pt., #111	20.00
Relish, 6" x 1¾", hdld., 2 pt., #115	20.00
Relish, 8" x 4½", pickle, 2 pt., #115	25.00
Relish, 8", 3 pt., hdld., #115	25.00
Relish, 9" x 1½", 2 pt. pickle, #115	25.00
Relish, 9" x 1½", 3 hdld, 3 pt., #115	30.00
Relish, 9" x 1½", 3 hdld., flared, #115	30.00
Relish, 10", 5 pt. tray, #30	60.00
Relish, 10½" x 1½", hdld., 5 pt., #111	65.00
Relish, 10½" x 1¼", 2 hdld, 3 pt., #115	55.00
Relish, 10½" x 7", #115	37.50
Relish, 11¾", tray, #115	45.00
Relish, 12", 4 pt., hdld., #111	40.00
Relish, 12", 5 pt., hdld., #111	50.00
Salt and pepper pr., #30	30.00
Salt and pepper pr., #115	40.00
Sandwich tray, 12" x 5¼", ctr. handle, #115	75.00
Saucer, #115	8.50
Stem, 3¾", 1 oz., cordial, #5111½	55.00
Stem, 3¾", 4½ oz., oyster cocktail, #5111½	22.50
Stem, 4", 5 oz., ice cream, #5111½	14.00
Stem, 4¼", 3 oz., cocktail, #115	22.50
Stem, 4½", 3½ oz., cocktail, #5111½	22.50
Stem, 5", 5 oz., saucer champagne, #5111½	18.00
Stem, 5¼", 3 oz., wine, #5111½	32.50
Stem, 5¼", 5 oz., ftd. juice, #5111½	24.00
Stem, 5¾", 10 oz., low luncheon goblet #5111½	17.50
Stem, 6", 4½ oz., claret, #5111½	40.00
Stem, 6½", 12 oz., ftd. ice tea, #5111½	32.50
Stem, 6¾", 10 oz., tall water goblet, #5111½	24.00
Stem, 6¾", 14 oz., ftd. ice tea, #5111½	35.00
Stem, cordial, #111	15.00
Sugar, 2½", individual, #115	14.00
Sugar, 3", 7 oz., #115	14.00
Sugar, 3", 10 oz., #111	15.00
Tray, 8" x 2", hdld. celery, #111	17.50
Tray, 8" x 4¾", individual sug/cr. #115	17.50
Tray, 8¾", celery, #91	30.00
Tray, 11", celery, #91	37.50
Tumbler, 2",1½ oz., whiskey, #5200	50.00
Tumbler, 2½" x 3⅜", sham, Teardrop, ftd.	55.00
Tumbler, 3", sham, #5200	30.00
Tumbler, 4¾", 10 oz., sham, #5200	35.00
Tumbler, 5½", 12 oz., sham, #5200	35.00
Tumbler, 6", 14 oz., sham, #5200	35.00
Tumbler, 8 oz., flat, #115	30.00
Urn, 4½" x 4½", #111	27.50
Urn, 4½" x 4½", #115	27.50
Urn, 4¾", rnd ft.	27.50
Urn, 5", #525	35.00
Urn, 5½", ring hdld, sq. ft.	55.00
Urn, 5½", sq. ft.	35.00
Urn, 6½", sq. hdld.	65.00
Urn, 7", #529	37.50
Vase, 4", flared rim, #115	25.00
Vase, 4½" x 4¾", #115	25.00
Vase, 5" x 5", crimped, #115	30.00
Vase, 6", #507	55.00
Vase, 8" x 4¾", cornucopia, #117	65.00
Vase, 8", ftd., #506	85.00
Vase, 8", ftd., #507	85.00
Vase, 8½" x 2¾", #505	90.00
Vase, 8½" x 6", #115	85.00
Vase, 9" x 4½", #505	90.00
Vase, 9", #509	85.00
Vase, 9", bud, #506	75.00
Vase, 9½" x 3½", #506	95.00
Vase, 10" x 4¾", #5200	85.00
Vase, 10", #507	90.00
Vase, 10, ftd., #111	100.00
Vase, 10", ftd., #505	100.00
Vase, 10", ftd., #506	100.00
Vase, 10½" x 12 x 9½", #126	125.00
Vase, 10½", #126	115.00
Vase, 11" x 5¼", #505	125.00
Vase, 11½ x 4½", #506	125.00
Vase, 12", flared #115	125.00
Vase, 12", ftd., #506	125.00
Vase, 12", ftd., #507	125.00

FLANDERS, Tiffin Glass Company, Mid 1910's – Mid 1930's

Colors: crystal, pink, yellow

Tiffin's Flanders is often confused with Cambridge's Gloria by novice collectors, and even some dealers. Refer to Gloria to see the differences.

New pieces in Flanders continue to be found. I now have a two handled consomme and an 11" rolled edge bowl in my possession. I have had reports of flat soups and cream soups but no confirmation on those pieces as yet. Shakers have been found in crystal and yellow and a Chinese "type" hurricane lamp has been found in crystal. (See Fuchsia for example).

Stemware normally found is #17024. This line usually has a crystal foot and stem with tops of crystal, pink, or yellow. Speaking of color combinations, these include green foot with pink stems; and pink tumblers as well as pitchers with crystal handle and foot. Round plates are line #8800 and each size plate has a different number. Scalloped plates are line #5831.

As awareness of Flanders pattern grows, the price continues to climb due to its limited supply. Pink is the collector's choice for now, but crystal and yellow are beginning to be noticed.

	Crystal	Pink	Yellow		Crystal	Pink	Yellow
Bowl, finger, w/liner.........	17.00	40.00	25.00	Plate, 8".............................	9.00	15.00	12.50
Bowl, 2 hdld., bonbon......	15.00	30.00	20.00	Plate, 10¼", dinner	30.00	65.00	45.00
Bowl, 12", flanged rim,				Relish, 3 pt........................	25.00	45.00	35.00
console	25.00	45.00	35.00	Salt & pepper, pr.	75.00		125.00
Candlestick, 2 styles.........	30.00	60.00	40.00	Saucer	5.00	10.00	8.00
Candy jar, w/cover, flat	75.00	125.00	100.00	Stem, claret	40.00	95.00	60.00
Candy jar, w/cover, ftd.	75.00	195.00	145.00	Stem, cordial.....................	50.00	85.00	65.00
Celery, 11".........................	20.00	40.00	30.00	Stem, cocktail	15.00	35.00	30.00
Cheese & cracker..............	35.00	85.00	65.00	Stem, oyster cocktail	12.00	30.00	20.00
Comport, 3½"....................	25.00	50.00	35.00	Stem, parfait......................	30.00	65.00	50.00
Comport, 6".......................	50.00	100.00	75.00	Stem, saucer champagne..	15.00	30.00	20.00
Creamer, flat.....................	40.00	115.00	70.00	Stem, sherbet	10.00	25.00	17.50
Creamer, ftd.	35.00	100.00	55.00	Stem, water	15.00	40.00	27.50
Cup, 2 styles.....................	30.00	60.00	45.00	Stem, wine	25.00	55.00	37.50
Decanter	150.00	275.00	225.00	Sugar, flat	40.00	110.00	65.00
Grapefruit, w/liner............	30.00	60.00	40.00	Sugar, ftd..........................	35.00	95.00	50.00
Hurricane lamp, Chinese				Tumbler, 2½ oz., ftd.	35.00	65.00	40.00
style...............................	135.00			Tumbler, 9 oz., ftd., water ..	12.00	30.00	20.00
Mayonnaise, w/liner.........	30.00	75.00	50.00	Tumbler, 10 oz., ftd...........	15.00	35.00	25.00
Nut cup, ftd., blown	30.00	50.00	40.00	Tumbler, 12 oz., ftd., tea...	20.00	40.00	27.50
Oil bottle & stopper	125.00	250.00	175.00	Vase, bud	30.00	65.00	45.00
Parfait, hdld.	50.00	125.00	75.00	Vase, ftd............................	75.00	175.00	125.00
Pitcher & cover	200.00	350.00	275.00	Vase, Dahlia style..............	100.00	225.00	165.00
Plate, 6"............................	4.00	12.00	9.00	Vase, fan...........................	75.00	150.00	90.00

FUCHSIA, Tiffin Glass Company, Late 1937 – 1940

Colors: crystal

A special thanks to Dale Mitchell for providing me with the listings and measurements for many additional pieces added below! Of course, I have helped add to his collection, too! (One good turn deserves another.) You can see the newly discovered cocktail shaker in *The Very Rare Glassware of the Depression Years* – 3rd Series.

Two other stemware lines for Fuchsia have been discovered. The normally found stem is #15083 and shown in the bottom photo. Also notice one of the most interesting stems in my cordial collection, an "S" like stem #17457. Other stems found in this line are listed below. The third stemware line is shown on the left in the top picture. These rounded top stems are a part of the stemware line #17453. I have only seen one small group of these; thus I do not know how readily they can be found.

The footed finger bowl is shown atop a salad plate and not the regular finger bowl liner. I have since found a flat finger bowl which will be shown in a later edition. You may find items not listed, so let me know what...(with photographs and measurements, please)!

	Crystal		Crystal
Ash tray, 2¼" x 3¾" w/cigarette rest	20.00	Relish, 9¼", square, 3 pt.	35.00
Bell, 5"	65.00	Relish, 10½" x 12½", hdld., 3 pt., #5902	55.00
Bowl, 2 hdld., bonbon #5831	25.00	Relish, 10½" x 12½", hdld., 5 pt.	65.00
Bowl, 4", finger, ftd., #041	40.00	Salt and pepper, pr.	75.00
Bowl, 4½" finger, w/#8814 liner	50.00	Saucer, #5831	7.50
Bowl, 5⁵⁄₁₆", 2 hdld., #5831	25.00	Stem, 4¹⁄₁₆", cordial, #15083	32.50
Bowl, 7¼", salad, #5902	30.00	Stem, 4⅛", sherbet, #15083	12.00
Bowl, 8⅜", 2 hdld., #5831	45.00	Stem, 4¼", cocktail, #15083	18.00
Bowl, 9¾", deep salad, #5902	50.00	Stem, 4⅝", 3½ oz., cocktail, #17453	32.50
Bowl, 10", salad, #5902	50.00	Stem, 4⅞", saucer champagne, hollow stem	50.00
Bowl, 11⅞", console	45.00	Stem, 5¹⁄₁₆", wine, #15083	30.00
Bowl, 11⅞", console, flared	65.00	Stem, 5¼", claret, #15083	18.00
Bowl, 12", flanged rim, console #5831	45.00	Stem, 5⅜", cocktail, "S" stem, #17457	35.00
Bowl, 12⅜", console, flared	75.00	Stem, 5⅜", cordial, "S" stem, #17457	85.00
Bowl, 13", crimped #5902	65.00	Stem, 5⅜", 7 oz., saucer champagne, #17453	25.00
Candlestick, 2-lite, w/pointed center, #5831	55.00	Stem, 5⅜", saucer champagne, #15083	15.00
Candlestick, 5", 2-lite, ball center	55.00	Stem, 5⅜", saucer champagne, "S" stem,	
Candlestick, 5⅝, 2-lite, w/fan center, #5902	55.00	#17457	35.00
Candlestick, single, #348	32.50	Stem, 5¹⁵⁄₁₆", parfait, #15083	25.00
Celery, 10", oval, #5831	32.50	Stem, 7⅜", 9 oz., water, #17453	35.00
Cigarette box, w/lid, 4" x 2¼", #9305	75.00	Stem, 7½", water, #15083	25.00
Cocktail shaker, 8", w/metal top	175.00	Stem, 7⅝", water, "S" stem, #17457	45.00
Comport, 6¼", #5831	30.00	Sugar, 2⅞", individual, #5831	35.00
Comport, 6½", w/beaded stem, #15082	35.00	Sugar, 3⅜", flat, w/beaded handle, #5902	27.50
Creamer, 2⅞", individual, #5831	35.00	Sugar, 4½", ftd., #5831	22.50
Creamer, 3⅜", flat w/beaded handle, #5902	27.50	Tray, sugar/creamer	32.50
Creamer, 4½", ftd., #5831	22.50	Tumbler, 2⁷⁄₁₆", 2 oz., bar, #506	50.00
Cup, #5831	47.50	Tumbler, 3⁵⁄₁₆", oyster cocktail, #14196	14.00
Hurricane, 12", Chinese style	100.00	Tumbler, 3⅜", old-fashioned, #580	30.00
Icer, with insert	100.00	Tumbler, 4⁵⁄₁₆", 5 oz., ftd., juice, #15083	18.00
Mayonnaise, flat, w/6¼" liner #5902	40.00	Tumbler, 5⅛", water, #517	25.00
Pitcher & cover, #194	325.00	Tumbler, 5⁵⁄₁₆", 9 oz., ftd., water, #15083	15.00
Plate, 6¼", bread and butter, #5902	8.00	Tumbler, 6⁵⁄₁₆", 12 oz., ftd., tea, #15083	30.00
Plate, 6⅜", 2 hdld., #5831	12.50	Vase, 6½", bud, #14185	30.00
Plate, 7", marmalade, 3-ftd., #310½	22.50	Vase, 8³⁄₁₆", flared, crimped	65.00
Plate, 7½", salad, #5831	15.00	Vase, 8¼", bud, #14185	35.00
Plate, 8", salad, #5902	17.50	Vase, 10½", bud, #14185	45.00
Plate, 8⅛", luncheon, #8833	22.50	Vase, 10¾", bulbous bottom, #5872	125.00
Plate, 9½", dinner, #5902	47.50	Vase, 10⅞", beaded stem, #15082	65.00
Plate, 10½", 2 hdld., cake, #5831	50.00	Vase, 11¾", urn, 2 hdld., trophy	95.00
Plate, 14¼", sandwich, #8833	35.00	Whipped cream, 3-ftd., #310	30.00
Relish, 6⅜", 3 pt., #5902	22.50		

GLORIA, (etching 1746), Cambridge Glass 3400 Line Dinnerware, Introduced 1930

Colors: crystal, yellow, Peach-Blo, green, Emerald green, amber, blue, Heatherbloom

Gloria is most often confused with Tiffin's Flanders. In fact, I just purchased a Flanders parfait at the Three Rivers Depression Glass Show a couple of weeks ago that was labelled Gloria. So look closely at these two pattern shots and notice that the flower on Gloria bends the stem. They are easily distinguished once you see them side by side.

Sets can be collected in amber, crystal, and yellow with work, but any other color will take infinite patience and beaucoup money. Heatherbloom and blue will cost up to 60% more than the prices below for other colors. I still have not been able to find a saucer for my Heatherbloom cup pictured.

The dark Emerald green vase sat in my shop for six months packed to ship to a customer. This brings up a real pet peeve for dealers. A customer calls and orders a piece of glassware and even sends a deposit to hold it. They never send the rest of the money or worse scenario, never send any. Meanwhile, some serious collector, cash in hand, is very upset that you will not sell him the item. You lose that customer also! I've taught dealers that you need to set time limits for phone orders!

	Crystal	Green, Pink/ Yellow		Crystal	Green, Pink/ Yellow
Basket, 6", 2 hdld. (sides up)	16.00	30.00	Comport, 5", 4 ftd.	17.00	37.50
Bowl, 3", indiv. nut, 4 ftd.	35.00	55.00	Comport, 6", 4 ftd.	19.00	35.00
Bowl, 3½", cranberry, 4 ftd.	17.50	40.00	Comport, 7", low	30.00	45.00
Bowl, 5", ftd., crimped edge, bonbon	14.00	22.00	Comport, 7", tall	35.00	75.00
Bowl, 5", sq. fruit, "saucer"	7.00	16.00	Comport, 9½", tall, 2 hdld., ftd. bowl	65.00	135.00
Bowl, 5½", bonbon, 2 hdld.	14.00	21.00	Creamer, ftd.	11.00	17.50
Bowl, 5½", bonbon, ftd.	12.00	19.00	Creamer, tall, ftd.	11.00	20.00
Bowl, 5½", flattened, ftd., bonbon	12.00	18.00	Cup, rnd. or sq.	15.00	25.00
Bowl, 5½", fruit, "saucer"	7.50	15.00	Cup, 4 ftd., sq.	25.00	60.00
Bowl, 6", rnd., cereal	12.00	25.00	Cup, after dinner (demitasse), rnd. or sq.	45.00	75.00
Bowl, 6", sq., cereal	12.00	22.00	Fruit cocktail, 6 oz., ftd. (3 styles)	9.00	15.00
Bowl, 8", 2 pt., 2 hdld., relish	15.00	23.00	Ice pail, metal handle w/tongs	37.50	75.00
Bowl, 8", 3 pt., 3 hdld., relish	20.00	34.00	Icer, w/insert	55.00	75.00
Bowl, 8¾", 2 hdld., figure, "8" pickle	17.50	30.00	Mayonnaise, w/liner & ladle, (4 ftd. bowl)	35.00	60.00
Bowl, 8¾", 2 pt., 2 hdld., figure "8" relish	20.00	32.00	Oil, w/stopper; tall, ftd., hdld.	85.00	165.00
Bowl, 9", salad, tab hdld.	20.00	55.00	Oyster cocktail, #3035, 4½ oz.	10.00	15.00
Bowl, 9½", 2 hdld., veg.	55.00	80.00	Oyster cocktail, 4½ oz., low stem	10.00	15.00
Bowl, 10", oblong, tab hdld., "baker"	32.00	70.00	Pitcher, 67 oz., middle indent	125.00	250.00
Bowl, 10", 2 hdld.	32.00	70.00	Pitcher, 80 oz., ball	135.00	235.00
Bowl, 11", 2 hdld., fruit	30.00	55.00	Pitcher, w/cover, 64 oz.	150.00	275.00
Bowl, 12", 4 ftd., console	25.00	50.00	Plate, 6", 2 hdld.	8.00	13.50
Bowl, 12", 4 ftd., flared rim	22.00	50.00	Plate, 6", bread/butter	6.00	9.00
Bowl, 12", 4 ftd., oval	30.00	65.00	Plate, 7½", tea	8.00	12.00
Bowl, 12", 5 pt., celery & relish	25.00	45.00	Plate, 8½"	9.00	14.00
Bowl, 13", flared rim	25.00	55.00	Plate, 9½", dinner	50.00	70.00
Bowl, cream soup, w/rnd. liner	18.00	35.00	Plate, 10", tab hdld. salad	15.00	30.00
Bowl, cream soup, w/sq. saucer	18.00	35.00	Plate, 11", 2 hdld.	15.00	25.00
Bowl, finger, flared edge, w/rnd. plate	14.00	26.00	Plate, 11", sq., ftd. cake	50.00	110.00
Bowl, finger, ftd.	15.00	30.00	Plate, 11½", tab hdld., sandwich	17.50	38.00
Bowl, finger, w/rnd. plate	20.00	35.00	Plate, 14", chop or salad	40.00	75.00
Butter, w/cover, 2 hdld.	110.00	265.00	Plate, sq., bread/butter	6.00	9.00
Candlestick, 6", ea.	17.50	32.50	Plate, sq., dinner	50.00	70.00
Candy box, w/cover, 4 ftd. w/tab hdld.	65.00	110.00	Plate, sq., salad	7.00	12.00
Cheese compote w/11½" cracker plate, tab hdld.	25.00	55.00	Plate, sq., service	22.00	45.00
Cocktail shaker, grnd. stopper, spout (like pitcher)	85.00	200.00	Platter, 11½"	45.00	95.00
			Salt & pepper, pr., short	25.00	55.00
Comport, 4", fruit cocktail	10.00	20.00	Salt & pepper, pr., w/glass top, tall	27.50	70.00

	Crystal	Green Pink/ Yellow		Crystal	Green Pink/ Yellow
Salt & pepper, ftd., metal tops..............	32.50	62.50	Tray, 4 pt., ctr. hdld., relish.................	30.00	45.00
Saucer, rnd...	2.00	4.00	Tray, 9", pickle, tab hdld.	15.00	25.00
Saucer, rnd. after dinner	5.00	10.00	Tumbler, #3035, 5 oz., high ftd.	11.00	20.00
Saucer, sq., after dinner (demitasse)....	5.00	15.00	Tumbler, #3035, 10 oz., high ftd.	12.00	22.00
Saucer, sq...	2.00	3.00	Tumbler, #3035, 12 oz., high ftd.	17.00	30.00
Stem, #3035, 2½ oz., wine	20.00	40.00	Tumbler, #3115, 5 oz., ftd., juice	12.00	20.00
Stem, #3035, 3 oz., cocktail	17.50	28.00	Tumbler, #3115, 8 oz., ftd.	12.00	20.00
Stem, #3035, 3½ oz., cocktail.............	17.00	27.00	Tumbler, #3115, 10 oz., ftd.	13.00	21.00
Stem, #3035, 4½ oz., claret	25.00	45.00	Tumbler, #3115, 12 oz., ftd.	17.00	30.00
Stem, #3035, 6 oz., low sherbet	10.00	15.00	Tumbler, #3120, 2½ oz., ftd. (used		
Stem, #3035, 6 oz., tall sherbet	11.00	17.50	w/cocktail shaker)	20.00	35.00
Stem, #3035, 9 oz., water	15.00	30.00	Tumbler, #3120, 5 oz., ftd.	12.00	20.00
Stem, #3035, 3½ oz., cocktail.............	17.00	28.00	Tumbler, #3120, 10 oz., ftd.	12.00	20.00
Stem, #3115, 9 oz., goblet	13.00	26.00	Tumbler, #3120, 12 oz., ftd.	17.00	30.00
Stem, #3120, 1 oz., cordial..................	50.00	110.00	Tumbler, #3120, 2½ oz., ftd. (used		
Stem, #3120, 4½ oz., claret	25.00	45.00	w/shaker)	20.00	35.00
Stem, #3120, 6 oz., low sherbet	10.00	15.00	Tumbler, #3130, 5 oz., ftd.	12.00	20.00
Stem, #3120, 6 oz., tall sherbet............	11.00	16.00	Tumbler, #3130, 10 oz., ftd.	13.00	20.00
Stem, #3120, 9 oz., water	15.00	25.00	Tumbler, #3130, 12 oz., ftd.	15.00	25.00
Stem, #3130, 2½ oz., wine	20.00	40.00	Tumbler, #3135, 5 oz., juice	12.00	20.00
Stem, #3130, 6 oz., low sherbet	10.00	15.00	Tumbler, #3135, 10 oz., water..............	12.00	20.00
Stem, #3130, 6 oz., tall sherbet............	11.00	16.00	Tumbler, #3135, 12 oz., tea	17.00	30.00
Stem, #3130, 8 oz., water	15.00	25.00	Tumbler, 12 oz., flat, (2 styles), one		
Stem, #3135, 1 oz., cordial..................	55.00	115.00	indent side to match 67 oz. pitcher.	15.00	30.00
Stem, #3135, 6 oz., low sherbet	11.00	15.00	Vase, 9", oval, 4 indent.......................	60.00	125.00
Stem, #3135, 6 oz., tall sherbet............	12.00	16.00	Vase, 10", keyhole base	40.00	95.00
Stem, #3135, 8 oz., water	15.00	26.00	Vase, 10", squarish top	45.00	100.00
Sugar, ftd..	11.00	18.00	Vase, 11"..	45.00	95.00
Sugar, tall, ftd.	11.00	19.00	Vase, 11", neck indent	50.00	100.00
Sugar shaker, w/glass top....................	125.00	250.00	Vase, 12", keyhole base, flared rim	50.00	110.00
Syrup, tall, ftd......................................	50.00	95.00	Vase, 12", squarish top	50.00	100.00
Tray, 11", ctr. hdld., sandwich	20.00	35.00	Vase, 14", keyhole base, flared rim	60.00	135.00
Tray, 2 pt., ctr. hdld., relish.................	22.00	35.00			

Note: See Pages 210-211 for stem identification.

GREEK KEY, A.H. Heisey & Co.

Colors: crystal; "Flamingo" pink punch bowl and cups only

	Crystal		Crystal
Bowl, finger	20.00	Pitcher, 1 pint	75.00
Bowl, jelly, w/cover, 2 hdld. ftd	145.00	Pitcher, 1 quart	85.00
Bowl, indiv., ftd., almond	25.00	Pitcher, 3 pint	125.00
Bowl, 4", nappy	20.00	Pitcher, ½ gal.	150.00
Bowl, 4", shallow, low ft., jelly	20.00	Oil bottle, 2 oz., squat, w/#8 stopper	90.00
Bowl, 4½", nappy	20.00	Oil bottle, 2 oz., w/#6 stopper	95.00
Bowl, 4½", scalloped, nappy	17.50	Oil bottle, 4 oz., squat, w/#8 stopper	80.00
Bowl, 4½", shallow, low ft., jelly	16.00	Oil bottle, 4 oz., w/#6 stopper	80.00
Bowl, 5", ftd., almond	35.00	Oil bottle, 6 oz., w/#6 stopper	100.00
Bowl, 5", ftd., almond, w/cover	90.00	Oil bottle, 6 oz., squat, w/#8 stopper	100.00
Bowl, 5", hdld., jelly	35.00	Plate, 4½"	10.00
Bowl, 5", low ft., jelly, w/cover	40.00	Plate, 5"	11.00
Bowl, 5", nappy	22.50	Plate, 5½"	12.00
Bowl, 5½", nappy	25.00	Plate, 6"	15.00
Bowl, 5½", shallow nappy, ftd.	55.00	Plate, 6½"	15.00
Bowl, 6", nappy	25.00	Plate, 7"	17.00
Bowl, 6", shallow nappy	27.50	Plate, 8"	20.00
Bowl, 6½", nappy	30.00	Plate, 9"	30.00
Bowl, 7", low ft., straight side	35.00	Plate, 10"	60.00
Bowl, 7", nappy	32.00	Plate, 16", orange bowl liner	65.00
Bowl, 8", low ft., straight side	40.00	Puff box, #1, w/cover	85.00
Bowl, 8", nappy	37.50	Puff box, #3, w/cover	95.00
Bowl, 8", scalloped nappy	42.00	Salt & pepper, pr.	90.00
Bowl, 8", shallow, low ft.	45.00	Sherbet, 4½ oz., ftd., straight rim	12.50
Bowl, 8½", shallow nappy	45.00	Sherbet, 4½ oz., ftd., flared rim	12.50
Bowl, 9", flat banana split	27.50	Sherbet, 4½ oz., high ft., shallow	12.50
Bowl, 9", ftd. banana split	25.00	Sherbet, 4½ oz., ftd., shallow	12.50
Bowl, 9", low ft., straight side	45.00	Sherbet, 4½ oz., ftd., cupped rim	12.50
Bowl, 9", nappy	40.00	Sherbet, 6 oz., low ft.	13.00
Bowl, 9", shallow, low ft.	45.00	Spooner, lg.	75.00
Bowl, 9½", shallow nappy	45.00	Spooner, 4½", (or straw jar)	75.00
Bowl, 10", shallow, low ft.	50.00	Stem, ¾ oz., cordial	235.00
Bowl, 11", shallow nappy	50.00	Stem, 2 oz., wine	150.00
Bowl, 12", orange bowl	55.00	Stem, 2 oz., sherry	140.00
Bowl, 12", punch, ftd.	175.00	Stem, 3 oz., cocktail	40.00
(Flamingo)	750.00	Stem, 3½ oz., burgundy	110.00
Bowl, 14", orange, flared rim	65.00	Stem, 4½ oz., saucer champagne	50.00
Bowl, 14½", orange, flared rim	76.50	Stem, 4½ oz., claret	120.00
Bowl, 15", punch, ftd.	165.00	Stem, 7 oz.	75.00
Bowl, 18", punch, shallow	165.00	Stem, 9 oz.	125.00
Butter, indiv. (plate)	30.00	Stem, 9 oz., low ft.	85.00
Butter/jelly, 2 hdld., w/cover	175.00	Straw jar, w/cover	300.00
Candy, w/cover, ½ lb.	135.00	Sugar	25.00
Candy, w/cover, 1 lb.	140.00	Sugar, oval, hotel	30.00
Candy, w/cover, 2 lb.	195.00	Sugar, rnd., hotel	27.50
Cheese & cracker set, 10"	80.00	Sugar & creamer, oval, individual	67.50
Compote, 5"	60.00	Tray, 9", oval celery	40.00
Compote, 5", w/cover	85.00	Tray, 12", oval celery	45.00
Creamer	25.00	Tray, 12½", French roll	100.00
Creamer, oval, hotel	30.00	Tray, 13", oblong	110.00
Creamer, rnd., hotel	27.50	Tray, 15", oblong	120.00
Cup, 4½ oz., punch	20.00	Tumbler, 2½ oz., (or toothpick)	300.00
Cup, punch, (Flamingo)	40.00	Tumbler, 5 oz., flared rim	20.00
Coaster	12.00	Tumbler, 5 oz., straight side	20.00
Egg cup, 5 oz.	60.00	Tumbler, 5½ oz., water	20.00
Hair receiver	80.00	Tumbler, 7 oz., flared rim	22.00
Ice tub, lg., tab hdld.	90.00	Tumbler, 7 oz., straight side	25.00
Ice tub, sm., tab hdld.	80.00	Tumbler, 8 oz., w/straight, flared, cupped,	
Ice tub, w/cover, hotel	95.00	shallow	35.00
Ice tub, w/cover, 5", individual w/5" plate	95.00	Tumbler, 10 oz., flared rim	37.00
Jar, 1 qt., crushed fruit, w/cover	300.00	Tumbler, 10 oz., straight wide	37.00
Jar, 2 qt., crushed fruit, w/cover	325.00	Tumbler, 12 oz., flared rim	40.00
Jar, lg. cover, horseradish	75.00	Tumbler, 12 oz., straight side	40.00
Jar, sm. cover, horseradish	65.00	Tumbler, 13 oz., straight side	42.00
Jar, tall celery	70.00	Tumbler, 13 oz., flared rim	42.00
Jar, w/knob cover, pickle	125.00	Water bottle	170.00

HERMITAGE, #2449, Fostoria Glass Company, 1932 – 1945

Colors: Amber, Azure (blue), crystal, Ebony, green, Topaz, Wisteria

My listings are from a Fostoria catalogue that had January 1, 1933, entered on the front page in pencil. Not all pieces were made in all colors. For example the 5" fruit, 6" cereal, and 7" soup were not made in green or Wisteria.

	Crystal	amber/green/Topaz	Azure/Wisteria
Ash tray holder, #2449	5.00	8.00	12.00
*Ash tray, #2449	3.00	5.00	8.00
Bottle, 3 oz., oil, #2449	17.50	35.00	
Bottle, 27 oz., bar w/stopper, #2449	45.00		
Bowl, 4½", finger, #2449½	4.00	6.00	10.00
Bowl, 5", fruit, #2449½	5.00	8.00	12.00
Bowl, 6", cereal, #2449½	6.00	9.00	14.00
Bowl, 6½", salad, #2449½	6.00	9.00	14.00
Bowl, 7", soup, #2449½	8.00	12.00	20.00
Bowl, 7½", salad, #2449½	8.00	12.00	20.00
Bowl, 8", deep, ped., ft., #2449	17.50	30.00	45.00
Bowl, 10", ftd., #2449	17.50	30.00	
Bowl, grapefruit w/crystal liner #2449	20.00	35.00	
Candle, 6", #2449	12.50	22.00	35.00
Coaster, 5⅝", #2449	5.00	7.50	11.00
Comport, 6", #2449	12.00	17.50	27.50
Creamer, ftd., #2449	4.00	6.00	10.00
Cup, ftd.,#2449	6.00	10.00	15.00
Decanter, 28 oz., w/stopper, #2449	35.00	50.00	75.00
Fruit cocktail, 2⅜", 5 oz., ftd., #2449	5.00	7.50	12.00
Ice tub, 6", #2449	17.50	30.00	45.00
Icer, #2449	10.00	15.00	25.00
Mayonnaise, 5⅝" w/7" plate, #2449	20.00	35.00	
Mug, 9 oz., ftd., #2449	12.50		
Mug, 12 oz., ftd., #2449	15.00		
Mustard w/cover & spoon, #2449	17.50	27.50	
Pitcher, pint, #2449	22.50	35.00	50.00
Pitcher, 3 pint, #2449	27.50	50.00	85.00
Plate, 6", #2449½	3.00	5.00	8.00
Plate, 7" ice dish liner	4.00	6.00	10.00
Plate, 7", #2449½	4.00	6.00	10.00
Plate, 7⅜", crescent salad, #2449	10.00	15.00	25.00
Plate, 8", #2449½	6.00	10.00	15.00
Plate, 9", #2449½	12.50	20.00	30.00
Plate, 12", sandwich, #2449		12.50	20.00
Relish, 6", 2 pt., #2449	6.00	10.00	15.00
Relish, 7¼", 3 pt., #2449	8.00	11.00	17.50
Relish, 8", pickle, #2449	8.00	11.00	17.50
Relish, 11", celery, #2449	10.00	15.00	25.00
Salt & pepper, 3⅜", #2449	20.00	35.00	55.00
Salt, indiv., #2449	4.00	6.00	10.00
Saucer, #2449	2.00	3.50	5.00
Sherbet, 3", 7 oz., low, ftd., #2449	6.00	8.00	12.50
Stem, 3¼", 5½ oz., high sherbet, #2449	8.00	11.00	17.50
Stem, 4⅝", 4 oz., claret, #2449	10.00	15.00	
Stem, 5¼", 9 oz., water goblet, #2449	10.00	15.00	25.00
Sugar, ftd., #2449	4.00	6.00	10.00
Tray, 6½", condiment, #2449	6.00	10.00	15.00
Tumbler, 2½", 2 oz., #2449½	4.00	6.00	10.00
Tumbler, 2½", 2 oz., ftd., #2449	5.00	8.00	
Tumbler, 3", 4 oz., cocktail, ftd., #2449	5.00	7.50	12.00
Tumbler, 3¼", 6 oz. old-fashioned, #2449½	6.00	9.00	15.00
Tumbler, 3⅞", 5 oz., #2449½	5.00	8.00	12.00
Tumbler, 4", 5 oz., ftd., #2449	5.00	8.00	12.00
Tumbler, 4⅛", 9 oz., ftd., #2449	6.00	10.00	15.00
Tumbler, 4¾", 9 oz., #2449½	6.00	10.00	15.00
Tumbler, 5¼", 12 oz., ftd., iced tea, #2449	10.00	15.00	25.00
Tumbler, 5⅞", 13 oz., #2449½	10.00	15.00	25.00
Vase, 6", ftd.	20.00	30.00	

* Ebony - $10.00

IMPERIAL HUNT SCENE, #718, Cambridge Glass Company, Late 1920's – 1930's

Colors: amber, black, crystal, Emerald green, green, pink, Willow blue

I have asked for years if anyone has ever seen an Imperial Hunt Scene cup and have always received the answer that they are pictured in the catalogue; so they must exist. Finally, cups in crystal #1402 Tally-Ho turned up at the recent Miami Depression Glass Show. Now, has anyone seen some crystal Tally-Ho saucers?

Last year a set of Willow Blue Hunt Scene was found on the East Coast and it now has a home on the West Coast. It is amazing how this glass does travel!

If your desire is to collect a pattern with an array of stems and tumblers – this is the one. I have difficulty in finding anything other than stems to photograph.

Black and dark Emerald green will fetch 15% to 25% higher prices than those listed.

	Crystal	Colors
Bowl, 6", cereal.	15.00	25.00
Bowl, 8".	35.00	60.00
Bowl, 8½", 3 pt.	25.00	45.00
Candlestick, 2-lite, keyhole.	17.50	35.00
Candlestick, 3-lite, keyhole.	27.50	55.00
Comport, 5½", #3085		30.00
Creamer, ftd.	15.00	30.00
Cup	45.00	
Decanter		225.00
Finger bowl, w/plate, #3085		35.00
Humidor, tobacco		350.00
Ice bucket.	40.00	75.00
Ice tub.	35.00	70.00
Mayonnaise, w/liner.	30.00	50.00
Pitcher, w/cover, 63 oz., #3085.		250.00
Pitcher, w/cover, 76 oz., #711.	150.00	225.00
Plate, 8".	12.00	22.00
Saucer.	10.00	
Stem, 1 oz., cordial, #1402.	55.00	
Stem, 2½ oz., wine, #1402.	45.00	
Stem, 3 oz., cocktail, #1402.	40.00	
Stem, 6 oz., tomato, #1402.	40.00	
Stem, 6½ oz., sherbet, #1402.	35.00	
Stem, 7½ oz., sherbet, #1402.	40.00	
Stem, 10 oz., water, #1402.	40.00	
Stem, 14 oz., #1402.	50.00	
Stem, 18 oz., #1402.	60.00	
Stem, 1 oz., cordial, #3085.		150.00
Stem, 2½ oz., cocktail, #3085.		40.00
Stem, 2½ oz., wine, #3085.		55.00
Stem, 4½ oz., claret, #3085.		65.00
Stem, 5½ oz., parfait, #3085.		60.00
Stem, 6 oz., low sherbet, #3085.		22.50
Stem, 6 oz., high sherbet, #3085.		27.50
Stem, 9 oz., water, #3085.		45.00
Sugar, ftd.	15.00	30.00
Tumbler, 2½ oz., flat, #1402.	25.00	
Tumbler, 5 oz., flat, #1402.	20.00	
Tumbler, 7 oz., flat, #1402.	20.00	
Tumbler, 10 oz., flat, #1402.	23.00	
Tumbler, 10 oz., flat, tall, #1402.	25.00	
Tumbler, 15 oz., flat, #1402.	35.00	
Tumbler, 2½ oz., ftd., #3085.		30.00
Tumbler, 5 oz., ftd., #3085.		25.00
Tumbler, 8 oz., ftd., #3085.		25.00
Tumbler, 10 oz., ftd., #3085.		30.00
Tumbler, 12 oz., ftd., #3085.		35.00

IPSWICH, Blank #1405, A.H. Heisey & Co.

Colors: crystal, "Flamingo" pink, "Sahara" yellow, "Moongleam" green, cobalt and "Alexandrite"

Ipswich prices have made some drastic increases since the last book. Economy, notwithstanding, Heisey prices are going in only one direction at the present moment and that is **up**!

If you find any colored piece of Ipswich, **other than those listed below**, it was made at Imperial and not Heisey. Even if it is marked Heisey, it was still manufactured at Imperial. Mostly, I get letters on (Alexandrite) candy jars which are actually Imperial's Heather color.

The only piece of Ipswich made in Alexandrite is the goblet. If you have any problems in determining whether a piece you have is Alexandrite or not, look in the back of this book on pages 212-213. We have been able to show this color more consistently than any other book ever has. You can also take an Alexandrite piece outside in natural light where it will look pinkish and then near a fluorescent bulb where it will change to a blue hue.

Note the candle vase in green which goes atop the candlestick centerpiece. Has anyone got the bottom?

	Crystal	Pink	Sahara	Green	Cobalt	Alexan
Bowl, finger w/underplate	20.00	55.00	60.00	70.00		
Bowl, 11", ftd., floral	45.00				250.00	
Candlestick, 6", 1-lite	75.00	205.00	150.00	200.00	350.00	
Candlestick centerpiece, ftd., vase, "A" prisms	95.00	275.00	300.00	450.00	500.00	
Candy jar, ½ lb., w/cover	130.00	225.00	250.00	300.00		
Cocktail shaker, 1 quart, strainer #86 stopper	225.00	600.00	700.00	800.00		
Creamer	24.00	47.50	37.50	42.50		
Stem, 4 oz., oyster cocktail	20.00					
Stem, 5 oz., saucer champagne	20.00					
Stem, 10 oz., goblet	25.00					750.00
Stem, 12 oz., schoppen	30.00					
Pitcher, ½ gal.	150.00	250.00	350.00	750.00		
Oil bottle, 2 oz., ftd., #86 stopper	75.00	185.00	150.00	200.00		
Plate, 7", square	20.00	25.00	25.00	35.00		
Plate, 8", square	20.00	30.00	30.00	40.00		
Sherbet, 4 oz.	9.00	17.50	22.50	30.00		
Sugar	24.00	42.50	37.50	42.50		
Tumbler, 5 oz., ftd.	30.00	40.00	40.00	50.00		
Tumbler, 8 oz., ftd.	30.00	40.00	40.00	60.00		
Tumbler, 10 oz., cupped rim	30.00	40.00	40.00	50.00		
Tumbler, 10 oz., straight rim	30.00	40.00	40.00	50.00		
Tumbler, 12 oz., ftd.	30.00	50.00	45.00	60.00		

JUNE, Fostoria Glass Company, 1928 – 1944

Colors: crystal, "Azure" blue, "Topaz" yellow, "Rose" pink

There is not enough room in this book to list all the line numbers for the items in June! If you will refer to Versailles, I have listed all the Fostoria line numbers for each piece. Since these are virtually the same listings, you can use the item number listings from Versailles if you need such information. There is other Fostoria information under Versailles you need to read also if you collect June!

Prices continue to increase, but some items are really wild. I attended a show recently where pink June water goblets were in three booths priced at $95.00, $75.00, and $55.00. None sold, but if you were shopping for them, which would you buy?

Prices for Rose June are now listed with the blue!

	Crystal	Rose, Blue	Topaz		Crystal	Rose, Blue	Topaz
Ash tray	23.00	45.00	32.00	Ice dish liner (tomato, crab, fruit)	5.00	20.00	10.00
Bottle, salad dressing, #2083 or #2375	165.00	450.00	275.00	Mayonnaise, w/liner	25.00	60.00	40.00
Bowl, baker, 9", oval	35.00	85.00	65.00	Oil, ftd.	200.00	500.00	300.00
Bowl, baker, 10", oval	40.00	100.00	75.00	Oyster cocktail, 5½ oz.	16.00	35.00	25.00
Bowl, bonbon	12.50	27.50	20.00	Parfait, 5¼"	30.00	95.00	55.00
Bowl, bouillon, ftd.	12.00	35.00	20.00	Pitcher	195.00	500.00	300.00
Bowl, finger, w/liner	32.50	50.00	25.00	Plate, canape	10.00	25.00	15.00
Bowl, mint, 3-ftd., 4½"	10.00	30.00	20.00	Plate, lemon	14.00	25.00	18.00
Bowl, 5", mint	11.00	22.00	18.00	Plate, 6", bread/butter	4.50	12.00	6.00
Bowl, 6", cereal	15.00	35.00	25.00	Plate, 6", finger bowl liner	4.50	10.00	6.00
Bowl, 6", nappy, 3-ftd., jelly	10.00	30.00	18.00	Plate, 7½", salad	5.00	9.00	8.00
Bowl, 7", soup	35.00	100.00	100.00	Plate, 7½, cream soup	4.00	12.00	7.50
Bowl, lg., dessert, hdld.	25.00	95.00	55.00	Plate, 8¾", luncheon	6.00	15.00	10.00
Bowl, 10"	30.00	95.00	55.00	Plate, 9½", sm. dinner	10.00	30.00	18.00
Bowl, 10", Grecian	35.00	85.00	50.00	Plate, 10", grill	30.00	75.00	60.00
Bowl, 11", centerpiece	25.00	60.00	40.00	Plate, 10", cake, hdld (no indent)	20.00	60.00	40.00
Bowl, 12", centerpiece, several types	25.00	85.00	45.00	Plate, 10", cheese with indent, hdld.	20.00	60.00	40.00
Bowl, 13", oval centerpiece, w/flower frog	45.00	125.00	65.00	Plate, 10¼", dinner	35.00	85.00	55.00
Candlestick, 2"	10.00	25.00	20.00	Plate, 13", chop	22.00	60.00	40.00
Candlestick, 3"	12.00	25.00	18.00	Plate, 14", torte			55.00
Candlestick, 3", Grecian	20.00	45.00	30.00	Platter, 12"	25.00	95.00	60.00
Candlestick, 5"	20.00	45.00	30.00	Platter, 15"	45.00	175.00	100.00
Candy, w/cover, 3 pt.		250.00		Relish, 8½", 3-part	15.00	35.00	22.00
Candy, w/cover, ½ lb., ¼ lb.			155.00	Sauce boat	40.00	275.00	95.00
Celery, 11½"	25.00	75.00	35.00	Sauce boat liner	15.00	75.00	30.00
Cheese & cracker set, #2368 or #2375	25.00	95.00	45.00	Saucer, after dinner	6.00	15.00	10.00
Comport, 5", #2400	18.00	50.00	27.50	Saucer	4.00	7.50	5.00
Comport, 6", #5298 or #5299	20.00	75.00	40.00	Shaker, ftd., pr.	60.00	165.00	110.00
Comport, 7", #2375	22.00	85.00	45.00	Sherbet, high, 6", 6 oz.	17.50	35.00	25.00
Comport, 8", #2400	40.00	100.00	55.00	Sherbet, low, 4¼", 6 oz.	15.00	30.00	20.00
Cream soup, ftd.	15.00	45.00	32.50	Sugar, ftd., straight or scalloped top	12.00	25.00	20.00
Creamer, ftd.	12.00	25.00	17.50	Sugar cover	50.00	200.00	125.00
Creamer, tea	20.00	55.00	40.00	Sugar pail	65.00	195.00	130.00
Cup, after dinner	20.00	75.00	40.00	Sugar, tea	20.00	55.00	40.00
Cup, ftd.	15.00	30.00	22.00	Sweetmeat	15.00	35.00	20.00
Decanter	400.00	1000.00	500.00	Tray, service and lemon		300.00	260.00
Goblet, claret, 6", 4 oz.	30.00	110.00	65.00	Tray, 11", ctr. hdld.	20.00	45.00	35.00
Goblet, cocktail, 5¼", 3 oz.	20.00	45.00	32.50	Tumbler, 2½ oz., ftd.	20.00	60.00	35.00
Goblet, cordial, 4", ¾ oz.	50.00	115.00	70.00	Tumbler, 5 oz., 4½", ftd.	15.00	35.00	22.50
Goblet, water, 8¼", 10 oz.	25.00	55.00	35.00	Tumbler, 9 oz., 5¼", ftd.	15.00	40.00	22.50
Goblet, wine, 5½", 3 oz.	25.00	90.00	50.00	Tumbler, 12 oz., 6", ftd.	20.00	50.00	30.00
Grapefruit	30.00	100.00	60.00	Vase, 8", 2 styles	75.00	225.00	145.00
Grapefruit liner	25.00	75.00	40.00	Vase, 8½", fan, ftd.	60.00	175.00	110.00
Ice bucket	47.50	110.00	75.00	Whipped cream bowl	10.00	20.00	14.00
Ice dish	22.50	55.00	40.00	Whipped cream pail	75.00	200.00	125.00

Note: See stemware identification on page 93.

KASHMIR, Fostoria Glass Company, 1930 – 1934

Colors: "Topaz" yellow, green; some blue

Kashmir is another of the patterns I can only find a piece here and there. Rarely do I see a lot of it for sale at one time except for yellow, which few people seem to notice. Both styles of after dinner cups are shown in the picture of blue. In the last book I said that finding blue Kashmir was a challenge; several new collectors have taken that challenge and are meeting with some success due to lack of competition from others.

Notice that I have found very little green in my travels. The next dare is to find some green! You may need some of that other "green" if you do!

	Yellow, Green	Blue		Yellow, Green	Blue
Ash tray	25.00	30.00	Plate, 10", dinner	35.00	50.00
Bowl, cream soup	22.00	25.00	Plate, 10", grill	35.00	50.00
Bowl, finger	15.00	20.00	Plate, cake, 10"	35.00	
Bowl, 5", fruit	13.00	15.00	Salt & pepper, pr.	100.00	150.00
Bowl, 6", cereal	25.00	30.00	Sandwich, center hdld	35.00	40.00
Bowl, 7", soup	25.00	35.00	Sauce boat, w/liner	75.00	100.00
Bowl, 8½", pickle	20.00	30.00	Saucer, rnd.	5.00	10.00
Bowl, 9", baker	37.50	45.00	Saucer, after dinner, sq.	5.00	
Bowl, 10"	40.00	45.00	Saucer, after dinner, rnd.	6.00	10.00
Bowl, 12", centerpiece	40.00	50.00	Stem, ¾ oz., cordial	85.00	110.00
Candlestick, 2"	15.00	17.50	Stem, 2½ oz., ftd.	25.00	35.00
Candlestick, 3"	20.00	25.00	Stem, 2 oz., ftd., whiskey	25.00	30.00
Candlestick, 5"	22.50	27.50	Stem, 2½ oz., wine	32.00	40.00
Candlestick, 9½"	40.00	60.00	Stem, 3 oz., cocktail	22.00	25.00
Candy, w/cover	75.00	95.00	Stem, 3½ oz., ftd., cocktail	22.00	25.00
Cheese and cracker set	65.00	85.00	Stem, 4 oz., claret	35.00	50.00
Comport, 6"	35.00	45.00	Stem, 4½ oz., oyster cocktail	16.00	18.00
Creamer, ftd.	17.50	20.00	Stem, 5½ oz., parfait	30.00	40.00
Cup	15.00	20.00	Stem, 5 oz., ftd., juice	15.00	25.00
Cup, after dinner, flat	35.00		Stem, 5 oz., low sherbet	13.00	20.00
Cup, after dinner, ftd.	35.00	50.00	Stem, 6 oz., high sherbet	17.50	22.50
Grapefruit	50.00		Stem, 9 oz., water	20.00	35.00
Grapefruit liner	40.00		Stem, 10 oz., ftd., water	22.00	30.00
Ice bucket	65.00	85.00	Stem, 11 oz.	22.50	
Oil, ftd.	250.00	400.00	Stem, 12 oz., ftd.	25.00	35.00
Pitcher, ftd.	250.00	350.00	Stem, 13 oz., ftd., tea	25.00	
Plate, 6", bread & butter	5.00	6.00	Stem, 16 oz., ftd., tea	35.00	
Plate, 7", salad, rnd.	6.00	7.00	Sugar, ftd.	15.00	20.00
Plate, 7", salad, sq.	6.00	7.00	Sugar lid	35.00	60.00
Plate, 8", salad	8.00	10.00	Vase, 8"	85.00	100.00
Plate, 9" luncheon	9.00	12.00			

Note: See stemware identification on page 93.

LARIAT, Blank #1540, A.H. Heisey & Co.

Colors: crystal; rare in black and amber

The cutting most often found on Lariat is Moonglo. This is shown on the stems on the right in the top picture. Notice the two styles of cordials there. One has a single loop of Lariat while the other is a double loop. The shaker shown in the bottom photo is a difficult piece to acquire; so be on the lookout for it.

	Crystal
Ash tray, 4"	10.00
Basket, 7½", bonbon	100.00
Basket, 8½", ftd.	165.00
Basket, 10", ftd.	195.00
Bowl, 7 quart, punch	110.00
Bowl, 4", nut, individual	20.00
Bowl, 7", 2 pt., mayo	20.00
Bowl, 7", nappy	15.00
Bowl, 8", flat, nougat	15.00
Bowl, 9½", camellia	22.00
Bowl, 10", hdld., celery	35.00
Bowl, 10½", 2 hdld., salad	32.00
Bowl, 10½", salad	32.00
Bowl, 11", 2 hdld., oblong, relish	25.00
Bowl, 12", floral or fruit	20.00
Bowl, 13", celery	22.00
Bowl, 13", gardenia	25.00
Bowl, 13", oval, floral	27.00
Candlestick, 1-lite	15.00
Candlestick, 2-lite	25.00
Candlestick, 3-lite	35.00
Candy box, w/cover, caramel	45.00
Candy, w/cover, 7"	50.00
Cheese, 5", ftd., w/cover	40.00
Cheese dish, w/cover, 8"	50.00
Cigarette box	42.00
Coaster, 4"	8.00
Compote, 10", w/cover	75.00
Creamer	15.00
Creamer & sugar, w/tray, indiv.	37.50
Cup	12.00
Cup, punch	6.00
Ice tub	75.00
Jar, w/cover, 12", urn	150.00
Lamp & globe, 7", black-out	100.00
Lamp & globe, 8", candle, handled	85.00
Mayonnaise, 5" bowl, 7" plate w/ladle set	55.00

	Crystal
Oil bottle, 4 oz., hdld., w/#133 stopper	100.00
Oil bottle, 6 oz., oval	65.00
Plate, 6", finger bowl liner	5.00
Plate, 7", salad	7.00
Plate, 8", salad	9.00
Plate, 11", cookie	25.00
Plate, 12", demi-torte, rolled edge	27.00
Plate, 13", deviled egg	150.00
Plate, 14", 2 hdld., sandwich	35.00
Plate, 21", buffet	90.00
Platter, 15", oval	40.00
Salt & pepper, pr.	200.00
Saucer	5.00
Stem, 1 oz., cordial, double loop	185.00
Stem, 1 oz., cordial blown, single loop	150.00
Stem, 2½ oz., wine, blown	25.00
Stem, 3½ oz., cocktail, pressed	15.00
Stem, 3½ oz., cocktail, blown	15.00
Stem, 3½ oz., wine, pressed	20.00
Stem, 4 oz., claret, blown	25.00
Stem, 4¼ oz., oyster cocktail or fruit	15.00
Stem, 4½ oz., oyster cocktail, blown	15.00
Stem, 5½ oz., sherbet/saucer champagne blown	15.00
Stem, 6 oz., low sherbet	10.00
Stem, 6 oz., sherbet/saucer champagne, pressed	12.50
Stem, 9 oz., pressed	20.00
Stem, 10 oz., blown	20.00
Sugar	15.00
Tray for sugar & creamer, 8" 2-handled	20.00
Tumbler, 5 oz., ftd., juice	15.00
Tumbler, 5 oz., ftd., juice, blown	15.00
Tumbler, 12 oz., ftd., ice tea	18.00
Tumbler, 12 oz., ftd., ice tea, blown	18.00
Vase, 7", ftd., fan	25.00
Vase, swung	125.00

LODESTAR, Pattern #1632, A.H. Heisey & Co.

Color: Dawn

This Heisey pattern is only called Lodestar in the Dawn color. If you find pieces in crystal, the pattern name becomes Satellite and the prices are entirely different than for this rarer Heisey color. Note the star-like design in each base design. The Dawn color is highly sought; be aware of its significance.

	Dawn
Ash tray	70.00
Bowl, 4½", sauce dish, #1626	35.00
Bowl, 5", mayonnaise	55.00
Bowl, 6¾", #1565	45.00
Bowl, 8"	45.00
Bowl, 11", crimped	95.00
Bowl, 12", deep floral	75.00
Candleblock, 2¾" tall, 1-lite star, #1543, pr., (Satellite)	275.00
Candlestick, 2" tall, 1-lite centerpiece, pr.	100.00
Candlestick, 5¾" tall, 2-lite, pr.	600.00
Candy jar, w/cover, 5"	135.00
Celery, 10"	60.00
Creamer	50.00
Creamer, w/handle	85.00
Jar, w/cover, 8", #1626	140.00
Pitcher, 1 qt., #1626	150.00
Plate, 8½"	65.00
Plate, 14"	85.00
Relish, 7½", 3 pt.	55.00
Salt and pepper, pr., #1485	250.00
Sugar	50.00
Sugar, w/handles	85.00
Tumbler, 6 oz., juice	35.00
Vase, 8", #1626	140.00
Vase, 8", crimped, #1626	175.00

MINUET, Etching #1530, QUEEN ANN Blank, #1509; TOUJOURS Blank, #1511; SYMPHONE Blank, #5010, et. al.; 1939 – 1950's

Colors: crystal

Minuet is one of the Heisey patterns that Cathy really likes. I guess it is the musical designs etched in the glass that she enjoys. (I bet I'll find out when she edits this for me!)

Stemware is fairly abundant, but serving pieces are hard to find. The cocktail icer shown in the last book sat on our table about fifteen minutes when we put it out for sale.

	Crystal
Bell, dinner, #3408	60.00
Bowl, finger, #3309	18.00
Bowl, 6", ftd., mint	15.00
Bowl, 6", ftd., 2 hdld., jelly	15.00
Bowl, 6½", salad dressings	25.00
Bowl, 7", salad dressings	27.50
Bowl, 7", triplex, relish	25.00
Bowl, 7½", sauce, ftd.	30.00
Bowl, 9½", 3 pt., "5 o'clock" relish	50.00
Bowl, 10", salad, #1511 TOUJOURS	50.00
Bowl, 11", 3 pt., "5 o'clock" relish	55.00
Bowl, 11", ftd., floral	45.00
Bowl, 12", oval, floral, #1511 TOUJOURS	50.00
Bowl, 12", oval, #1514	50.00
Bowl, 13", floral, #1511 TOUJOURS	45.00
Bowl, 13", pickle & olive	30.00
Bowl, 13½", shallow salad	60.00
Candelabrum, 1-lite w/prisms	95.00
Candelabrum, 2-lite, bobeche & prisms	150.00
Candlestick, 1-lite, #112	25.00
Candlestick, 2-lite, #1511 TOUJOURS	125.00
Candlestick, 3-lite, #142 CASCADE	65.00
Candlestick, 5", 2-lite, #134 TRIDENT	35.00
Centerpiece vase & prisms #1511 TOUJOURS	175.00
Cocktail icer, w/liner #3304 UNIVERSAL	100.00
Comport, 5½", #5010	35.00
Comport, 7½", #1511 TOUJOURS	50.00
Creamer, #1511 TOUJOURS	50.00
Creamer, dolp. ft.	40.00
Creamer, indiv., #1509 QUEEN ANN	35.00
Creamer, indiv., #1511 TOUJOURS	35.00
Cup	35.00
Ice bucket, dolp. ft.	135.00
Marmalade, w/cover, #1511 TOUJOURS (apple shape)	85.00
Mayonnaise, 5½", dolp. ft.	40.00
Mayonnaise, ftd., #1511 TOUJOURS	40.00
Pitcher, 73 oz., #4164	225.00
Plate, 7", mayonnaise liner	10.00

	Crystal
Plate, 7", salad	10.00
Plate, 7", salad, #1511 TOUJOURS	12.00
Plate, 8", luncheon	15.00
Plate, 8", luncheon, #1511 TOUJOURS	20.00
Plate, 10½", service	50.00
Plate, 12", rnd., 2 hdld., sandwich	40.00
Plate, 13", floral, salver, #1511 TOUJOURS	45.00
Plate, 14", torte, #1511 TOUJOURS	45.00
Plate, 15", sand., #1511 TOUJOURS	50.00
Plate, 16", snack rack, w/#1477 center	75.00
Salt & pepper, pr. (#10)	50.00
Saucer	10.00
Stem, #5010, SYMPHONE, 1 oz., cordial	135.00
Stem, #5010, 2½ oz., wine	65.00
Stem, #5010, 3½ oz., cocktail	30.00
Stem, #5010, 4 oz., claret	30.00
Stem, #5010, 4½ oz., oyster cocktail	15.00
Stem, #5010, 6 oz., saucer champagne	15.00
Stem, #5010, 6 oz., sherbet	12.00
Stem, #5010, 9 oz., water	30.00
Sugar, indiv., #1511 TOUJOURS	35.00
Sugar, indiv., #1509 QUEEN ANN	35.00
Sugar dolp. ft., #1509 QUEEN ANN	40.00
Sugar, #1511 TOUJOURS	50.00
Tray, 12", celery, #1511 TOUJOURS	27.50
Tray, 15", social hour	60.00
Tray for indiv. sugar & creamer	20.00
Tumbler, #5010, 5 oz., fruit juice	30.00
Tumbler, #5010, 9 oz., low ftd., water	35.00
Tumbler, #5010, 12 oz., tea	40.00
Tumbler, #2351, 12 oz., tea	30.00
Vase, 5", #5013	40.00
Vase, 5½", ftd., #1511 TOUJOURS	50.00
Vase, 6", urn, #5012	65.00
Vase, 7½", urn, #5012	75.00
Vase, 8", #4196	75.00
Vase, 9", urn, #5012	80.00
Vase, 10", #4192	80.00
Vase, 10", #4192, SATURN optic	95.00

MT. VERNON, Cambridge Glass Company, late 1920's – 1940's

Colors: amber, crystal, Carmen, Royal Blue, Heatherbloom, Emerald green (light and dark); rare in Violet

The range of colors in Mt. Vernon gives collectors a wide choice. Large sets can be accumulated in only amber and crystal. Red, cobalt blue, and Heatherbloom are found, but not in large quantities that collectors would like to see. These colors are nearly impossible to acquire in sets. Note the Violet sherbet shown in the top photograph. This color is rare in dinnerware lines!

	Amber/Crystal
Ash tray, 3½", #63	8.00
Ash tray, 4", #68	12.00
Ash tray, 6" x 4½", oval, #71	12.00
Bonbon, 7", ftd., #10	12.50
Bottle bitters, 2½ oz., #62	55.00
Bottle, 7 oz., sq., toilet, #18	65.00
Bowl, finger, #23	10.00
Bowl, 4½", ivy ball or rose, ftd., #12	27.50
Bowl, 5¼", fruit, #6	10.00
Bowl, 6", cereal, #32	12.50
Bowl, 6", preserve, #76	12.00
Bowl, 6½", rose, #106	18.00
Bowl, 8", pickle, #65	17.50
Bowl, 8½", 4 pt., 2 hdld., sweetmeat, #105	30.00
Bowl, 10", 2 hdld., #39	20.00
Bowl, 10½", deep, #43	30.00
Bowl, 10½", salad, #120	25.00
Bowl, 11", oval, 4 ftd., #136	27.50
Bowl, 11", oval, #135	25.00
Bowl, 11½", belled, #128	30.00
Bowl, 11½", shallow, #126	30.00
Bowl, 11½", shallow cupped, #61	30.00
Bowl, 12", flanged, rolled edge, #129	32.50
Bowl, 12", oblong, crimped, #118	32.50
Bowl, 12", rolled edge, crimped, #117	32.50
Bowl, 12½", flanged, rolled edge, #45	32.50
Bowl, 12½", flared, #121	32.00
Bowl, 12½", flared, #44	32.00
Bowl, 13", shallow, crimped, #116	35.00
Box, 3", w/cover, round, #16	25.00
Box, 4", w/cover, sq., #17	30.00
Box, 4½", w/cover, ftd., round, #15	35.00
Butter tub, w/cover, #73	60.00
Cake stand, 10½" ftd., #150	35.00
Candelabrum, 13½", #38	45.00
Candlestick, 4", #130	10.00
Candlestick, 5", 2-lite, #110	20.00
Candlestick, 8", #35	25.00
Candy, w/cover, 1 lb., ftd., #9	50.00
Celery, 10½", #79	15.00
Celery, 11", #98	17.50
Celery, 12", #79	20.00
Cigarette box, 6", w/cover, oval, #69	27.50
Cigarette holder, #66	15.00
Coaster, 3", plain, #60	5.00
Coaster, 3", ribbed, #70	5.00
Cocktail icer, 2 pc., #85	22.50
Cologne, 2½ oz., w/stopper, #1340	35.00
Comport, 4½", #33	12.00
Comport, 5½", 2 hdld., #77	15.00
Comport, 6", #34	15.00
Comport, 6½", #97	17.50
Comport, 6½", belled, #96	22.50
Comport, 7½" #11	25.00
Comport, 8", #81	25.00
Comport, 9", oval, 2 hdld., #100	27.50
Comport, 9½", #99	27.50
Creamer, ftd., #8	10.00
Creamer, indiv., #4	10.00
Creamer, #86	10.00
Cup, #7	6.50
Decanter, 11 oz., #47	50.00
Decanter, 40 oz., w/stopper, #52	70.00

	Amber/Crystal
Honey jar, w/cover (marmalade), #74	30.00
Ice bucket, w/tongs, #92	35.00
Lamp, 9" hurricane, #1607	70.00
Mayonnaise, divided, 2 spoons, #107	25.00
Mug, 14 oz., stein, #84	27.50
Mustard, w/cover, 2½ oz., #28	22.00
Pickle, 6", 1 hdld., #78	12.00
Pitcher, 50 oz., #90	75.00
Pitcher, 66 oz., #13	80.00
Pitcher, 80 oz., ball, #95	90.00
Pitcher, 86 oz., #91	110.00
Plate, finger bowl liner, #23	4.00
Plate, 6", bread & butter, #4	3.00
Plate, 6⅜", bread & butter, #19	4.00
Plate, 8½", salad, #5	7.00
Plate, 10½", dinner, #40	27.50
Plate, 11½", hdld., #37	20.00
Relish, 6", 2 pt., 2 hdld., #106	12.00
Relish, 8", 2 pt., hdld., #101	17.50
Relish, 8", 3 pt., 3 hdld., #103	20.00
Relish, 11", 3 part, #200	25.00
Relish, 12", 2 part, #80	30.00
Relish, 12", 5 part, #104	30.00
Salt, indiv., #24	7.00
Salt, oval, 2 hdld., #102	12.00
Salt & pepper, pr., #28	22.50
Salt & pepper, pr., short, #88	20.00
Salt & pepper, tall, #89	25.00
Salt dip, #24	9.00
Sauce boat & ladle, tab hdld., #30-445	55.00
Saucer, #7	7.50
Stem, 3 oz., wine, #27	13.50
Stem, 3½ oz., cocktail, #26	9.00
Stem, 4 oz., oyster cocktail, #41	9.00
Stem, 4½ oz., claret, #25	13.50
Stem, 4½ oz., low sherbet, #42	7.50
Stem, 6½ oz., tall sherbet, #2	10.00
Stem, 10 oz., water, #1	15.00
Sugar, ftd., #8	10.00
Sugar, indiv., #4	12.00
Sugar, #86	10.00
Tray, for indiv., sugar & creamer, #4	10.00
Tumbler, 1 oz., ftd., cordial, #87	22.00
Tumbler, 2 oz., whiskey, #55	10.00
Tumbler, 3 oz., ftd., juice, #22	9.00
Tumbler, 5 oz., #56	12.00
Tumbler, 5 oz., ftd., #21	12.00
Tumbler, 7 oz., old-fashioned, #57	15.00
Tumbler, 10 oz., ftd., water, #3	15.00
Tumbler, 10 oz., table, #51	12.00
Tumbler, 10 oz., tall, #58	12.00
Tumbler, 12 oz., barrel shape, #13	15.00
Tumbler, 12 oz., ftd., tea, #20	17.00
Tumbler, 14 oz., barrel shape, #14	20.00
Tumbler, 14 oz., tall, #59	22.00
Urn, w/cover (same as candy), #9	50.00
Vase, 5", #42	15.00
Vase, 6", crimped, #119	20.00
Vase, 6", ftd., #50	25.00
Vase, 6½", squat, #107	27.50
Vase, 7", #58	30.00
Vase, 7", ftd., #54	35.00
Vase, 10", ftd., #46	50.00

NAVARRE, (Plate Etching #327) Fostoria Glass Company, 1937 – 1980

Colors: crystal; all other colors found made very late

As of now, I am going to stick to pricing the older pieces of Navarre. Colors in pink, blue, and green were all made in the 1970's as were additional crystal pieces not originally made in the late 1930's and the 1940's. The later pieces included carafes, roemer wines, continental champagnes and brandies. You can find all of these later pieces in my new book *Collectible Glassware from the 40's, 50's & 60's....*

Most of these later pieces are signed "Fostoria" although some only carried a sticker. I am mentioning this to make you aware of the colors made in Navarre. Some of the Depression era glass shows do not allow this glass to be sold since it was so recently manufactured.

Navarre is extremely popular on the West Coast. Prices there are higher as is the case of Fostoria's Chintz. These patterns were more expensive originally due to shipping costs, but today the prices on the East Coast are rapidly catching up and it is the Midwest that has more reasonable pricing!

	Crystal		Crystal
Bell, dinner	30.00	Plate, #2440, 7½", salad	15.00
Bowl, #2496, 4", square, hdld.	10.00	Plate, #2440, 8½", luncheon	17.50
Bowl, #2496, 4⅜", hdld.	11.00	Plate, #2440, 9½", dinner	39.50
Bowl, #869, 4½", finger	37.50	Plate, #2496, 10", hdld., cake	47.50
Bowl, #2496, 4⅝", tri-cornered	15.00	Plate, #2440, 10½" oval cake	45.00
Bowl, #2496, 5", hdld., ftd.	17.50	Plate, #2496, 14", torte	55.00
Bowl, #2496, 6", square, sweetmeat	17.00	Plate, #2464, 16", torte	85.00
Bowl, #2496, 6¼", 3 ftd., nut	17.50	Relish, #2496, 6", 2 part, square	30.00
Bowl, #2496, 7⅜", ftd., bonbon	25.00	Relish, #2496, 10" x 7½", 3 part	45.00
Bowl, #2496, 10", oval, floating garden	50.00	Relish, #2496, 10", 4 part	50.00
Bowl, #2496, 10½", hdld., ftd.	60.00	Relish, #2419, 13¼", 5 part	85.00
Bowl, #2470½, 10½", ftd.	55.00	Salt & pepper, #2364, 3¼", flat, pr.	55.00
Bowl, #2496, 12", flared	60.00	Salt & pepper, #2375, 3½", ftd., pr.	95.00
Bowl, #2545, 12½", oval, "Flame"	52.50	Salad dressing bottle, #2083, 6½"	300.00
Candlestick, #2496, 4"	17.50	Sauce dish, #2496, div. mayo., 6½"	35.00
Candlestick, #2496, 4½", double	32.50	Sauce dish, #2496, 6½" x 5¼"	100.00
Candlestick, #2472, 5", double	40.00	Sauce dish liner, #2496, 8" oval	25.00
Candlestick, #2496, 5½"	27.50	Saucer, #2440	5.00
Candlestick, #2496, 6", triple	42.50	Stem, #6106, 1 oz., cordial, 3⅞"	45.00
Candlestick, #2545, 6¾", double, "Flame"	47.50	Stem, #6106, 3¼ oz., wine, 5½"	35.00
Candlestick, #2482, 6¾", triple	42.50	Stem, #6106, 3½ oz., cocktail, 6"	25.00
Candy, w/cover, #2496, 3 part	100.00	Stem, #6106, 4 oz., oyster cocktail, 3⅝"	25.00
Celery, #2440, 9"	27.50	Stem, #6106, 4½ oz., claret, 6½"	37.50
Celery, #2496, 11"	37.50	Stem, #6106, 6 oz., low sherbet, 4⅜"	22.50
Comport, #2496, 3¼", cheese	25.00	Stem, #6106, 6 oz., saucer champagne,	
Comport, #2400, 4½"	27.50	5⅝"	23.50
Comport, #2496, 4¾"	30.00	Stem, #6106, 10 oz., water, 7⅝"	30.00
Cracker, #2496, 11" plate	40.00	Sugar, #2440, 3⅝", ftd.	17.50
Creamer, #2440, 4¼", ftd.	20.00	Sugar, #2496, individual	15.00
Creamer, #2496, individual	17.50	Syrup, #2586, metal cut-off top, 5½"	250.00
Cup, #2440	17.50	Tid bit, #2496, 8¼", 3 ftd., turned up edge	22.00
Ice bucket, #2496, 4⅜" high	85.00	Tray, #2496½", for ind. sugar/creamer	20.00
Ice bucket, #2375, 6" high	135.00	Tumbler, #6106, 5 oz., ftd., juice, 4⅝"	22.50
Mayonnaise, #2375, 3 piece	65.00	Tumbler, #6106, 10 oz., ftd., water, 5⅜"	22.50
Mayonnaise, #2496½", 3 piece	65.00	Tumbler, #6106, 13 oz., ftd., tea, 5⅞"	30.00
Pickle, #2496, 8"	25.00	Vase, #4108, 5"	75.00
Pickle, #2440, 8½"	27.50	Vase, #4121, 5"	75.00
Pitcher, #5000, 48 oz., ftd.	310.00	Vase, #4128, 5"	75.00
Plate, #2440, 6", bread/butter	10.00	Vase, #2470, 10", ftd.	135.00

NEW ERA, #4044, A.H. Heisey Co., 1934 – 1941; 1944 – 1957 (stems, celery tray, and candlesticks)

Colors: crystal, frosted crystal, some cobalt with crystal stem and foot.

New Era is being sought by "Art Deco" collectors. The double branched candelabra with the New Era bobeches is a prize worthy of any mantle. These are not hard to find, but very desirable to own. Dinner plates without scratches and after dinner cups and saucers will probably keep you searching for a long time!

	Crystal		Crystal
Ash tray or indiv. nut	30.00	Stem, 1 oz. cordial	45.00
Bottle, rye w/ stopper	120.00	Stem, 3 oz. wine	35.00
Bowl, 11" floral	25.00	Stem, 3½ oz., high, cocktail	10.00
Candelabra, 2-lite w/2 #4044 bobeche		Stem, 3½ oz. oyster cocktail	10.00
& prisms	55.00	Stem, 4 oz. claret	15.00
Creamer	35.00	Stem, 6 oz. champagne	12.50
Cup	10.00	Stem, 10 oz. goblet	15.00
Cup, after dinner	50.00	Stem, low, 6 oz. sherbet	10.00
Pilsner, 8 oz.	25.00	Sugar	35.00
Pilsner, 12 oz.	30.00	Tray, 13" celery	30.00
Plate, 5½" x 4½" bread & butter	12.00	Tumbler, 5 oz. ftd. soda	7.00
Plate, 9"x 7"	20.00	Tumbler, 8 oz. ftd. soda	10.00
Plate, 10" x 8"	35.00	Tumbler, 12 oz. ftd. soda	12.50
Relish, 13" 3-part	25.00	Tumbler, 14 oz. ftd. soda	15.00
Saucer	5.00	Tumbler, low, footed 10 oz.	10.00
Saucer, after dinner	10.00		

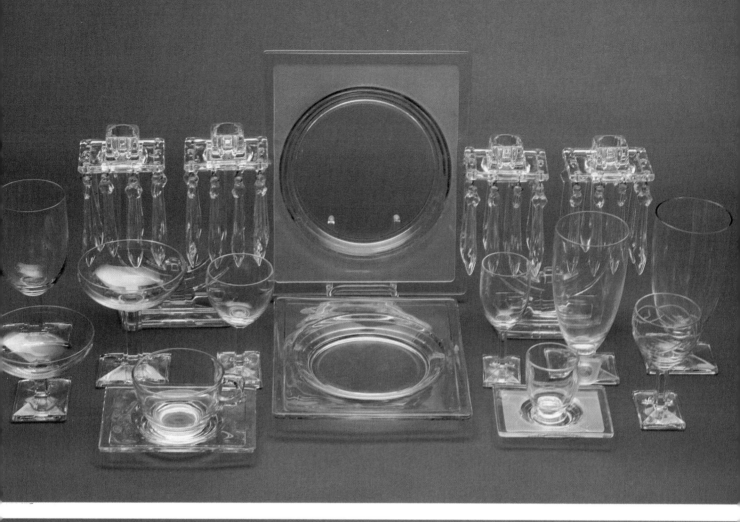

OCTAGON, Blank #1231 – Ribbed; also Blank #500 and Blank #1229, A.H. Heisey & Co.

Colors: crystal, "Flamingo" pink, "Sahara" yellow, "Moongleam" green, "Hawthorne" orchid, "Marigold," a deep, amber/yellow, and "Dawn"

Octagon is one of those Heisey patterns that everyone recognizes, since it is almost always marked; yet few collectors buy it. True, it is one of the plainer patterns, but it does come in a multitude of colors! The piece in the prices below that jumps out at you is the Dawn colored 12", 4-part, tray. Otherwise, it is priced reasonably and is usually just sitting around waiting for a new home.

	Crystal	Flam.	Sahara	Moon.	Hawth.	Marigold
Basket, 5", #500.	60.00	140.00	170.00	190.00	220.00	
Bonbon, 6", sides up, #1229	5.00	10.00	15.00	20.00	25.00	
Bowl, cream soup, 2 hdld.	10.00	20.00	25.00	30.00	40.00	
Bowl, 5½", jelly, #1229	7.00	12.00	15.00	17.00	20.00	
Bowl, 6", mint, #1229	7.00	12.00	15.00	17.00	20.00	
Bowl, 6", #500	14.00	20.00	22.00	25.00	35.00	
Bowl, 6½", grapefruit	10.00	20.00	22.00	25.00	35.00	
Bowl, 8", ftd., #1229 comport	15.00	25.00	35.00	45.00	55.00	
Bowl, 9", flat soup	10.00	15.00	20.00	27.50	30.00	
Bowl, 9", vegetable	15.00	20.00	25.00	30.00	50.00	
Candlestick, 3", 1-lite	10.00	25.00	27.00	30.00	40.00	
Cheese dish, 6", 2 hdld., #1229	7.00	10.00	10.00	12.00	15.00	
Creamer #500	7.00	20.00	30.00	35.00	40.00	
Creamer, hotel	10.00	15.00	15.00	20.00	30.00	
Cup, after dinner	5.00	15.00	15.00	20.00	42.00	
Cup #1231	5.00	15.00	20.00	20.00	35.00	
Dish, frozen dessert, #500	10.00	15.00	15.00	15.00	30.00	50.00
Ice tub, #500	25.00	65.00	75.00	75.00	90.00	135.00
Mayonnaise, 5½", ftd., #1229	10.00	25.00	30.00	35.00	45.00	
Plate, cream soup liner	3.00	5.00	7.00	9.00	12.00	
Plate, 6"	4.00	6.00	8.00	10.00	12.00	
Plate, 7", bread	5.00	7.00	9.00	11.00	13.00	
Plate, 8", luncheon	6.00	8.00	10.00	12.00	14.00	
Plate, 10", sand., #1229	15.00	20.00	25.00	30.00	35.00	
Plate, 10", muffin, #1229 sides up	15.00	25.00	30.00	35.00	40.00	
Plate, 10½"	17.00	25.00	30.00	35.00	45.00	
Plate, 10½", ctr. hdld., sandwich	22.00	35.00	40.00	45.00	60.00	
Plate, 12", muffin, #1229 sides up	20.00	27.00	30.00	35.00	45.00	
Plate, 13", hors d'oeuvre, #1229	15.00	25.00	28.00	35.00	45.00	
Plate, 14"	22.00	25.00	30.00	35.00	45.00	
Platter, 12¾" oval	20.00	25.00	30.00	40.00	50.00	
Saucer, after dinner	2.00	5.00	6.00	6.00	12.00	
Saucer, #1231	2.00	5.00	6.00	7.00	9.00	
Sugar #500	7.00	20.00	30.00	35.00	40.00	
Sugar, hotel	10.00	15.00	15.00	20.00	30.00	
Tray, 6", oblong, #500	5.00	10.00	12.00	12.00	20.00	
Tray, 9", celery	5.00	10.00	15.00	15.00	25.00	
Tray, 12", celery	7.00	15.00	17.00	17.00	35.00	**(Dawn)**
Tray, 12", 4 pt., #500 variety	25.00	75.00	95.00	135.00	200.00	300.00

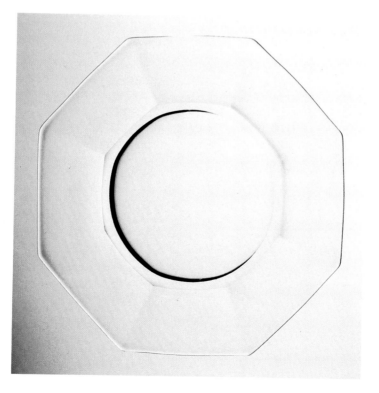

OLD COLONY, Empress Blank #1401; Caracassone Blank #3390; and Old Dominion Blank #3380, A.H. Heisey & Co., 1930 – 1939

Colors: crystal, "Flamingo" pink, "Sahara" yellow, "Moongleam" green, "Marigold," a deep, amber/yellow, and cobalt

	Crystal	Flam.	Sahara	Moon.	Marigold
Bouillon cup, 2 hdld., ftd.	12.50	18.00	20.00	24.00	
Bowl, finger, #4075	5.50	10.00	11.00	14.00	18.00
Bowl, ftd., finger, #3390	5.50	16.00	21.00	27.50	
Bowl, 4½", nappy	7.00	10.00	12.50	15.00	
Bowl, 5", ftd., 2 hdld.	12.50	17.50	22.50	27.50	
Bowl, 6", ftd., 2 hdld., jelly	15.00	20.00	25.00	32.50	
Bowl, 6", dolp. ftd., mint	16.00	22.00	27.50	35.00	
Bowl, 7", triplex, dish	15.00	22.00	25.00	28.00	
Bowl, 7½", dolp. ftd., nappy	22.00	60.00	65.00	75.00	
Bowl, 8", nappy	25.00	35.00	40.00	42.50	
Bowl, 8½", ftd., floral, 2 hdld.	32.00	47.00	57.50	67.50	
Bowl, 9", 3 hdld.	36.00	75.00	90.00	95.00	
Bowl, 10", rnd., 2 hdld., salad	32.00	47.50	57.50	65.00	
Bowl, 10", sq., salad, 2 hdld.	30.00	45.00	55.00	65.00	
Bowl, 10", oval, dessert, 2 hdld.	30.00	40.00	50.00	62.50	
Bowl, 10", oval, veg.	30.00	34.00	42.00	50.00	
Bowl, 11", floral, dolp. ft.	32.00	70.00	80.00	95.00	
Bowl, 13", ftd., flared	30.00	35.00	40.00	45.00	
Bowl, 13", 2 pt., pickle & olive	12.50	20.00	22.50	27.50	
Cigarette holder, #3390 (Cobalt $100.00)	16.00	47.50	42.50	55.00	
Comport, 7", oval, ftd.	40.00	75.00	80.00	85.00	
Comport, 7", ftd., #3368	30.00	57.50	62.50	85.00	95.00
Cream soup, 2 hdld.	12.00	20.00	22.00	27.00	
Creamer, dolp. ft.	17.50	32.00	45.00	50.00	
Creamer, indiv.	15.00	30.00	40.00	37.50	
Cup, after dinner	12.00	25.00	35.00	50.00	
Cup	10.00	26.00	32.00	38.00	
Decanter, 1 pt.	150.00	300.00	275.00	525.00	
Flagon, 12 oz., #3390	25.00	55.00	55.00	85.00	
Grapefruit, 6"	15.00	23.00	30.00	35.00	
Grapefruit, ftd., #3380	10.00	16.00	18.00	20.00	30.00
Ice tub, dolp. ft.	42.50	110.00	115.00	135.00	
Mayonnaise, 5½", dolp. ft.	36.00	55.00	70.00	80.00	
Oil, 4 oz., ftd.	42.50	70.00	105.00	120.00	
Pitcher, 3 pt., #3390	90.00	245.00	210.00	400.00	
Pitcher, 3 pt., dolp. ft.	85.00	195.00	200.00	210.00	
Plate, bouillon	5.00	8.00	12.00	15.00	
Plate, cream soup	5.00	8.00	12.00	15.00	
Plate, 4½", rnd.	3.00	6.00	7.00	8.00	
Plate, 6", rnd.	6.00	12.00	15.00	18.00	
Plate, 6", sq.	6.00	12.00	15.00	18.00	
Plate, 7", rnd.	8.00	14.00	18.00	20.00	
Plate, 7", sq.	8.00	14.00	18.00	20.00	
Plate, 8", rnd.	10.00	17.00	22.00	27.00	
Plate, 8", sq.	10.00	17.00	22.00	27.00	
Plate, 9", rnd.	15.00	22.00	25.00	28.00	
Plate, 10½", rnd.	28.50	60.00	70.00	75.00	
Plate, 10½", sq.	27.50	50.00	65.00	70.00	
Plate, 12", rnd.	31.00	57.50	70.00	75.00	
Plate, 12", 2 hdld., rnd., muffin	31.00	57.50	70.00	75.00	
Plate, 12", 2 hdld., rnd., sand.	31.00	57.50	70.00	75.00	
Plate, 13", 2 hdld., sq., sand.	35.00	40.00	45.00	50.00	
Plate, 13", 2 hdld., sq., muffin	35.00	40.00	45.00	50.00	
Platter, 14", oval	25.00	35.00	40.00	45.00	
Salt & pepper, pr.	52.50	80.00	110.00	130.00	
Saucer, sq.	4.00	8.00	10.00	10.00	
Saucer, rnd.	4.00	8.00	10.00	10.00	
Stem, #3380, 1 oz., cordial	75.00	135.00	135.00	155.00	375.00
Stem, #3380, 2½ oz., wine	18.00	40.00	35.00	50.00	75.00
Stem, #3380, 3 oz., cocktail	13.00	34.00	25.00	40.00	60.00
Stem, #3380, 4 oz., oyster/cocktail	8.00	13.00	15.00	17.00	25.00
Stem, #3380, 4 oz., claret	20.00	50.00	40.00	55.00	65.00
Stem, #3380, 5 oz., parfait	10.00	15.00	15.00	17.00	40.00
Stem, #3380, 6 oz., champagne	8.00	13.00	15.00	17.00	25.00
Stem, #3380, 6 oz., sherbet	6.00	11.00	13.00	15.00	25.00

	Crystal	Flam.	Sahara	Moon.	Marigold
Stem, #3380, 10 oz., short soda	7.00	18.00	15.00	22.00	30.00
Stem, #3380, 10 oz., tall soda		21.00	18.00	25.00	32.50
Stem, #3390, 1 oz., cordial	50.00	130.00	125.00	165.00	
Stem, #3390, 2½ oz., wine	12.00	20.00	27.50	35.00	
Stem, #3390, 3 oz., cocktail	7.00	15.00	20.00	25.00	
Stem, #3390, 3 oz., oyster/cocktail	7.00	15.00	20.00	25.00	
Stem, #3390, 4 oz., claret	12.00	22.50	27.50	32.50	
Stem, #3390, 6 oz., champagne	10.00	20.00	25.00	30.00	
Stem, #3390, 6 oz., sherbet	10.00	20.00	25.00	30.00	
Stem, #3390, 11 oz., low water	8.00	20.00	25.00	30.00	
Stem, #3390, 11 oz., tall water	10.00	22.00	27.00	32.00	
Sugar, dolp. ft.	17.50	30.00	45.00	50.00	
Sugar, indiv.	12.50	27.50	32.50	35.00	
Tray, 10", celery	14.00	20.00	25.00	30.00	
Tray, 12", ctr. hdld., sand.	35.00	65.00	75.00	85.00	
Tray, 12", ctr. hdld., sq.	35.00	65.00	75.00	85.00	
Tray, 13", celery	17.00	20.00	26.00	30.00	
Tray, 13", 2 hdld., hors d'oeuvre	30.00	36.00	45.00	55.00	
Tumbler, dolp. ft.	90.00	135.00	165.00	195.00	
Tumbler, #3380, 1 oz., ftd., bar	22.00	37.50	42.50	52.50	55.00
Tumbler, #3380, 2 oz., ftd., bar	12.00	20.00	20.00	25.00	35.00
Tumbler, #3380, 5 oz., ftd., bar	7.00	12.00	12.00	17.00	25.00
Tumbler, #3380, 8 oz., ftd., soda	10.00	21.00	18.00	25.00	32.50
Tumbler, #3380, 10 oz., ftd., soda	12.00	23.00	20.00	25.00	32.50
Tumbler, #3380, 12 oz., ftd., tea	13.00	25.00	22.00	27.00	35.00
Tumbler, #3390, 2 oz., ftd.	7.00	18.00	22.50	28.00	
Tumbler, #3390, 5 oz., ftd., juice	7.00	15.00	20.00	25.00	
Tumbler, #3390, 8 oz., ftd., soda	10.00	22.00	25.00	30.00	
Tumbler, #3390, 12 oz., ftd., tea	12.00	24.00	27.00	30.00	
Vase, 9", ftd.	75.00	130.00	150.00	175.00	

OLD SANDWICH, Blank #1404, A.H. Heisey & Co.

Colors: crystal, "Flamingo" pink, "Sahara" yellow, "Moongleam" green, cobalt, amber

Moongleam is the most desirable color to own. Sahara and crystal also have their devotees. Cobalt blue is rare as you can see by the prices listed!

	Crystal	Flam.	Sahara	Moon.	Cobalt
Ash tray, individual	7.00	35.00	25.00	45.00	35.00
Beer mug, 12 oz.	35.00	180.00	210.00	400.00	240.00
Beer mug, 14 oz.	45.00	200.00	225.00	425.00	250.00
* Beer mug, 18 oz.	40.00	240.00	250.00	450.00	275.00
Bottle, catsup, w/#3 stopper (like lg. cruet)	50.00	150.00	150.00	200.00	
Bowl, finger	12.00	50.00	60.00	60.00	
Bowl, ftd., popcorn, cupped	45.00	60.00	60.00	80.00	
Bowl, 11", rnd., ftd., floral	25.00	50.00	50.00	60.00	
Bowl, 12", oval, ftd., floral	27.00	50.00	60.00	70.00	
Candlestick, 6"	35.00	80.00	80.00	100.00	235.00
Cigarette holder	50.00	65.00	60.00	65.00	
Comport, 6"	37.50	85.00	90.00	95.00	
Creamer, oval	10.00	20.00	22.00	25.00	
Creamer, 12 oz.	32.00	165.00	170.00	175.00	300.00
Creamer, 14 oz.	35.00	175.00	180.00	185.00	
Creamer, 18 oz.	40.00	185.00	190.00	195.00	
Cup	40.00	65.00	65.00	65.00	
Decanter, 1 pint, w/#98 stopper	75.00	185.00	200.00	225.00	425.00
Floral block, #22	15.00	25.00	30.00	35.00	
Oil bottle, 2½ oz., #85 stopper	65.00	100.00	95.00	140.00	
Parfait, 4½ oz.	10.00	15.00	20.00	25.00	
Pilsner, 8 oz.	14.00	28.00	32.00	38.00	
Pilsner, 10 oz.	16.00	32.00	37.00	42.00	
Pitcher, ½ gallon, ice lip	75.00	155.00	160.00	180.00	
Pitcher, ½ gallon, reg.	75.00	150.00	155.00	175.00	
Plate, 6", sq., grnd. bottom	5.00	8.00	10.00	13.00	
Plate, 7", sq.	7.00	20.00	20.00	25.00	
Plate, 8", sq.	9.00	25.00	25.00	30.00	
Salt & pepper, pr.	40.00	65.00	75.00	85.00	
Saucer	10.00	15.00	15.00	15.00	
Stem, 2½ oz., wine	18.00	45.00	45.00	55.00	
Stem, 3 oz., cocktail	9.00	15.00	18.00	20.00	
Stem, 4 oz., claret	10.00	20.00	23.00	27.50	150.00
Stem, 4 oz., oyster cocktail	8.00	25.00	25.00	30.00	
Stem, 4 oz., sherbet	6.00	12.00	15.00	18.00	
Stem, 5 oz., saucer champagne	9.00	27.50	28.00	32.00	
Stem, 10 oz., low ft.	9.00	25.00	30.00	35.00	
Sugar, oval	10.00	20.00	22.00	25.00	
Sundae, 6 oz.	18.00	30.00	30.00	35.00	
Tumbler, 1½ oz., bar, grnd. bottom	17.50	70.00	60.00	70.00	95.00
Tumbler, 5 oz., juice	5.00	13.00	17.50	22.00	
Tumbler, 6½ oz., toddy	8.00	16.00	20.00	22.00	
Tumbler, 8 oz., grnd. bottom, cupped & straight rim	9.00	17.00	22.00	27.50	
Tumbler, 10 oz.	10.00	17.00	22.00	27.50	
Tumbler, 10 oz., low ft.	10.00	35.00	37.00	40.00	
Tumbler, 12 oz., ftd., iced tea	12.00	22.00	30.00	40.00	
Tumbler, 12 oz., iced tea	12.00	22.00	30.00	40.00	

*Amber; 300.00

ORCHID, (Etching #1507) ON WAVERLY BLANK #1519, and QUEEN ANN BLANK #1509,
A.H. Heisey & Co. 1940 – 1957

Colors: crystal

Orchid has slowed somewhat in its heretofore selling frenzy and Heisey's Rose has taken over as the "hot" property for now.

I hope you enjoy the 1945 advertisement shown here as well as the others throughout the book.

You can see the difference between the Queen Ann and Waverly lemon dishes under Queen Ann on page 151. The Waverly Orchid lemon is rarely seen while the Queen Ann Orchid lemon dish is commonly seen! Price reflects the difference!

The Universal #3304 cocktail icer and the Fern #1495 mayonnaise and liner are shown separately as pattern shots. Each of these items is extremely hard to find and very desirable to own.

	Crystal
Ash tray, 3".	27.50
Basket, 8½", LARIAT	450.00
Bell, dinner, #5022 or #5025	125.00
Bottle, 8 oz., French dressings	165.00
Bowl, finger, #3309 or #5025	65.00
Bowl, 4½", nappy, QUEEN ANN	37.50
Bowl, 5½", ftd., mint, QUEEN ANN	35.00
Bowl, 6", jelly, 2 hdld, QUEEN ANN	30.00
Bowl, 6" oval, lemon, w/cover, QUEEN ANN	275.00
Bowl, 6", oval, lemon, w/cover, WAVERLY	795.00
Bowl, 6½", ftd., honey; cheese, QUEEN ANN	32.50
Bowl, 6½", ftd., jelly, WAVERLY	40.00
Bowl, 6½", 2 pt., oval, dressings, WAVERLY	47.50
Bowl, 7", lily, QUEEN ANN	85.00
Bowl, 7", salad	45.00
Bowl, 7", 3 pt., rnd., relish	45.00
Bowl, 7", ftd., honey; cheese, WAVERLY	50.00
Bowl, 7", ftd., jelly	40.00
Bowl, 7", ftd., oval, nut, WAVERLY	85.00
Bowl, 8", mint, ftd., QUEEN ANN	60.00
Bowl, 8", nappy, QUEEN ANN	65.00
Bowl, 8", 2 pt., oval, dressings, ladle	52.50
Bowl, 8", pt., rnd., relish	57.50
Bowl, 8½", flared, QUEEN ANN	65.00
Bowl, 8½", floral, 2 hdld., ftd., QUEEN ANN	57.50
Bowl, 9", 4 pt., rnd., relish	65.00
Bowl, 9", ftd., fruit or salad	100.00
Bowl, 9", gardenia, QUEEN ANN	60.00
Bowl, 9", salad, WAVERLY	135.00
Bowl, 9½", crimped floral, QUEEN ANN	65.00
Bowl, 9½" epergne	450.00
Bowl, 10", crimped	65.00
Bowl, 10", deep salad	100.00
Bowl, 10", gardenia	70.00
Bowl, 10½", ftd., floral	90.00
Bowl, 11", shallow, rolled edge	70.00
Bowl, 11", 3 ftd., floral, seahorse ft.	135.00
Bowl, 11", 3 pt., oblong, relish	67.50
Bowl, 11", 4 ftd., oval	80.00
Bowl, 11", flared	55.00
Bowl, 11", floral	55.00

	Crystal
Bowl, 11", ftd., floral	95.00
Bowl, 12", crimped, floral, WAVERLY	55.00
Bowl, 13", floral	65.00
Bowl, 13", crimped, floral, WAVERLY	85.00
Bowl, 13", gardenia	65.00
Butter, w/cover, ¼ lb., CABOCHON	300.00
Butter, w/cover, 6", WAVERLY	165.00
Candleholder, 6", deep epernette, WAVERLY	300.00
Candlestick, 1-lite, MERCURY	32.50
Candlestick, 1-lite, QUEEN ANN w/prisms	115.00
Candlestick, 2-lite, FLAME	135.00
Candlestick, 5", 2-lite, TRIDENT	50.00
Candlestick, 2-lite, WAVERLY	50.00
Candlestick, 3-lite, CASCADE	75.00
Candlestick, 3-lite, WAVERLY	87.50
Candy box, w/cover, 6", low ft.	150.00
Candy, w/cover, 5", high ft., WAVERLY	175.00
Candy, w/cover, 6", bow knot finial	160.00
Cheese (comport) & cracker (11½") plate	110.00
Cheese & cracker, 14" plate	130.00
Chocolate, w/cover, 5", WAVERLY	175.00
Cigarette box, w/cover, 4", PURITAN	125.00
Cigarette holder, #4035	60.00
Cigarette holder, w/cover	125.00
Cocktail icer, w/liner, UNIVERSAL, #3304	200.00
Cocktail shaker, pt., #4225	265.00
Cocktail shaker, qt., #4036 or #4225	210.00
Comport, 5½", blown	87.50
Comport, 6", low ft., WAVERLY	45.00
Comport, 6½", low ft., WAVERLY	47.50
Comport, 7", ftd., oval	115.00
Creamer, individual	22.50
Creamer, ftd.	25.00
Cup, WAVERLY or QUEEN ANN	37.50
Decanter, oval, sherry, pt.	225.00
Decanter, pt., ftd. #4036	310.00
Decanter, pt., #4036½	235.00
Ice bucket, ftd., QUEEN ANN	265.00
Ice bucket, 2 hdld., WAVERLY	275.00
Marmalade, w/cover	200.00
Mayonnaise and liner, #1495, FERN	235.00

"It's Heisey, Honey!

and this has been a 'Heisey family' since I was young as you!"

In the fall of 1895, Heisey craftsmen produced the first gleaming samples that introduced our crystal to the nation. The "gay nineties" took hand-wrought Heisey Crystal to its heart—and every succeeding decade has found it in even greater favor with all who love fine things. Today Heisey Crystal is offered from dealers in a multitude of pieces and patterns—in tableware and in decorative crystal. Each precious piece has the grace, the sparkling loveliness, the hand-wrought craftsmanship that have heightened the name of "Heisey families" for all of fifty years. It may be seen at leading stores throughout the nation. A. H. Heisey & Co., Newark, Ohio.

Heisey's

HAND · WROUGHT CRYSTAL

ORCHID, (Etching #1507) ON WAVERLY BLANK #1519 amd QUEEN ANN BLANK #1509,
A.H. Heisey & Co. 1940 – 1957 (continued)

	Crystal
Mayonnaise, 5½", 1 hdl.	40.00
Mayonnaise, 5½", ftd.	40.00
Mayonnaise, 5½", 1 hdl., div.	42.50
Mayonnaise, 6½", 1 hdl.	50.00
Mayonnaise, 6½", 1 hdl., div.	52.50
Mustard, w/cover, QUEEN ANN	135.00
Oil, 3 oz., ftd.	155.00
Pitcher, 73 oz.	425.00
Pitcher, 64 oz., ice tankard	500.00
Plate, 6"	12.50
Plate, 7", mayonnaise	15.00
Plate, 7", salad	18.00
Plate, 8", salad, WAVERLY	21.50
Plate, 10½", dinner	130.00
Plate, 11", demi-torte	50.00
Plate, 11", sandwich	50.00
Plate, 12", ftd., salver, WAVERLY	195.00
Plate, 12", rnd sandwich, hdld.	50.00
Plate, 14", ftd., cake or salver	265.00
Plate, 14", torte, rolled edge	55.00
Plate, 14", torte, WAVERLY	45.00
Plate, 14", sandwich, WAVERLY	65.00
Plate, 15", sandwich, WAVERLY	65.00
Plate, 15½", QUEEN ANN	95.00
Salt & pepper, pr.	60.00
Salt & pepper, ftd., pr., WAVERLY	65.00
Saucer, WAVERLY or QUEEN ANN	12.50
Stem, #5022 or #5025, 1 oz., cordial	135.00

	Crystal
Stem, #5022 or #5025, 2 oz., sherry	110.00
Stem, #5022 or #5025, 3 oz., wine	75.00
Stem, #5022 or #5025, 4 oz., oyster cocktail	55.00
Stem, #5025, 4 oz., cocktail	40.00
Stem, #5022 or #5025, 4½ oz., claret	125.00
Stem, #5022 or #5025, 6 oz., saucer champagne	30.00
Stem, #5022 or #5025, 6 oz., sherbet	25.00
Stem, #5022 or #5025, 10 oz., low water goblet	35.00
Stem, #5022 or #5025, 10 oz., water goblet	42.50
Sugar, individual	25.00
Sugar, ftd.	25.00
Toast, w/dome	300.00
Tray, indiv., creamer/sugar, QUEEN ANN	85.00
Tray, 12", celery	45.00
Tray, 13", celery	47.50
Tumbler, #5022 or #5025, 5 oz., fruit	50.00
Tumbler, #5022 or #5025, 12 oz., iced tea	60.00
Vase, 4", ftd., violet, WAVERLY	90.00
Vase, 6", crimped top	110.00
Vase, 7", ftd., fan	85.00
Vase, 7", ftd.	85.00
Vase, 8", ftd., bud	165.00
Vase, 8", sq., ftd., bud	185.00
Vase, 10", sq., ftd., bud	250.00
Vase, 14"	600.00

PLANTATION, Blank #1567, A.H. Heisey & Co.

Colors: crystal; rare in amber

The photograph on the right was originally scheduled to be on the cover, but it did not work out; so I hope you enjoy it here. Plantation is gaining in popularity with collectors!

	Crystal
Ash tray, 3½"..	30.00
Bowl, 9 qt., Dr. Johnson, punch..................	300.00
Bowl, 5", nappy	15.00
Bowl, 5½", nappy	15.00
Bowl, 6½", 2 hdld., jelly...............................	18.00
Bowl, 6½", flared, jelly................................	18.00
Bowl, 6½", ftd., honey, cupped....................	45.00
Bowl, 8", 4 pt., rnd., relish........................	60.00
Bowl, 8½", 2 pt., dressing............................	45.00
Bowl, 9", salad	85.00
Bowl, 9½", crimped, fruit or flower.............	85.00
Bowl, 9½", gardenia.....................................	85.00
Bowl, 11", 3 part, relish...............................	60.00
Bowl, 11½", ftd., gardenia	80.00
Bowl, 12", crimped, fruit or flower..............	60.00
Bowl, 13", celery	35.00
Bowl, 13", 2 part, celery...............................	35.00
Bowl, 13", 5 part, oval relish........................	65.00
Bowl, 13", gardenia	45.00
Bowl, 13", punch	500.00
Butter, ¼ lb., oblong, w/cover......................	85.00
Butter, 5", rnd., (or cov. candy)	95.00
Candelabrum, w/two #1503 bobeche & 10	
"A" prisms..	110.00
Candle block, hurricane type.......................	95.00
Candle block, 1-lite	85.00
Candle holder, 5", ftd., epergne	75.00
Candlestick, 1-lite	75.00
Candlestick, 2-lite	50.00
Candlestick, 3-lite	80.00
Candy box, w/cover, 7"	115.00
Candy, w/cover, 5", tall, ftd..........................	165.00
Cheese, w/cover, 5", ftd................................	85.00
Coaster, 4"	45.00
Comport, 5"...	30.00
Comport, 5", w/cover, deep...........................	75.00
Creamer, ftd.	25.00
Cup..	15.00

	Crystal
Cup, punch	25.00
Marmalade, w/cover	100.00
Mayonnaise, 4½", rolled ft.	55.00
Mayonnaise, 5¼", w/liner	45.00
Oil bottle, 3 oz., w/#125 stopper	85.00
Pitcher, ½ gallon, ice lip, blown	300.00
Plate, coupe (rare)	225.00
Plate, 7", salad	15.00
Plate, 8", salad	20.00
Plate, 10½", demi-torte	40.00
Plate, 13", ftd., cake salver	125.00
Plate, 14", sandwich....................................	45.00
Plate, 18", buffet	55.00
Plate, 18", punch bowl liner	95.00
Salt & pepper, pr...	45.00
Saucer	5.00
Stem, 1 oz., cordial.......................................	100.00
Stem, 3 oz., wine, blown...............................	50.00
Stem, 3½ oz., cocktail, pressed	30.00
Stem, 4 oz., fruit/oyster cocktail..................	20.00
Stem, 4½ oz., claret, blown	30.00
Stem, 4½ oz., claret, pressed.........................	30.00
Stem, 4½ oz., oyster cocktail, blown	25.00
Stem, 6½ oz., sherbet/saucer champagne,	
blown	25.00
Stem, 10 oz., pressed....................................	25.00
Stem, 10 oz., blown......................................	25.00
Sugar, ftd...	25.00
Syrup bottle, w/drip, cut top	75.00
Tray, 8½", condiment/sugar & creamer........	22.50
Tumbler, 5 oz., ftd., juice, pressed..............	35.00
Tumbler, 5 oz., ftd., juice, blown	35.00
Tumbler, 10 oz., pressed	45.00
Tumbler, 12 oz., ftd., iced tea, pressed........	45.00
Tumbler, 12 oz., ftd., iced tea, blown	45.00
Vase, 5", ftd., flared	40.00
Vase, 9", ftd., flared	65.00

tradition in crystal...

Plantation Ivy...
hospitality's
traditional warmth
captured in
boldly etched
hand blown crystal

the finest in glassware, made in America by hand

Heisey
HAND-WROUGHT CRYSTAL

PLEAT & PANEL, Blank #1170, A.H. Heisey & Co.

Colors: crystal, "Flamingo" pink, "Moongleam" green

Pleat and Panel is another easily recognized Heisey pattern because most pieces carry the familiar H in diamond mark. Stems are marked on the stem itself and not the foot; so look there if you can not find a mark. This is not one of Heisey's higher priced patterns which lends it to being a good starting pattern for beginning collectors.

	Crystal	Flam.	Moongleam
Bowl, 4", chow chow	5.00	10.00	12.00
Bowl, 4½", nappy	5.00	10.00	12.00
Bowl, 5", 2 hdld., bouillon	7.00	12.00	15.00
Bowl, 5", 2 hdld., jelly	9.00	12.00	15.00
Bowl, 5", lemon, w/cover	10.00	25.00	30.00
Bowl, 6½", grapefruit/cereal	5.00	12.50	15.00
Bowl, 8", nappy	10.00	30.00	35.00
Bowl, 9", oval, vegetable	12.50	30.00	35.00
Cheese & cracker set, 10½", tray, w/compote	25.00	75.00	80.00
Compotier, w/cover, 5", hi. ftd.	35.00	60.00	70.00
Creamer, hotel	10.00	25.00	30.00
Cup	7.00	15.00	17.50
Marmalade, 4¾"	10.00	22.00	25.00
Oil bottle, 3 oz., w/pressed stopper	20.00	50.00	55.00
Pitcher, 3 pint, ice lip	45.00	130.00	140.00
Pitcher, 3 pint	45.00	130.00	140.00
Plate, 6"	4.00	8.00	8.00
Plate, 6¾", bouillon underliner	4.00	8.00	8.00
Plate, 7", bread	4.00	8.00	10.00
Plate, 8", luncheon	5.00	12.50	15.00
Plate, 10¾", dinner	15.00	40.00	45.00
Plate, 14", sandwich	15.00	30.00	35.00
Platter, 12", oval	15.00	35.00	40.00
Saucer	3.00	5.00	5.00
Sherbet, 5 oz., footed	4.00	8.00	10.00
Stem, 5 oz., saucer champagne	5.00	10.00	12.00
Stem, 7½ oz., low foot	10.00	15.00	20.00
Stem, 8 oz.	12.00	20.00	25.00
Sugar w/lid, hotel	10.00	25.00	30.00
Tray, 10", compartmented spice	10.00	25.00	30.00
Tumbler, 8 oz., ground bottom	5.00	12.00	15.00
Tumbler, 12 oz., tea, ground bottom	7.00	15.00	20.00
Vase, 8"	20.00	50.00	55.00

PORTIA, Cambridge Glass Company, 1932 – Early 1950's

Colors: crystal, yellow, Heatherbloom, green, amber

	Crystal		Crystal
Basket, 2 hdld. (upturned sides)	16.00	Saucer, sq. or rnd.	3.00
Basket, 7", 1 hdld.	195.00	Set: 3 pc. frappe (bowl, 2 plain inserts)	45.00
Bowl, 3½", cranberry	20.00	Stem, #3121, 1 oz., cordial	55.00
Bowl, 3½" sq., cranberry	20.00	Stem, #3121, 1 oz., low ftd., brandy	40.00
Bowl, 5¼", 2 hdld., bonbon	15.00	Stem, #3121, 2½ oz., wine	27.50
Bowl, 6", 2 pt., relish	16.00	Stem, #3121, 3 oz., cocktail	20.00
Bowl, 6", ftd., 2 hdld., bonbon	16.00	Stem, #3121, 4½ oz., claret	35.00
Bowl, 6", grapefruit or oyster	17.00	Stem, #3121, 4½ oz., oyster cocktail	15.00
Bowl, 6½", 3 pt., relish	18.00	Stem, #3121, 5 oz., parfait	35.00
Bowl, 7", 2 pt., relish	16.00	Stem, #3121, 6 oz., low sherbet	13.50
Bowl, 7", ftd., bonbon, tab hdld.	22.00	Stem, #3121, 6 oz., tall sherbet	15.00
Bowl, 7", pickle or relish	22.00	Stem, #3121, 10 oz., goblet	22.50
Bowl, 9", 3 pt., celery & relish, tab hdld.	30.00	Stem, #3124, 3 oz., cocktail	15.00
Bowl, 9½", ftd., pickle (like corn bowl)	22.00	Stem, #3124, 3 oz., wine	25.00
Bowl, 10", flared, 4 ftd.	35.00	Stem, #3124, 4½ oz., claret	27.50
Bowl, 11", 2 pt., 2 hdld., "figure 8" relish	27.50	Stem, #3124, 7 oz., low sherbet	14.00
Bowl, 11", 2 hdld.	35.00	Stem, #3124, 7 oz., tall sherbet	15.00
Bowl, 12", 3 pt., celery & relish, tab hdld.	35.00	Stem, #3124, 10 oz., goblet	18.00
Bowl, 12", 5 pt., celery & relish	37.50	Stem, #3126, 1 oz., cordial	55.00
Bowl, 12", flared, 4 ftd.	45.00	Stem, #3126, 1 oz., low ft., brandy	40.00
Bowl, 12", oval, 4 ftd., "ears" handles	45.00	Stem, #3126, 2½ oz., wine	27.50
Bowl, finger, w/liner #3124	30.00	Stem, #3126, 3 oz., cocktail	17.50
Bowl, seafood (fruit cocktail w/liner)	40.00	Stem, #3126, 4½ oz., claret	35.00
Candlestick, 5"	20.00	Stem, #3126, 4½ oz., low ft., oyster cocktail	12.50
Candlestick, 6", 2-lite, "fleur-de-lis"	35.00	Stem, #3126, 7 oz., low sherbet	14.00
Candlestick, 6", 3-lite	45.00	Stem, #3126, 7 oz., tall sherbet	15.00
Candy box, w/cover, rnd.	65.00	Stem, #3126, 9 oz., goblet	20.00
Cigarette holder, urn shape	55.00	Stem, #3130, 1 oz., cordial	55.00
Cocktail icer, 2 pt.	60.00	Stem, #3130, 2½ oz., wine	25.00
Cocktail shaker, w/stopper	90.00	Stem, #3130, 3 oz., cocktail	17.50
Cocktail shaker, 80 oz., hdld. ball		Stem, #3130, 4½ oz., claret	35.00
w/chrome top	135.00	Stem, #3130, 4½ oz., fruit/oyster cocktail	15.00
Cologne, 2 oz., hdld. ball w/stopper	75.00	Stem, #3130, 7 oz., low sherbet	14.00
Comport, 5½"	27.50	Stem, #3130, 7 oz., tall sherbet	15.00
Comport, 5⅜", blown	35.00	Stem, #3130, 9 oz., goblet	22.50
Creamer, hdld. ball	25.00	Sugar, ftd., hdld. ball	22.50
Creamer, indiv.	12.50	Sugar, indiv.	11.50
Cup, ftd. sq.	18.00	Tray, 11", celery	27.50
Decanter, 29 oz. ftd., sherry, w/stopper	165.00	Tumbler, #3121, 2½ oz., bar	30.00
Hurricane lamp, candlestick base	145.00	Tumbler, #3121, 5 oz., ftd., juice	16.00
Hurricane lamp, keyhole base,		Tumbler, #3121, 10 oz., ftd., water	16.50
w/prisms	125.00	Tumbler, #3121, 12 oz., ftd., tea	25.00
Ice bucket, w/chrome handle	65.00	Tumbler, #3124, 3 oz.	13.00
Ivy ball, 5¼"	35.00	Tumbler, #3124, 5 oz., juice	12.50
Mayonnaise, div. bowl, w/liner &		Tumbler, #3124, 10 oz., water	15.00
2 ladles	40.00	Tumbler, #3124, 12 oz., tea	22.00
Mayonnaise, w/liner & ladle	40.00	Tumbler, #3126, 2½ oz.	30.00
Oil, 6 oz., loop hdld., w/stopper	60.00	Tumbler, #3126, 5 oz., juice	14.00
Oil, 6 oz., hdld. ball, w/stopper	65.00	Tumbler, #3126, 10 oz., water	15.00
Pitcher, ball	125.00	Tumbler, #3126, 12 oz., tea	22.00
Pitcher, Doulton	295.00	Tumbler, #3130, 5 oz., juice	16.00
Plate, 6", 2 hdld.	15.00	Tumbler, #3130, 10 oz., water	15.00
Plate, 6½", bread/butter	7.50	Tumbler, #3130, 12 oz., tea	22.00
Plate, 8", salad	12.50	Tumbler, 12 oz., "roly-poly"	25.00
Plate, 8", ftd., 2 hdld.	17.50	Vase, 5", globe	40.00
Plate, 8", ftd., bonbon, tab hdld.	20.00	Vase, 6", ftd.	40.00
Plate, 8½", sq.	15.00	Vase, 8", ftd.	50.00
Plate, 10½", dinner	60.00	Vase, 9", keyhole ft.	60.00
Plate, 13", 4 ftd., torte	35.00	Vase, 10", bud	40.00
Plate, 13½", 2 hdld., cake	35.00	Vase, 11", flower	50.00
Plate, 14", torte	35.00	Vase, 11", pedestal ft.	55.00
Puff box, 3½", ball shape, w/lid	95.00	Vase, 12", keyhole ft.	75.00
Salt & pepper, pr., flat	25.00	Vase, 13", flower	85.00

PROVINCIAL, Blank #1506, A.H. Heisey & Co.

Colors: crystal, "Limelight" green

"Limelight" green or Zircon prices for Provincial are escalating! Many collectors are beginning to turn to the crystal. If you find pieces other than these two colors shown, you are seeing colors made by Imperial after they purchased the Heisey moulds in 1957. Some of these other colored pieces still have Heisey marks (H in diamond), but they were made at Imperial after the Heisey plant closed.

	Crystal	Limelight Green
Ash tray, 3" square	12.50	
Bonbon dish, 7", 2 hdld., upturned sides	12.00	37.50
Bowl, 5 quart, punch	100.00	
Bowl, individual, nut/jelly	15.00	35.00
Bowl, 4½", nappy	10.00	60.00
Bowl, 5", 2 hdld., nut/jelly	12.00	
Bowl, 5½", nappy	12.00	40.00
Bowl, 5½", round, hdld., nappy	15.00	
Bowl, 5½", tri-corner, hdld., nappy	15.00	55.00
Bowl, 10", 4 part, relish	40.00	195.00
Bowl, 12", floral	30.00	
Bowl, 13", gardenia	35.00	
Box, 5½", footed, candy, w/cover	75.00	500.00
Butter dish, w/cover	85.00	
Candle, 1-lite, block	25.00	
Candle, 3-lite	50.00	
Candle, 3-lite, #4233, 5", vase	65.00	
Cigarette box w/cover	45.00	
Cigarette lighter	25.00	
Coaster, 4"	8.00	
Creamer, footed	20.00	95.00
Creamer & sugar, w/tray, individual	65.00	
Cup, punch	10.00	
Ice jug, ½ gal.	90.00	
Mayonnaise, 7" (plate, ladle, bowl)	40.00	150.00
Mustard	75.00	
Oil bottle, 4 oz., #1 stopper	45.00	
Oil & vinegar bottle, (french dressing)	60.00	
Plate, 5", footed, cheese	10.00	
Plate, 7", 2 hdld., snack	12.00	
Plate, 7", bread	10.00	
Plate, 8", luncheon	15.00	50.00
Plate, 14", torte	30.00	
Plate, 18", buffet	37.50	165.00
Salt & pepper, pr.	25.00	
Stem, 3½ oz., oyster cocktail	15.00	
Stem, 3½ oz., wine	20.00	
Stem, 5 oz., sherbet/champagne	10.00	
Stem, 10 oz.	20.00	
Sugar, footed	20.00	95.00
Tray, 13", oval, celery	22.00	
Tumbler, 5 oz., footed, juice	12.00	50.00
Tumbler, 8 oz.	15.00	
Tumbler, 9 oz., footed	15.00	65.00
Tumbler, 12 oz., footed, iced tea	17.00	75.00
Tumbler, 13", flat, ice tea	20.00	
Vase, 3½", violet	20.00	85.00
Vase, 4", pansy	25.00	
Vase, 6", sweet pea	35.00	

QUEEN ANN, Blank #1401, A.H. Heisey & Co.

Queen Ann is the pattern name given to Empress when it was made in crystal. Pictured here for comparison is the Empress lemon dish and the Waverly lemon dish. The Waverly lemon dish shown here with Orchid etching is rare!

	Crystal		Crystal
Ash tray.	30.00	Marmalade, w/cover, dolp. ftd.	50.00
Bonbon, 6"	10.00	Mayonnaise, 5½", ftd., w/ladle	20.00
Bowl, cream soup	15.00	Mustard, w/cover	30.00
Bowl, cream soup, w/sq. liner	20.00	Oil bottle, 4 oz.	35.00
Bowl, frappe, w/center	20.00	Plate, bouillon liner	4.00
Bowl, nut, dolphin ftd., indiv.	15.00	Plate, cream soup liner	5.00
Bowl, 4½", nappy	5.00	Plate, 4½"	5.00
Bowl, 5", preserve, 2 hdld.	12.00	Plate, 6"	5.00
Bowl, 6", ftd., jelly, 2 hdld.	12.00	Plate, 6", square	5.00
Bowl, 6", dolp. ftd., mint	14.00	Plate, 7"	8.00
Bowl, 6", grapefruit, sq. top, grnd. bottom	9.00	Plate, 7", square	7.00
Bowl, 6½", oval, lemon, w/cover	35.00	Plate, 8", square	10.00
Bowl, 7", 3 pt., relish, triplex	12.50	Plate, 8"	9.00
Bowl, 7", 3 pt., relish, ctr. hand.	20.00	Plate, 9"	12.00
Bowl, 7½", dolp. ftd., nappy	25.00	Plate, 10½"	40.00
Bowl, 7½", dolp. ftd., nasturtium	30.00	Plate, 10½", square	40.00
Bowl, 8", nappy	22.00	Plate, 12"	25.00
Bowl, 8½", ftd., floral, 2 hdld	30.00	Plate, 12", muffin, sides upturned	30.00
Bowl, 9", floral, rolled edge	22.00	Plate, 12", sandwich, 2 hdld.	25.00
Bowl, 9", floral, flared	30.00	Plate, 13", hors d'oeuvre, 2 hdld.	28.00
Bowl, 10", 2 hdld., oval dessert	30.00	Plate, 13", square, 2 hdld.	28.00
Bowl, 10", lion head, floral	250.00	Platter, 14"	25.00
Bowl, 10", oval, veg.	27.00	Salt & pepper, pr.	50.00
Bowl, 10", square, salad, 2 hdld.	30.00	Saucer, square	3.00
Bowl, 10", triplex, relish	20.00	Saucer, after dinner	2.00
Bowl, 11", dolphin ftd., floral	32.00	Saucer	3.00
Bowl, 13", pickle/olive, 2 pt.	15.00	Stem, 2½ oz., oyster cocktail	15.00
Bowl, 15", dolp. ftd., punch	400.00	Stem, 4 oz., saucer champagne	20.00
Candlestick, 3", 3 ftd	45.00	Stem, 4 oz., sherbet	15.00
Candlestick, low, 4 ftd., w/2 hdld.	15.00	Stem, 9 oz., Empress stemware, unusual	30.00
Candlestick, 6", dolphin ftd.	50.00	Sugar, indiv.	15.00
Candy, w/cover, 6", dolphin ftd.	40.00	Sugar, dolphin ftd., 3 hdld.	10.00
Comport, 6", ftd.	25.00	Tray, condiment & liner for indiv. sugar/creamer	15.00
Comport, 6", square	40.00	Tray, 10", 3 pt., relish	18.00
Comport, 7", oval	35.00	Tray, 10", 7 pt., hors d'oeuvre	50.00
Compotier, 6", dolphin ftd.	70.00	Tray, 10", celery	12.00
Creamer, dolphin ftd.	15.00	Tray, 12", ctr. hdld., sand.	30.00
Creamer, indiv.	15.00	Tray, 12", sq. ctr. hdld., sand.	32.50
Cup	12.00	Tray, 13", celery	16.00
Cup, after dinner	15.00	Tray, 16", 4 pt., buffet relish	30.00
Cup, bouillon, 2 hdld.	16.00	Tumbler, 8 oz., dolp. ftd., unusual	75.00
Cup, 4 oz., custard or punch	12.00	Tumbler, 8 oz., grnd. bottom	15.00
Cup, #1401½, has rim as demi-cup	20.00	Tumbler, 12 oz., tea, grnd. bottom	18.00
Grapefruit, w/square liner	15.00	Vase, 8", flared	45.00
Ice tub, w/metal handles	40.00		
Jug, 3 pint, ftd.	70.00		

RIDGELEIGH, Blank #1469, A.H. Heisey & Co.

Colors: crystal, "Sahara," "Zircon," rare

	Crystal
Ash tray, round	5.00
Ash tray, square	4.00
Ash tray, 4", round	12.00
Ash tray, 6", square	20.00
Ash trays, bridge set (heart, diamond, spade, club)	35.00
Basket, bonbon	11.00
Bottle, rock & rye, w/#104 stopper	110.00
Bottle, 4 oz., cologne	85.00
Bottle, 5 oz., bitters, w/tube	65.00
Bowl, indiv., nut	9.00
Bowl, oval, indiv., jelly	12.50
Bowl, indiv., nut, 2 part	10.50
Bowl, 4½", nappy, bell or cupped	7.00
Bowl, 4½", nappy, scalloped	7.00
Bowl, 5", lemon, w/cover	35.00
Bowl, 5", nappy, straight	6.50
Bowl, 5", nappy, square	6.50
Bowl, 6", 2 hdld., divided, jelly	12.75
Bowl, 6", 2 hdld., jelly	14.00
Bowl, 7", 2 part, oval, relish	12.75
Bowl, 8", centerpiece	22.00
Bowl, 8", nappy, square	35.00
Bowl, 9", nappy, square	27.50
Bowl, 9", salad	30.00
Bowl, 10", flared, fruit	35.00
Bowl, 10", floral	35.00
Bowl, 11", centerpiece	35.00
Bowl, 11", punch	90.00
Bowl, 11½", floral	35.00
Bowl, 12", oval, floral	35.00
Bowl, 12", flared, fruit	35.00
Bowl, 13", cone, floral	40.00
Bowl, 14", oblong, floral	50.00
Bowl, 14", oblong, swan hdld., floral	110.00
Box, 8", floral	25.00
Candle block, 3"	18.00
Candle vase, 6"	25.00
Candlestick, 2", 1-lite	20.00
Candlestick, 2-lite, bobeche & "A" prisms	75.00
Candlestick, 7", w/bobeche & "A" prisms	110.00
Cheese, 6", 2 hdld.	11.00
Cigarette box, w/cover, oval	55.00
Cigarette box, w/cover, 6"	30.00
Cigarette holder, oval, w/2 comp. ashtrays	50.00
Cigarette holder, round	7.50
Cigarette holder, square	7.50
Cigarette holder, w/cover	20.00
Coaster or cocktail rest	5.00
Cocktail shaker, 1 qt., w/#1 strainer & #86 stopper	195.00
Comport, 6", low ft., flared	16.00
Comport, 6", low ft., w/cover	30.00
Creamer	20.00
Creamer, indiv.	15.00
Cup	8.00
Cup, beverage	12.00
Cup, punch	10.00
Decanter, 1 pint, w/#95 stopper	150.00
Ice tub, 2 hdld.	60.00
Marmalade, w/cover	50.00
Mayonnaise	35.00

	Crystal
Mustard, w/cover	40.00
Oil bottle, 3 oz., w/#103 stopper	50.00
Pitcher, ½ gallon	175.00
Pitcher, ½ gallon, ice lip	175.00
Plate, oval, hors d'oeuvres	50.00
Plate, 2 hdld., ice tub liner	15.00
Plate, 6", round	7.00
Plate, 6", scalloped	5.00
Plate, 6", square	10.00
Plate, 7", square	12.00
Plate, 8", round	12.00
Plate, 8", square	22.00
Plate, 13½", sandwich	40.00
Plate, 13½", ftd., torte	40.00
Plate, 14", salver	40.00
Salt & pepper, pr.	30.00
Salt dip, indiv.	13.00
Saucer	5.00
Soda, 12 oz., cupped or flared	30.00
Stem, cocktail, pressed	22.00
Stem, claret, pressed	32.00
Stem, oyster cocktail, pressed	15.00
Stem, sherbet, pressed	12.00
Stem, saucer champagne, pressed	20.00
Stem, wine, pressed	32.00
Stem, 1 oz., cordial, blown	150.00
Stem, 2 oz., sherry, blown	85.00
Stem, 2½ oz., wine, blown	75.00
Stem, 3½ oz., cocktail, blown	30.00
Stem, 4 oz., claret, blown	45.00
Stem, 4 oz., oyster cocktail, blown	25.00
Stem, 5 oz., saucer champagne, blown	20.00
Stem, 5 oz., sherbet, blown	15.00
Stem, 8 oz., luncheon, low stem	25.00
Stem, 8 oz., tall stem	30.00
Sugar	20.00
Sugar, indiv.	12.50
Tray, for indiv. sugar & creamer	12.50
Tray, 10½", oblong	30.00
Tray, 11", 3 part, relish	40.00
Tray, 12", celery & olive, divided	35.00
Tray, 12", celery	35.00
Tumbler, 2½ oz., bar, pressed	30.00
Tumbler, 5 oz., juice, blown	24.00
Tumbler, 5 oz., soda, ftd., pressed	22.00
Tumbler, 8 oz., (#1469¾), pressed	18.00
Tumbler, 8 oz., old-fashioned, pressed	20.00
Tumbler, 8 oz., soda, blown	21.00
Tumbler, 10 oz., (#1469¾), pressed	20.00
Tumbler, 12 oz., ftd., soda, pressed	30.00
Tumbler, 12 oz., soda, (#1469¾) pressed	30.00
Tumbler, 13 oz., iced tea, blown	22.00
Vase, #1 indiv., cuspidor shape	25.00
Vase, #2 indiv., cupped top	22.00
Vase, #3 indiv., flared rim	27.50
Vase, #4 indiv., fan out top	35.00
Vase, #5 indiv., scalloped top	25.00
Vase, 3½"	22.00
Vase, 6" (also flared)	17.50
Vase, 8"	55.00
Vase, 8", triangular (#1469¾)	35.00

ROMANCE, Etching #341, Fostoria Glass Company, 1942–1986

Colors: crystal

Romance is sometimes confused with Fostoria's June because of the "bow" in the design. Although I will be placing this pattern in the next edition of my new book *Collectible Glassware from the 40's, 50's & 60's...*, I am introducing it here for new collectors to become familiar with now. Pricing has been "hit and miss"; here goes a compilation of several collectors' and dealers' ideas of pricing which they have kindly shared with me.

	Crystal		Crystal
Ash tray, 2⅝", indiv., #2364	12.50	Plate, 9", #2337	45.00
Bowl, 6", baked apple #2364	15.00	Plate, 11", sandwich, #2364	35.00
Bowl, 8", soup, rimmed, #2364	22.50	Plate, 11¼", cracker, #2364	22.50
Bowl, 9", salad, #2364	37.50	Plate, 14", torte, #2364	40.00
Bowl, 9¼", ftd. blown, #6023	65.00	Plate, 16", torte, #2364	55.00
Bowl, 10", 2 hdld, #2594	42.50	Plate, crescent salad, #2364	40.00
Bowl, 10½", salad, #2364	40.00	Relish, 8", pickle, #2364	22.50
Bowl, 11", shallow, oblong, #2596	45.00	Relish, 10", 3 pt., #2364	25.00
Bowl, 12", ftd. #2364	50.00	Relish, 11", celery, #2364	27.50
Bowl, 12", lily pond, #2364	45.00	Salt & pepper, 2⅝", #2364	45.00
Bowl, 13", fruit, #2364	50.00	Saucer, #2350	5.00
Bowl, 13½", hdld., oval, #2594	50.00	Stem, 3⅞", ¾ oz., cordial, #6017	40.00
Candlestick, 4", #2324	17.50	Stem, 4½", 6 oz., low sherbet, #6017	14.00
Candlestick, 5", #2596	22.50	Stem, 4⅞", 3½ oz., cocktail, #6017	21.50
Candlestick, 5½", #2594	25.00	Stem, 5½", 3 oz., wine, #6017	27.50
Candlestick, 5½", 2 lite, #6023	27.50	Stem, 5½", 6 oz., champagne, #6017	17.50
Candlestick, 8", 3 lite, #2594	37.50	Stem, 5⅞", 4 oz., claret, #6017	30.00
Candy w/ lid, rnd., blown, #2364	67.50	Stem, 7⅜", 9 oz., goblet, #6017	25.00
Cigarette holder, 2", blown, #2364	32.50	Sugar, 3⅛", ftd., #2350½	16.50
Comport, 3¼", cheese, #2364	22.50	Tray, 11¼", ctr. hdld., #2364	32.50
Comport, 5", #6030	22.50	Tumbler, 3⅝", 4 oz., ftd., oyster	
Comport, 8", #2364	35.00	cocktail, #6017	17.50
Creamer, 3¼", ftd., #2350½	17.50	Tumbler, 4¾", 5 oz., ftd., #6017	17.50
Cup, ftd., #2350½	20.00	Tumbler, 5½", 9 oz., ftd., #6017	20.00
Ice tub, 4¾", #4132	57.50	Tumbler, 6", 12 oz., ftd., #6017	25.00
Ladle, mayonnaise, #2364	5.00	Vase, 5", #4121	35.00
Mayonnaise, 5", #2364	22.50	Vase, 6", ftd. bud, #6021	35.00
Pitcher, 8⅞", 53 oz., ftd., #6011	225.00	Vase, 6", ftd., #4143	45.00
Plate, 6", #2337	8.00	Vase, 6", grnd. bottom, #2619½	45.00
Plate, 6¾", mayonnaise liner, #2364	10.00	Vase, 7½", ftd., #4143	57.50
Plate, 7", #2337	10.00	Vase, 7½", grnd. bottom, #2619½	55.00
Plate, 8", #2337	15.00	Vase, 9½", grnd. bottom, #2619½	75.00
		Vase, 10", #2614	65.00
		Vase, 10", ftd., #2470	85.00

ROSALIE, or #731, Cambridge Glass Company, Late 1920's – 1930's

Colors: blue, green, Heatherbloom, pink, red, amber, bluebell, crystal, topaz

Rosalie is another Cambridge pattern which keeps you searching for new items. I am amazed at the variety of pieces and colors that keep turning up. Pink, green, and amber seem to be the only colors in which one can accrue a large set, but with persistence you might find enough blue Rosalie.

Many of my unusual finds in this pattern end up in a collection in Seattle.

Notice the center handled tray in green in the bottom photo. Not only does it have Rosalie etching on the inside, but it has Apple Blossom around the edge! Why two etchings on one piece?

	Blue Pink Green	Amber		Blue Pink Green	Amber
Bottle, French dressing	110.00	75.00	Gravy, double, w/platter	135.00	85.00
Bowl, bouillon, 2 hdld.	25.00	15.00	Ice bucket or pail	65.00	45.00
Bowl, cream soup	22.50	18.00	Icer, w/liner	50.00	40.00
Bowl, finger, w/liner	35.00	25.00	Ice tub	60.00	50.00
Bowl, finger, ftd., w/liner	37.50	30.00	Marmalade	100.00	75.00
Bowl, 3½", cranberry	25.00	20.00	Mayonnaise, ftd., w/liner	55.00	25.00
Bowl, 3⅝", w/cover, 3 pt.	45.00	35.00	Nut, 2½", ftd.	55.00	45.00
Bowl, 5½", fruit	15.00	10.00	Pitcher, 62 oz., #955	215.00	160.00
Bowl, 5½", 2 hdld., bonbon	20.00	12.00	Plate, 6¾", bread/butter	7.00	5.00
Bowl, 6¼", 2 hdld., bonbon	22.50	15.00	Plate, 7", 2 hdld.	15.00	7.00
Bowl, 7", basket, 2 hdld.	25.00	15.00	Plate, 7½", salad	10.00	6.00
Bowl, 8½", soup	40.00	30.00	Plate, 8⅜"	15.00	10.00
Bowl, 8½", 2 hdld.	25.00	15.00	Plate, 9½", dinner	55.00	30.00
Bowl, 8½", w/cover, 3 pt.	67.50	35.00	Plate, 11", 2 hdld.	30.00	20.00
Bowl, 10"	37.50	25.00	Platter, 12"	65.00	35.00
Bowl, 10", 2 hdld.	39.00	27.00	Platter, 15"	95.00	65.00
Bowl, 11"	40.00	25.00	Relish, 9", 2 pt.	25.00	15.00
Bowl, 11", basket, 2 hdld.	45.00	35.00	Relish, 11", 2 pt.	35.00	20.00
Bowl, 11½"	65.00	45.00	Salt dip, 1½", ftd.	45.00	35.00
Bowl, 12", decagon	95.00	75.00	Saucer	5.00	4.00
Bowl, 13", console	50.00		Stem, 1 oz., cordial, #3077	85.00	60.00
Bowl, 14", decagon	225.00	165.00	Stem, 3½ oz., cocktail, #3077	20.00	15.00
Bowl, 15", oval console	75.00	60.00	Stem, 6 oz., low sherbet, #3077	15.00	12.00
Bowl, 15", oval, flanged	85.00	65.00	Stem, 6 oz., high sherbet, #3077	18.00	14.00
Bowl, 15½", oval	95.00	70.00	Stem, 9 oz., water goblet, #3077	25.00	20.00
Candlestick, 4", 2 styles	30.00	20.00	Stem, 10 oz., goblet, #801	30.00	20.00
Candlestick, 5", keyhole	35.00	25.00	Sugar, ftd.	16.00	13.00
Candlestick, 6", 3-lite keyhole	55.00	35.00	Sugar shaker	225.00	195.00
Candy and cover, 6"	95.00	60.00	Tray for sugar shaker/creamer	30.00	20.00
Celery, 11"	35.00	20.00	Tray, ctr. hdld., for sugar/creamer	20.00	14.00
Cheese & cracker, 11" plate	65.00	40.00	Tray, 11", ctr. hdld.	30.00	20.00
Comport, 5½", 2 hdld.	30.00	15.00	Tumbler, 2½ oz., ftd., #3077	35.00	25.00
Comport, 5¾"	30.00	15.00	Tumbler, 5 oz., ftd., #3077	25.00	20.00
Comport, 6", ftd., almond	40.00	25.00	Tumbler, 8 oz., ftd. #3077	25.00	16.00
Comport, 6½", low ft.	40.00	25.00	Tumbler, 10 oz., ftd., #3077	27.00	20.00
Comport, 6½", high ft.	40.00	25.00	Tumbler, 12 oz., ftd., #3077	35.00	25.00
Comport, 6¾"	45.00	30.00	Vase, 5½", ftd.	45.00	27.50
Creamer, ftd.	17.00	12.00	Vase, 6"	55.00	40.00
Creamer, ftd., tall, ewer	30.00	20.00	Vase, 6½", ftd.	75.00	45.00
Cup	35.00	25.00			

ROSE, Etching #1515, on WAVERLY Blank #1519, A.H. Heisey & Co., 1949 - 1957

Colors: crystal

Heisey's Rose pattern has taken over the number one spot from Orchid in collector demand. Sorry, I purchased a cocktail icer too late to include in this book. They are truly hard to find. Pitchers have become more plentiful, but dinner plates are almost nonexistent at the present. Maybe a large cache will turn up!

	Crystal
Ash tray, 3"	37.50
Bell, dinner, #5072	145.00
Bottle, 8 oz., French dressing, blown, #5031	195.00
Bowl, finger, #3309	75.00
Bowl, 5½", ftd., mint	35.00
Bowl, 5¾", ftd., mint, CABOCHON	75.00
Bowl, 6", ftd., mint, QUEEN ANN	45.00
Bowl, 6", jelly, 2 hdld., ftd., QUEEN ANN	42.50
Bowl, 6", oval, lemon, w/cover, WAVERLY	295.00
Bowl, 6½", 2 pt., oval, dressing, WAVERLY	65.00
Bowl, 6½", ftd., honey/cheese, WAVERLY	60.00
Bowl, 6½", ftd., jelly, WAVERLY	45.00
Bowl, 6½", lemon, w/cover, WAVERLY	167.50
Bowl, 7", ftd., honey, WAVERLY	60.00
Bowl, 7", ftd., jelly, WAVERLY	45.00
Bowl, 7", lily, QUEEN ANN	50.00
Bowl, 7", relish, 3 pt., round, WAVERLY	67.50
Bowl, 7", salad, WAVERLY	55.00
Bowl, 7", salad dressings, QUEEN ANN	50.00
Bowl, 9", ftd., fruit or salad, WAVERLY	145.00
Bowl, 9", salad, WAVERLY	95.00
Bowl, 9", 4 pt., rnd, relish, WAVERLY	90.00
Bowl, 9½", crimped, floral, WAVERLY	65.00
Bowl, 10", gardenia, WAVERLY	70.00
Bowl, 10", crimped, floral, WAVERLY	70.00
Bowl, 11", 3 pt., relish, WAVERLY	77.50
Bowl, 11", 3 ftd., floral, WAVERLY	140.00
Bowl, 11", floral, WAVERLY	67.50
Bowl, 11", oval, 4 ftd., WAVERLY	150.00
Bowl, 12", crimped, floral, WAVERLY	65.00
Bowl, 13", crimped, floral, WAVERLY	110.00
Bowl, 13", floral, WAVERLY	80.00
Bowl, 13", gardenia, WAVERLY	80.00
Butter, w/cover, 6", WAVERLY	175.00
Butter, w/cover, ¼ lb., CABOCHON	275.00
Candlestick, 1-lite, #112	40.00
Candlestick, 2-lite, FLAME	65.00
Candlestick, 3-lite, #142, CASCADE	77.50
Candlestick, 3-lite, WAVERLY	90.00
Candlestick, 5", 2-lite, #134, TRIDENT	65.00
Candlestick, 6", epergnette, deep, WAVERLY	350.00
Candy, w/cover, 5", ftd., WAVERLY	160.00
Candy, w/cover, 6", low, bowknot cover	165.00
Candy, w/cover, 6¼", #1951, CABOCHON	145.00
Celery tray, 12", WAVERLY	55.00
Celery tray, 13", WAVERLY	65.00
Cheese compote, 4½", & cracker (11" plate) WAVERLY	145.00
Cheese compote, 5½", & cracker (12" plate) QUEEN ANNE	145.00
Chocolate, w/cover, 5", WAVERLY	150.00
Cigarette holder, #4035	95.00

	Crystal
Cocktail icer, w/liner, #3304, UNIVERSAL	250.00
Cocktail shaker, #4225, COBEL	125.00
Comport, 6½", low ft., WAVERLY	60.00
Comport, 7", oval, ftd., WAVERLY	130.00
Creamer, ftd., WAVERLY	27.50
Creamer, indiv., WAVERLY	25.00
Cup, WAVERLY	65.00
Decanter, 1 pt., #4036½, #101 stopper	195.00
Hurricane lamp, w/12" globe, #5080	325.00
Hurricane lamp, w/12" globe, PLANTATION	325.00
Ice bucket, dolp. ft., QUEEN ANN	275.00
Ice tub, 2 hdld., WAVERLY	275.00
Mayonnaise, 5½", 2 hdld., WAVERLY	55.00
Mayonnaise, 5½", div., 1 hdld., WAVERLY	55.00
Mayonnaise, 5½", ftd., WAVERLY	60.00
Oil, 3 oz., ftd., WAVERLY	165.00
Pitcher, 73 oz., #4164	550.00
Plate, 7", salad, WAVERLY	20.00
Plate, 7", mayonnaise, WAVERLY	20.00
Plate, 8", salad, WAVERLY	30.00
Plate, 10½", dinner	155.00
Plate, 10½", service, WAVERLY	75.00
Plate, 11", sandwich, WAVERLY	50.00
Plate, 11", demi-torte, WAVERLY	65.00
Plate, 12", ftd., salver, WAVERLY	225.00
Plate, 15", ftd., cake, WAVERLY	300.00
Plate, 14", torte, WAVERLY	90.00
Plate, 14", sandwich, WAVERLY	90.00
Plate, 14", ctr. hdld., sandwich, WAVERLY	200.00
Salt & pepper, ftd., pr., WAVERLY	65.00
Saucer, WAVERLY	15.00
Stem, #5072, 1 oz., cordial	145.00
Stem, #5072, 3 oz., wine	110.00
Stem, #5072, 3½ oz., oyster cocktail, ftd.	27.50
Stem, #5072, 4 oz., claret	110.00
Stem, #5072, 4 oz., cocktail	45.00
Stem, #5072, 6 oz., sherbet	27.50
Stem, #5072, 6 oz., saucer champagne	35.00
Stem, #5072, 9 oz., water	45.00
Sugar, indiv., WAVERLY	25.00
Sugar, ftd., WAVERLY	25.00
Tumbler, #5072, 5 oz., ftd., juice	45.00
Tumbler, #5072, 12 oz., ftd., tea	50.00
Tray, indiv. creamer/sugar, QUEEN ANN	55.00
Vase, 3½", ftd., violet, WAVERLY	95.00
Vase, 4", ftd., violet, WAVERLY	100.00
Vase, 7", ftd., fan, WAVERLY	100.00
Vase, 8", #4198	110.00
Vase, 8", sq., ftd., urn	110.00
Vase, 10", #4198	185.00
Vase, 10", sq., ftd, urn	120.00
Vase, 12", sq., ftd., urn	195.00

ROSE POINT, Cambridge Glass Company, 1936 – 1953

Colors: crystal; some crystal with gold

After all the work to update listings in the last book (a week of sixteen hour days) I have added over twenty additional pieces to the Rose Point listing this time!

Speaking of photography, I have reduced the number of pieces in each picture and tried to get the patterns to show more clearly. If the book's pictures mass print as well as the copies I am working from today, then it should show remarkable improvement from the light blue backgrounds we used last book.

The most unusual piece of Rose Point to show up in the last two years is an 18" crimped pan bowl which can be seen in the *Very Rare Glassware of the Depression Years - 3rd Series.*

Notice the pressed Rose Point stems with etched Rose Point tops, and the punch bowl set. Throughout the photographs are many unusual and rare pieces, but in order to show them, I have little space to mention them. Enjoy!

	Crystal		Crystal
Ash tray, stack set on metal pole, #1715	195.00	Bowl, 9½", ftd., w/hdl. (#3500/115)	120.00
Ash tray, 2½", sq. #721	32.50	Bowl, 9½", 2 hdld. (#3400/34)	67.50
Ash tray, 3¼" (#3500/124)	32.50	Bowl, 9½", 2 part, blown (#225)	350.00
Ash tray, 3¼", sq. (#3500/129)	55.00	Bowl, 2 hdld. (#3400/1185)	70.00
Ash tray, 3½" (#3500/125)	35.00	Bowl, 10", 2 hdld. (#3500/28)	77.50
Ash tray, 4" (#3500/126)	40.00	Bowl, 10", 4 tab ftd., flared (#3900/54)	60.00
Ash tray, 4", oval (#3500/130)	80.00	Bowl, 10½", crimp edge, #1351	80.00
Ash tray, 4¼" (#3500/127)	45.00	Bowl, 10½", flared (#3400/168)	65.00
Ash tray, 4½" (#3500/128)	50.00	Bowl, 10½", 3 part, #222	175.00
Ash tray, 4½", oval (#3500/131)	62.50	Bowl, 10½", 3 part (#1401/122)	235.00
Basket, 3", favor (#3500/79)	265.00	Bowl, 11", ftd. (#3500/16)	90.00
Basket, 5", 1 hdld. (#3500/51)	185.00	Bowl, 11", ftd., fancy edge (#3500/19)	120.00
Basket, 6", 1 hdld. (#3500/52)	225.00	Bowl, 11", 4 ftd., oval (#3500/109)	300.00
Basket, 6", 2 hdld. (#3400/1182)	35.00	Bowl, 11", 4 ftd., shallow, fancy edge	
Basket, 6", sq., ftd., 2 hdld (#3500/55)	37.50	(#3400/48)	75.00
Basket, 7", 1 hdld., #119	375.00	Bowl, 11", fruit (#3400/1188)	80.00
Basket, 7", wide (#3500/56)	50.00	Bowl, 11", low foot (#3400/3)	135.00
Basket, sugar, w/handle and tongs (#3500/13)	245.00	Bowl, 11", tab hdld. (#3900/34)	67.50
Bell, dinner, #3121	135.00	Bowl, 11½", ftd., w/tab hdl. (#3900/28)	70.00
Bowl, 3", 4 ftd., nut (#3400/71)	67.50	Bowl, 12", crimped, pan (Pristine #136)	250.00
Bowl, 3½", bonbon, cupped, deep (#3400/204)	75.00	Bowl, 10", salad (Pristine #427)	125.00
Bowl, 3½", cranberry (#3400/70)	80.00	Bowl, 12", 4 ftd., oval (#3400/1240)	95.00
Bowl, 5", hdld. (#3500/49)	35.00	Bowl, 12", 4 ftd., oval, w/"ears" hdl.	
Bowl, 5" fruit (#3500/10)	42.50	(#3900/65)	77.50
Bowl, 5" fruit, blown #1534	70.00	Bowl, 12", 4 ftd., fancy rim oblong (#3400/160)	77.50
Bowl, 5¼" fruit (#3400/56)	42.50	Bowl, 12", 4 ftd., flared (#3400/4)	65.00
Bowl, 5½", nappy (#3400/56)	42.50	Bowl, 12", 4 tab ftd., flared (#3900/62)	67.50
Bowl, 5½", 2 hdld., bonbon (#3400/1179)	32.00	Bowl, 12", ftd., (#3500/17)	100.00
Bowl, 5½", 2 hdld., bonbon (#3400/1180)	30.00	Bowl, 12", ftd., oblong (#3500/118)	145.00
Bowl, 6", bonbon, crimped (#3400/203)	85.00	Bowl, 12", ftd., oval w/hdl. (#3500/21)	175.00
Bowl, 6", bonbon, cupped, shallow (#3400/205)	80.00	Bowl, 12½", flared, rolled edge (#3400/2)	135.00
Bowl, 6", cereal (#3400/53)	57.50	Bowl, 12½", 4 ftd., #993	80.00
Bowl, 6", cereal (#3400/10)	55.00	Bowl, 13", #1398	100.00
Bowl, 6", cereal (#3500/11)	55.00	Bowl, 13", 4 ftd., narrow, crimped (#3400/47)	115.00
Bowl, 6", hdld. (#3500/50)	42.50	Bowl, 13", flared (#3400/1)	65.00
Bowl, 6", 2 hdld. (#1402/89)	40.00	Bowl, 14", 4 ftd., crimp edge, oblong, #1247	125.00
Bowl, 6", 2 hdld., ftd., bonbon (#3500/54)	35.00	Bowl, 18", crimped, pan, (Pristine #136)	550.00
Bowl, 6", 4 ftd., fancy rim (#3400/136)	135.00	Bowl, cream soup, w/liner (#3400)	135.00
Bowl, 6½" bonbon, crimped (#3400/202)	85.00	Bowl, cream soup, w/liner (#3500/2)	145.00
Bowl, 7", bonbon, crimped, shallow		Bowl, finger, w/liner, #3106	75.00
(#3400/201)	100.00	Bowl, finger, w/liner, #3121	75.00
Bowl, 7", tab hdld., ftd., bonbon (#3900/130)	35.00	Butter, w/cover, round, #506	175.00
Bowl, 8", ram's head, squared (#3500/27)	295.00	Butter, w/cover, 5" (#3400/52)	165.00
Bowl, 8½", rimmed soup, #361	250.00	Butter dish, ¼ lb. (#3900/52)	275.00
Bowl, 8½", 3 part, #221	140.00	Candelabrum, 2-lite w/bobeches & prisms,	
Bowl, 9", 4 ftd., (#3400/135)	195.00	#1268	120.00
Bowl, 9", ram's head (#3500/25)	325.00	Candelabrum, 2-lite (#3500/94)	90.00
Bowl, 9½", pickle (like corn), #477	50.00	Candelabrum, 3-lite, #1338	55.00

	Crystal
Candelabrum, 5½", 3-lite w/#19 bobeche & #1 prisms, #1545	95.00
Candelabrum, 6½", 2-lite, w/bobeches & prisms, (Martha #496)	150.00
Candle, torchere, cup ft. (#3500/90)	165.00
Candle, torchere, flat ft. (#3500/88)	150.00
Candlestick, (Pristine #500)	110.00
Candlestick, sq. base & lites (#1700/501)	150.00
Candlestick, 2½" (#3500/108)	30.00
Candlestick, 3½", #628	35.00
Candlestick, 4", #627	50.00
Candlestick, 4", ram's head (#3500/74)	90.00
Candlestick, 5", 1-lite keyhole (#3400/646)	30.00
Candlestick, 5", inverts to comport (#3900/68)	50.00
Candlestick, 5½", 2-lite (Martha #495)	50.00
Candlestick, 6" (#3500/31)	85.00
Candlestick, 6", 2-lite keyhole (#3400/647)	37.50
Candlestick, 6", 2-lite (#3900/72)	42.50
Candlestick, 6", 3-lite (#3900/74)	47.50
Candlestick, 6", 3-lite keyhole (#3400/638)	45.00
Candlestick, 6", 3-tiered lite, #1338	65.00
Candlestick, 6½", Calla Lily, #499	90.00
Candlestick, 7", #3121	70.00
Candlestick, 7½", w/prism (Martha #497)	125.00
Candy box, w/cover, 5", apple shape, #316	800.00
Candy box, w/cover, 5⅜", #1066 stem	145.00
Candy box, w/cover, 5⅜", tall stem, (#3121/3)	135.00
Candy box, w/cover, 5⅜", short stem, (#3121/4)	150.00
Candy box, w/cover, blown, 5⅜" (#3500/103)	150.00
Candy box, w/cover, 6", ram's head (#3500/78)	225.00
Candy box, w/rose finial, 6", 3 ftd., #300	250.00
Candy box, w/cover, 7" (#3400/9)	130.00
Candy box, w/cover, 7", round, 3 pt. #103	150.00
Candy box, w/cover, 8", 3 pt. (#3500/57)	72.50
Candy box, w/cover, rnd. (#3900/165)	95.00
Celery, 12" (#3400/652)	45.00
Celery, 12" (#3500/652)	47.50
Celery, 12", 5 pt. (#3400/67)	55.00
Celery, 14", 4 pt., 2 hdld. (#3500/97)	135.00
Celery & relish, 9", 3 pt. (#3900/125)	47.50
Celery & relish, 12", 3 pt. (#3900/126)	57.50
Celery & relish, 12", 5 pt. (#3900/120)	65.00
Cheese (5" comport) & cracker (13" plate) (#3900/135)	110.00
Cheese (5½" comport) & cracker (11½" plate) (#3400/6)	110.00
Cheese (6" comport) & cracker (12" plate) (#3500/162)	130.00
Cheese dish, w/cover, 5", #980	400.00
Cigarette box, w/cover, #615	120.00
Cigarette box, w/cover, #747	150.00
Cigarette holder, oval, w/ash tray ft., #1066	150.00
Cigarette holder, round, w/ash tray ft., #1337	135.00
Coaster, 3½", #1628	50.00
Cocktail icer, 2 pc. (#3600)	70.00
Cocktail shaker, metal top (#3400/157)	150.00
Cocktail shaker, metal top (#3400/175)	120.00
Cocktail shaker, 12 oz., metal top, #97	275.00
Cocktail shaker, 32 oz., w/glass stopper, #101	160.00
Cocktail shaker, 46 oz., metal top, #98	135.00
Cocktail shaker, 48 oz., glass stopper, #102	150.00
Comport, 5" (#3900/135)	40.00

	Crystal
Comport, 5", 4 ftd., (#3400/74)	67.50
Comport, 5½", scalloped edge (#3900/136)	52.50
Comport, 5⅜", blown (#3500/101)	62.50
Comport, 5⅜", blown, 3121 stem	60.00
Comport, 5⅜", blown, 1066 stem	65.00
Comport, 6" (#3500/36)	115.00
Comport, 6" (#3500/111)	135.00
Comport, 6", 4 ftd., (#3400/13)	37.50
Comport, 7", 2 hdld. (#3500/37)	110.00
Comport, 7", keyhole (#3400/29)	125.00
Comport, 7", keyhole, low (#3400/28)	80.00
Creamer (#3400/68)	20.00
Creamer (#3500/14)	22.00
Creamer, flat #137	110.00
Creamer, flat, #944	130.00
Creamer, ftd., (#3400/16)	85.00
Creamer, ftd., (#3900/41)	20.00
Creamer, indiv. (#3500/15) pie crust edge	25.00
Creamer, indiv. (#3900/40) scalloped edge	20.00
Cup, 3 styles (#3400/54, #3500/1, #3900/17)	30.00
Cup, 5 oz., punch, #488	37.50
Cup, after dinner (#3400/69)	225.00
Decanter, 12 oz., ball, w/stopper (#3400/119)	225.00
Decanter, 14 oz., ftd., #1320	395.00
Decanter, 26 oz., sq., #1380	395.00
Decanter, 28 oz., tall, #1372	550.00
Decanter, 28 oz., w/stopper, #1321	275.00
Decanter, 32 oz., ball, w/stopper (#3400/92)	350.00
Dressing bottle, flat, #1263	265.00
Dressing bottle, ftd., #1261	295.00
Epergne (candle w/vases) (#3900/75)	195.00
Grapefruit, w/liner, #187	110.00
Hat, 5", #1704	400.00
Hat, 6", #1703	400.00
Hat, 8", #1702	450.00
Hat, 9", #1701	500.00
Honey dish, w/cover (#3500/139)	265.00
Hot plate or trivet	65.00
Hurricane lamp, w/prisms, #1613	300.00
Hurricane lamp, candlestick base, #1617	175.00
Hurricane lamp, keyhole base, w/prisms, #1603	195.00
Hurricane lamp, 8", etched chimney, #1601	210.00
Hurricane lamp, 10", etched chimney & base, #1604	250.00
Ice bucket (#1402/52)	185.00
Ice bucket, w/chrome hand. (#3900/671)	125.00
Ice pail, #1705	210.00
Ice pail (#3400/851)	110.00
Ice tub, (Pristine), #671	175.00
Icer, cocktail, #968 or #18	70.00
Marmalade, 8 oz., #147	130.00
Marmalade, w/cover, 7 oz., ftd., #157	165.00
Mayonnaise (sherbet type w/ladle) #19	52.50
Mayonnaise, div., w/liner & 2 ladles (#3900/111)	75.00
Mayonnaise, 3 pc. (#3400/11)	67.50
Mayonnaise, 3 pc. (#3900/129)	65.00
Mayonnaise, w/liner & ladle (#3500/59)	75.00
Mustard, 3 oz., #151	130.00
Mustard, 4½ oz., ftd., #1329	295.00
Oil, 2 oz., ball, w/stopper (#3400/96)	65.00

	Crystal		Crystal
Oil, 6 oz., ball, w/stopper (#3400/99)	110.00	Relish, 7½", 3 pt., center hdld. (#3500/71)	125.00
Oil, 6 oz., hdld (#3400/193)	82.50	Relish, 7½", 4 pt. (#3500/70)	37.50
Oil, 6 oz., hdld., #193	173.00	Relish, 7½", 4 pt., 2 hdld. (#3500/62)	55.00
Oil, 6 oz., loop hdld., w/stopper (#3900/100)	110.00	Relish, 8", 3 pt., 3 hdld. (#3400/91)	37.50
Oil, 6 oz., w/stopper, ftd., hdld. (#3400/161)	195.00	Relish, 10", 2 hdld. (#3500/85)	70.00
Pickle, 9" (#3400/59)	60.00	Relish, 10", 3 pt., 2 hdld. (#3500/86)	52.50
Pickle or relish, 7", (#3900/123)	35.00	Relish, 10", 3 pt., 4 ftd., 2 hdld. (#3500/64)	52.50
Pitcher, 20 oz., (#3900/117)	225.00	Relish, 10", 4 pt., 4 ftd., (#3500/65)	62.50
Pitcher, 20 oz. w/ice lip, #70	225.00	Relish, 10", 4 pt., 2 hdld. (#3500/87)	60.00
Pitcher, 32 oz. (#3900/118)	275.00	Relish, 11", 2 pt., 2 hdld. (#3400/89)	77.50
Pitcher, 32 oz. martini (slender) w/metal insert, (#3900/114)	400.00	Relish, 11", 3 pt. (#3400/200)	57.50
Pitcher, 60 oz., martini, #1408	1,750.00	Relish, 12", 5 pt. (#3400/67)	62.50
Pitcher, 76 oz. (#3900/115)	185.00	Relish, 12", 5 pt., (Pristine #419)	200.00
Pitcher, 76 oz., ice lip (#3400/100)	195.00	Relish, 12", 6 pc. (#3500/67)	200.00
Pitcher, 76 oz., ice lip (#3400/152)	275.00	Relish, 14", w/cover, 4 pt., 2 hdld. (#3500/142)	400.00
Pitcher, 80 oz., ball (#3400/38)	185.00	Relish, 15", 4 pt., hdld. (#3500/113)	175.00
Pitcher, 80 oz., ball (#3900/116)	195.00	Salt & pepper, egg shape, pr., #1468	80.00
Pitcher, 80 oz., Doulton (#3400/141)	275.00	Salt & pepper, individual, rnd., glass base, pr., #1470	80.00
Pitcher, nite set, 2 pc., w/tumbler insert top, #103	525.00	Salt & pepper, individual, w/chrome tops, pr., #360	65.00
Plate, 6", bread/butter (#3400/60)	13.50	Salt & pepper, lg., rnd., glass base, pr., #1471	80.00
Plate, 6", bread/butter (#3500/3)	15.00	Salt & pepper, w/chrome tops, pr., #395	150.00
Plate, 6", 2 hdld. (#3400/1181)	20.00	Salt & pepper, w/chrome tops, pr. (#3400/37)	150.00
Plate, 6⅛" canape #693	150.00	Salt & pepper, w/chrome tops, pr., ftd. (#3400/77)	50.00
Plate, 6½", bread/butter (#3900/20)	13.50	Salt & pepper w/chrome tops, pr., flat (#3900/1177)	40.00
Plate, 7½" (#3500/4)	15.00	Sandwich tray, 11", center handled (#3400/10)	135.00
Plate, 7½", salad (#3400/176)	15.00	Saucer, after dinner (#3400/69)	50.00
Plate, 8", salad (#3900/22)	20.00	Saucer, 3 styles (#3400, #3500, #3900)	5.00
Plate, 8", 2 hdld., ftd., (#3500/161)	40.00	Stem, #3104, 3½ oz., cocktail	250.00
Plate, 8", tab hdld., ftd., bonbon (#3900/131)	35.00	Stem, #3106, ¾ oz., brandy	100.00
Plate, 8½", breakfast (#3400/62)	20.00	Stem, #3106, 1 oz., cordial	100.00
Plate, 8½", salad (#3500/5)	20.00	Stem, #3106, 1 oz., pousse cafe	110.00
Plate, 9½" crescent salad #485	225.00	Stem, #3106, 2 oz., sherry	40.00
Plate, 9½", luncheon (#3400/63)	40.00	Stem, #3106, 2½ oz., wine	40.00
Plate, 10½", dinner (#3400/64)	125.00	Stem, #3106, 3 oz., cocktail	30.00
Plate, 10½" dinner (#3900/24)	125.00	Stem, #3106, 4½ oz., claret	45.00
Plate, 11", 2 hdld. (#3400/35)	50.00	Stem, #3106, 5 oz., oyster cocktail	30.00
Plate, 12", 4 ftd., service (#3900/26)	70.00	Stem, #3106, 7 oz., high sherbet	30.00
Plate, 12", ftd. (#3500/39)	90.00	Stem, #3106, 7 oz., low sherbet	25.00
Plate, 12½", 2 hdld. (#3400/1186)	65.00	Stem, #3106, 10 oz., water goblet	35.00
Plate, 13", rolled edge, ftd. (#3900/33)	70.00	Stem, #3121, 1 oz., brandy	110.00
Plate, 13", 4 ftd., torte (#3500/110)	120.00	Stem, #3121, 1 oz., cordial	70.00
Plate, 13", ftd., cake (Martha #170)	225.00	Stem, #3121, 3 oz., cocktail	32.50
Plate, 13", torte (#3500/38)	165.00	Stem, #3121, 3½ oz., wine	57.50
Plate, 13½", #242	135.00	Stem, #3121, 4½ oz., claret	85.00
Plate, 13½", rolled edge, #1397	70.00	Stem, #3121, 4½ oz., low oyster cocktail	37.50
Plate, 13½", tab hdld., cake (#3900/35)	70.00	Stem, #3121, 5 oz., low ft. parfait	75.00
Plate, 14", rolled edge (#3900/166)	60.00	Stem, #3121, 6 oz., low sherbet	20.00
Plate, 14", service (#3900/167)	75.00	Stem, #3121, 6 oz., tall sherbet	22.00
Plate, 14", torte (#3400/65)	120.00	Stem, #3121, 10 oz., water	30.00
Plate, 18", punch bowl liner (Martha #129)	450.00	Stem, #3500, 1 oz., cordial	67.50
Punch bowl, 15", Martha #478	3,100.00	Stem, #3500, 2½ oz., wine	57.50
Punch set, 15-pc. (Martha)	4,000.00	Stem, #3500, 3 oz., cocktail	35.00
Relish, 5½", 2 pt. (#3500/68)	25.00	Stem, #3500, 4½ oz., claret	75.00
Relish, 5½", 2 pt., hdld. (#3500/60)	30.00	Stem, #3500, 4½ oz., low oyster cocktail	37.50
Relish, 6", 2 pt. (#3400/90)	32.50	Stem, #3500, 5 oz., low ft. parfait	75.00
Relish, 6", 2 pt., 1 hdl. (#3400/1093)	80.00	Stem, #3500, 7 oz., low ft. sherbet	18.00
Relish, 6½", 3 pt. (#3500/69)	32.50	Stem, #3500, 7 oz., tall sherbet	24.00
Relish, 6½", 3 pt., hdld. (#3500/61)	37.50		
Relish, 7", 2 pt. (#3900/124)	37.50		

ROSE POINT, Cambridge Glass Company, 1936 – 1953 (continued)

	Crystal		Crystal
Stem, #3500, 10 oz. water	30.00	Tumbler, #3500, 5 oz., low ft., juice	32.50
Stem, #37801, 4 oz., cocktail	45.00	Tumbler, #3500, 10 oz., low ft., water	26.00
Stem, #7801, 4 oz. cocktail, plain stem	40.00	Tumbler, #3500, 13 oz., low ftd	35.00
Stem, #7966, 1 oz., cordial, plain ft.	125.00	Tumbler, #3500, 12 oz., tall ft., ice tea	32.50
Stem, #7966, 2 oz., sherry, plain ft.	90.00	Tumbler, #7801, 5 oz., ftd.	35.00
Sugar (#3400/68)	20.00	Tumbler, #7801, 12 oz., ftd., ice tea	50.00
Sugar (#3500/14)	20.00	Tumbler, #3900/117, 5 oz.	45.00
Sugar, flat, #137	105.00	Tumbler, #3400/115, 13 oz.	45.00
Sugar, flat, #944	130.00	Urn, 10", w/cover (#3500/41)	450.00
Sugar, ftd. (#3400/16)	80.00	Urn, 12", w/cover (#3500/42)	595.00
Sugar, ftd. (#3900/41)	20.00	Vase, 5", #1309	67.50
Sugar, indiv. (#3500/15) pie crust edge	22.50	Vase, 5", globe (#3400/102)	70.00
Sugar, indiv. (#3900/40) scalloped edge	21.50	Vase, 5", ftd., #6004	45.00
Syrup, w/drip stop top, #1670	350.00	Vase, 6", high ftd., flower, #6004	50.00
Tray, 6", 2 hdld., sq. (#3500/91)	165.00	Vase, 6", #572	125.00
Tray, 12", 2 hdld., oval, service (#3500/99)	195.00	Vase, 6½", globe (#3400/103)	80.00
Tray, 12", rnd. (#3500/67)	140.00	Vase, 7", ivy, ftd., ball, #1066	210.00
Tray, 13", 2 hdld., rnd. (#3500/72)	140.00	Vase, 8", #1430	135.00
Tray, sugar/creamer, (#3900/37)	25.00	Vase, 8", flat, flared, #797	120.00
Tumbler, #498, 2 oz., straight side	95.00	Vase, 8", ftd. (#3500/44)	110.00
Tumbler, #498, 5 oz., straight side	45.00	Vase, 8", high ftd., flower, #6004	55.00
Tumbler, #498, 8 oz., straight side	45.00	Vase, 9", ftd., keyhole, #1237	85.00
Tumbler, #498, 10 oz., straight side	45.00	Vase, 9", ftd., #1620	110.00
Tumbler, #498, 12 oz., straight side	50.00	Vase, 9½" ftd., keyholde, #1233	75.00
Tumbler, #3000, 3½ oz., cone, ftd.	90.00	Vase, 10", ball bottom, #400	150.00
Tumbler, #3000, 5 oz., cone, ftd.	100.00	Vase, 10", bud, #1528	80.00
Tumbler, #3106, 3 oz., ftd.	25.00	Vase, 10", cornucopia (#3900/575)	165.00
Tumbler, #3106, 5 oz., ftd.	25.00	Vase, 10", flat, #1242	115.00
Tumbler, #3106, 9 oz., ftd.	25.00	Vase, 10", ftd., #1301	75.00
Tumbler, #3106, 12 oz., ftd.	30.00	Vase, 10", ftd., #6004	75.00
Tumbler, #3121, 2½ oz., ftd.	62.50	Vase, 10", ftd. (#3500/45)	145.00
Tumbler, #3121, 5 oz., low ft., juice	32.50	Vase, 10", slender, #274	55.00
Tumbler, #3121, 10 oz., low ft., water	27.50	Vase, 11", ftd., flower, #278	110.00
Tumbler, #3121, 12 oz., low ft., ice tea	32.50	Vase, 11", ped. ftd., flower, #1299	125.00
Tumbler, #3400/1341, 1 oz., cordial	90.00	Vase, 12", ftd., #6004	85.00
Tumbler, #3400/92, 2½ oz.	95.00	Vase, 12", ftd., keyhole, #1234	85.00
Tumbler, #3400/38, 5 oz.	85.00	Vase, 12", ftd., keyhole, #1238	125.00
Tumbler, #3400/38, 12 oz.	50.00	Vase, 13", ftd., flower, #279	175.00
Tumbler, #3900/115, 13 oz.	40.00	Vase 18", #1336	1,750.00
Tumbler, #3500, 2½ oz., ftd.	52.50	Vase, sweet pea, #629	225.00

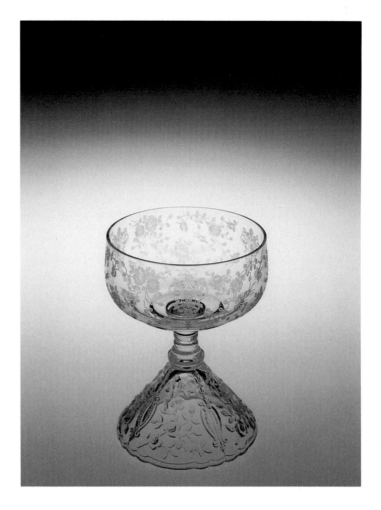

ROYAL, Plate Etching #273, Fostoria Glass Company, 1925 – 1932

Colors: amber, black, blue, green

Although some production of Royal supposedly continued until 1934, the January 1, 1933, Fostoria Catalogue no longer listed pieces as being for sale. I am adjusting my cutoff date for production to 1932 until someone can prove otherwise. If you ever have access to a May, 1928, copy of *House and Garden*, there is an interesting Fostoria advertisement there.

Royal is a Fostoria pattern that is often confused with Vesper since both designs are similar and both are found in the same colors on the #2350 blank. There are more collectors for Vesper at the present time because that pattern has been more publicized than Royal. That may be changing as new collectors are finding that the less expensive Royal is comparable to Vesper in many ways.

Several pieces to search for include the covered cheese, cologne bottles, and the pitchers. Both the amber and green can be collected in sets; but only a few pieces can be found in blue and black. Fostoria's blue color found with Royal etching was called "Blue" as opposed to the "Azure" blue which is the lighter color found with June etching. Refer to Fairfax pattern (page 90) for an example of these two differing shades of blue.

	*Amber, Green		*Amber, Green
Ash tray, #2350, 3½"	22.50	Ice bucket, #2378	45.00
Bowl, #2350, bouillon, flat	11.00	Mayonnaise, #2315	25.00
Bowl, #2350½, bouillon, ftd.	12.50	Pickle, 8", #2350	20.00
Bowl, #2350, cream soup, flat	15.00	Pitcher, #1236	350.00
Bowl, #2350½, cream soup, ftd.	17.50	Pitcher, #5000, 48 oz.	250.00
Bowl, #869, 4½", finger	16.00	Plate, 8½", deep soup/underplate	35.00
Bowl, #2350, 5½", fruit	11.00	Plate, #2350, 6", bread/butter	3.00
Bowl, #2350, 6½", cereal	15.00	Plate, #2350, 7½", salad	4.00
Bowl, #2267, 7", ftd.	30.00	Plate, #2350, 8½", luncheon	8.00
Bowl, #2350, 7¾", soup	18.00	Plate, #2321, 8¾, Maj Jongg (canape)	32.50
Bowl, #2350, 8", nappy	30.00	Plate, #2350, 9½", small dinner	13.00
Bowl, #2350, 9", nappy	32.00	Plate, #2350, 10½", dinner	27.50
Bowl, #2350, 9", oval, baker	37.50	Plate, #2350, 13", chop	27.50
Bowl, #2324, 10", ftd.	40.00	Plate, #2350, 15", chop	40.00
Bowl, #2350, 10", salad	35.00	Platter, #2350, 10½"	30.00
Bowl, #2350, 10½", oval, baker	45.00	Platter, #2350, 12"	40.00
Bowl, #2315, 10½", ftd.	45.00	Platter, #2350, 15½"	75.00
Bowl, #2329, 11", console	22.00	Salt and pepper, #5100, pr.	60.00
Bowl, #2297, 12", deep	22.00	Sauce boat, w/liner	125.00
Bowl, #2329, 13", console	30.00	Saucer, #2350/#2350½	3.00
Bowl, #2324, 13", ftd.	45.00	Saucer, #2350, demi	5.00
Bowl, #2371, 13", oval, w/flower frog	95.00	Server, #2287, 11", center hdld.	25.00
Butter, w/cover #2350	225.00	Stem, #869, ¾ oz., cordial	65.00
Candlestick, #2324, 4"	14.00	Stem, #869, 2¾ oz., wine	27.50
Candlestick, #2324, 9"	45.00	Stem, #869, 3 oz., cocktail	22.50
Candy, w/cover, #2331, 3 part	60.00	Stem, #869, 5½ oz., oyster cocktail	15.00
Candy, w/cover, ftd., ½ lb.	145.00	Stem, #869, 5½ oz., parfait	30.00
Celery, #2350, 11"	25.00	Stem, #869, 6 oz., low sherbet	12.50
Cheese, w/cover/plate #2276 (plate 11")	110.00	Stem, #869, 6 oz., high sherbet	16.00
Cologne, #2322, tall	30.00	Stem, #869, 9 oz., water	20.00
Cologne, #2323, short	25.00	Sugar, flat, w/lid	150.00
Cologne/powder jar combination	195.00	Sugar, #2315, ftd., flat	17.00
Comport, #1861½, 6", jelly	25.00	Sugar, #2350½, ftd.	12.00
Comport, #2327, 7"	28.00	Sugar lid, #2350½	95.00
Comport, #2358, 8" wide	30.00	Tumbler, #869, 5 oz., flat	22.50
Creamer, flat	14.00	Tumbler, #859, 9 oz., flat	25.00
Creamer, #2315½, ftd., fat	18.00	Tumbler, #859, 12 oz., flat	30.00
Creamer, #2350½, ftd.	13.00	Tumbler, #5000, 2½ oz., ftd.	27.50
Cup, #2350, flat	12.00	Tumbler, #5000, 5 oz., ftd.	14.00
Cup, #2350½, ftd.	13.00	Tumbler, #5000, 9 oz., ftd.	16.00
Cup, #2350, demi	22.50	Tumbler, #5000, 12 oz., ftd.	25.00
Egg cup, #2350	25.00	Vase, #2324, urn, ftd.	75.00
Grapefruit, w/insert	70.00	Vase, #2292, flared	90.00

* Add 50% more for blue or black!

SANDWICH, #41, Duncan & Miller Glass Company, 1924 – 1955

Colors: crystal, amber, pink, green, red, cobalt blue

Lancaster Colony is making some of this for their lines today. The bright blue, green and amberina are from Duncan moulds and were sold by Montgomery Ward in the early 1970's. Tiffin also made some Sandwich pieces in milk glass. Stemware abounds and it is the serving pieces that are in demand. This older stemware is as economical to use as newly made stemware.

	Crystal		Crystal
Ash tray, 2½" x 3¾", rect.	10.00	Bowl, 10", lily, vertical edge	50.00
Ash tray, 2⅓", sq.	8.00	Bowl, 11", cupped nut	50.00
Basket, 6½", w/loop hdld.	115.00	Bowl, 11½", crimped flower	50.00
Basket, 10", crimped, w/loop hdl.	155.00	Bowl, 11½", gardenia	45.00
Basket, 10", oval, w/loop hdl.	155.00	Bowl, 11½", ftd., crimped fruit	55.00
Basket, 11½", w/loop hdl.	200.00	Bowl, 12", fruit, flared edge	45.00
Bonbon, 5", heart shape, w/ring hdl.	15.00	Bowl, 12", shallow salad	40.00
Bonbon, 5½", heart shape, hdld.	15.00	Bowl, 12", oblong console	40.00
Bonbon, 6", heart shape, w/ring hdl.	20.00	Bowl, 12", epergne, w/ctr. hole	65.00
Bonbon, 7½", ftd., w/cover	37.50	Butter, w/cover, ¼ lb.	37.50
Bowl, 2½", salted almond	8.00	Cake stand, 11½", ftd., rolled edge	90.00
Bowl, 3½", nut	8.50	Cake stand, 12", ftd., rolled edge, plain pedestal	75.00
Bowl, 4", finger	12.50	Cake stand, 13", ftd., plain pedestal	75.00
Bowl, 5½", hdld.	15.00	Candelabra, 10", 1-lite, w/bobeche & prisms	70.00
Bowl, 5½", ftd., grapefruit, w/rim liner	15.00	Candelabra, 10", 3-lite, w/bobeche & prisms	150.00
Bowl, 5½", ftd., grapefruit, w/fruit cup liner	15.00	Candelabra, 16", 3-lite, w/bobeche & prisms	210.00
Bowl, 5", 2 pt., nappy	12.00	Candlestick, 4", 1-lite	14.00
Bowl, 5", ftd., crimped ivy	25.00	Candlestick, 4", 1-lite, w/bobeche & stub. prisms	30.00
Bowl, 5", fruit	10.00	Candlestick, 5", 3-lite	35.00
Bowl, 5", nappy, w/ring hdl.	12.00	Candlestick, 5", 3-lite, w/bobeche & stub. prisms	90.00
Bowl, 6", 2 pt., nappy	14.00	Candlestick, 5", 2-lite, w/bobeche & stub. prisms	70.00
Bowl, 6", fruit salad	12.00	Candlestick, 5", 2-lite	25.00
Bowl, 6", grapefruit, rimmed edge	15.00		
Bowl, 6", nappy, w/ring hdl.	17.50		
Bowl, 10", salad, deep	65.00		
Bowl, 10", 3 pt., fruit	75.00		

	Crystal
Candy, 6" square	325.00
Candy box, w/cover, 5", flat	35.00
Candy jar, w/cover, 8½", ftd	50.00
Cheese, w/cover (cover 4¾", plate 8")	95.00
Cheese/cracker (3" compote, 13" plate)	45.00
Cigarette box, w/cover, 3½"	22.00
Cigarette holder, 3", ftd	27.50
Coaster, 5"	12.00
Comport, 2¼"	15.00
Comport, 3¼", low ft., crimped candy	20.00
Comport, 3¼", low ft., flared candy	17.50
Comport, 4¼", ftd	20.00
Comport, 5", low ft	20.00
Comport, 5½", ftd., low crimped	25.00
Comport, 6", low ft., flared	22.50
Condiment set (2 cruets; 3¾" salt & pepper; 4 pt. tray)	90.00
Creamer, 4", 7 oz., ftd	9.00
Cup, 6 oz., tea	10.00
Epergne, 9", garden	90.00
Epergne, 12", 3 pt., fruit or flower	195.00
Jelly, 3", indiv	7.00
Mayonnaise set, 3 pc.: ladle, 5" bowl, 7" plate	32.00
Oil bottle, 5¾"	35.00
Pan, 6¾" x 10½", oblong, camelia	55.00
Pitcher, 13 oz., metal top	55.00
Pitcher, w/ice lip, 8", 64 oz	125.00
Plate, 3", indiv. jelly	6.00
Plate, 6", bread/butter	6.00
Plate, 6½", finger bowl liner	8.00
Plate, 7", dessert	7.50
Plate, 8", mayonnaise liner, w/ring	5.00
Plate, 8", salad	10.00
Plate, 9½", dinner	32.50
Plate, 11½", hdld., service	35.00
Plate, 12", torte	45.00
Plate, 12", ice cream, rolled edge	50.00
Plate, 12", deviled egg	60.00
Plate, 13", salad dressing, w/ring	32.00
Plate, 13", service	50.00
Plate, 13", service, rolled edge	55.00
Plate, 13", cracker, w/ring	27.50
Plate, 16", lazy susan, w/turntable	90.00
Plate, 16", hostess	90.00
Relish, 5½", 2 pt., rnd., ring hdl	15.00
Relish, 6", 2 pt., rnd., ring hdl	17.00
Relish, 7", 2 pt., oval	20.00
Relish, 10", 4 pt., hdld	25.00

	Crystal
Relish, 10", 3 pt., oblong	27.50
Relish, 10½", 3 pt., oblong	27.50
Relish, 12", 3 pt.	37.50
Salad dressing set: (2 ladles; 5" ftd. mayonnaise; 13" plate w/ring)	80.00
Salad dressing set: (2 ladles; 6" ftd. div. bowl; 8" plate w/ring)	65.00
Salt & pepper, 2½", w/glass tops, pr.	18.00
Salt & pepper, 2½", w/metal tops, pr.	18.00
Salt & pepper, 3¾", w/metal top (on 6" tray), 3 pc.	30.00
Saucer, 6", w/ring	4.00
Stem, 2½", 6 oz., ftd., fruit cup/jello	11.00
Stem, 2¾", 5 oz., ftd., oyster cocktail	15.00
Stem, 3½", 5 oz., sundae (flared rim)	12.00
Stem, 4¼", 3 oz., cocktail	15.00
Stem, 4¼", 5 oz., ice cream	12.50
Stem, 4¼", 3 oz., wine	20.00
Stem, 5¼", 4 oz., ftd., parfait	25.00
Stem, 5¼", 5 oz., champagne	20.00
Stem, 6", 9 oz., goblet	18.50
Sugar, 3¼", ftd., 9 oz.	8.00
Sugar, 5 oz.	7.50
Sugar (cheese) shaker, 13 oz., metal top	65.00
Tray, oval (for sugar/creamer)	10.00
Tray, 6" mint, rolled edge, w/ring hdl.	17.50
Tray, 7", oval, pickle	15.00
Tray, 7", mint, rolled edge, w/ring hdl.	20.00
Tray, 8", oval	18.00
Tray, 8", for oil/vinegar	20.00
Tray, 10", oval, celery	18.00
Tray, 12", fruit epergne	45.00
Tray, 12", ice cream, rolled edge	45.00
Tumbler, 3¾", 5 oz., ftd., juice	12.00
Tumbler, 4¾", 9 oz., ftd., water	14.00
Tumbler, 5¼", 13 oz., flat, iced tea	20.00
Tumbler, 5¼", 12 oz., ftd., iced tea	17.50
Urn, w/cover, 12", ftd	115.00
Vase, 3", ftd., crimped	17.50
Vase, 3", ftd., flared rim	15.00
Vase, 4", hat shape	20.00
Vase, 4½", flat base, crimped	25.00
Vase, 5", ftd., flared rim	22.50
Vase, 5", ftd., crimped	25.00
Vase, 5", ftd., fan	35.00
Vase, 7½", epergne, threaded base	50.00
Vase, 10", ftd	55.00

173

SATURN, Blank #1485, A.H. Heisey & Co.

Colors: crystal, "Zircon" or "Limelight" green, "Dawn"

Zircon prices continue to skyrocket in Saturn!
Shakers in "Zircon" are quite rare as you can see by the price. "Limelight" and "Zircon" are the same color. Originally made in 1937, this color was called "Zircon." In 1955, it was made again by Heisey, but called "Limelight."

	Crystal	Zircon/ Limelight
Ash tray	9.00	110.00
Bitters bottle, w/short tube, blown	35.00	
Bowl, baked apple	7.00	65.00
Bowl, finger	5.00	
Bowl, rose, lg.	40.00	
Bowl, 4½", nappy	5.00	
Bowl, 5", nappy	7.00	
Bowl, 5", whipped cream	15.00	150.00
Bowl, 7", pickle	15.00	
Bowl, 9", 3 part, relish	17.50	
Bowl, 10", celery	15.00	
Bowl, 11", salad	40.00	140.00
Bowl, 12", fruit, flared rim	35.00	100.00
Bowl, 13", floral, rolled edge	37.00	
Bowl, 13", floral	37.00	
Candelabrum, w/"e" ball drops, 2-lite	125.00	500.00
Candle block, 2-lite	95.00	325.00
Candlestick, 3", ftd., 1-lite	30.00	500.00
Comport, 7"	30.00	350.00
Creamer	15.00	140.00
Cup	9.00	150.00
Hostess Set, 8 pc. (low bowl w/ftd. ctr. bowl, 3 toothpick holders & clips)	45.00	300.00
Marmalade, w/cover	45.00	500.00
Mayonnaise	8.00	80.00
Mustard, w/cover and paddle	45.00	325.00
Oil bottle, 2 oz., w/#1 stopper	55.00	350.00
Pitcher, 70 oz., w/ice lip, blown	65.00	500.00
Pitcher, juice	40.00	300.00
Plate, 6"	3.00	35.00
Plate, 7", bread	5.00	45.00
Plate, 8", luncheon	7.00	55.00
Plate, 13", torte	25.00	
Plate, 15", torte	30.00	
Salt & pepper, pr.	45.00	550.00
Saucer	5.00	30.00
Stem, 3 oz., cocktail	10.00	60.00
Stem, 4 oz., fruit cocktail or oyster cocktail	8.00	75.00
Stem, 4½ oz., sherbet	5.00	70.00
Stem, 5 oz., parfait	10.00	110.00
Stem, 6 oz., saucer champagne	5.00	95.00
Stem, 10 oz.	12.00	90.00
Sugar	12.50	90.00
Sugar shaker (pourer)	75.00	
Sugar, w/cover, no handles	25.00	
Tray, tidbit, 2 sides turned as fan	25.00	80.00
Tumbler, 5 oz., juice	7.00	120.00
Tumbler, 7 oz., old-fashioned	10.00	
Tumbler, 8 oz., old-fashioned	10.00	
Tumbler, 9 oz., luncheon	12.00	
Tumbler, 10 oz.	17.50	70.00
Tumbler, 12 oz., soda	10.00	150.00
Vase, violet	22.00	85.00
Vase, 8½", flared	25.00	175.00
Vase, 8½", straight	25.00	175.00

SEVILLE, Fostoria Glass Company, 1926 – 1931

Colors: amber, green

Fostoria's Seville is a pattern that would be a good starting point for someone wanting to collect an inexpensive pattern. It probably will not stay that way for long as there is not that much to go around. Green would be easier to collect than amber. The butter dish, pitcher, and candy jars are all difficult to find; be on the lookout for them.

	Amber	Green		Amber	Green
Ash tray, #2350, 4"	17.50	22.50	Grapefruit, #945½, blown	40.00	45.00
Bowl, #2350, fruit, 5½"	10.00	12.00	Grapefruit, #945½, liner, blown	30.00	35.00
Bowl, #2350, cereal, 6½"	16.00	18.00	Grapefruit, #2315, molded	22.50	25.00
Bowl, #2350, soup, 7¾"	17.50	20.00	Ice bucket, #2378	50.00	52.00
Bowl, #2315, low foot, 7"	16.00	18.00	Pickle, #2350, 8"	13.50	15.00
Bowl, #2350, vegetable	20.00	25.00	Pitcher, #5084, ftd.	225.00	250.00
Bowl, #2350, nappy, 9"	30.00	35.00	Plate, #2350, bread and butter, 6"	3.50	4.00
Bowl, #2350, oval, baker, 9"	25.00	30.00	Plate, #2350, salad, 7½"	5.00	5.50
Bowl, #2315, flared, 10½", ftd.	25.00	30.00	Plate, #2350, luncheon, 8½"	6.00	6.50
Bowl, #2350, oval, baker, 10½"	35.00	40.00	Plate, #2321, Maj Jongg (canape),		
Bowl, 10", ftd.	35.00	40.00	8¾"	30.00	35.00
Bowl, #2350, salad, 10"	30.00	35.00	Plate, #2350, sm. dinner, 9½"	12.00	13.50
Bowl, #2329, rolled edge, console,			Plate, #2350, dinner, 10½"	32.50	40.00
11"	27.50	32.50	Plate, #2350, chop, 13¾"	30.00	35.00
Bowl, #2297, deep, flared, 12"	30.00	32.50	Plate, #2350, round, 15"	35.00	40.00
Bowl, #2371, oval, console, 13"	35.00	40.00	Plate, #2350, cream soup liner	5.00	6.00
Bowl, #2329, rolled edge, console,			Platter, #2350, 10½"	22.50	25.00
13"	30.00	32.50	Platter, #2350, 12"	35.00	40.00
Bowl, #2350, bouillon, flat	13.50	15.00	Platter, #2350, 15"	65.00	75.00
Bowl, #2350½, bouillon, ftd.	14.00	16.00	Salt and pepper shaker, #5100, pr.	60.00	65.00
Bowl, #2350, cream soup, flat	14.50	16.00	Sauce boat liner, #2350	25.00	27.50
Bowl, #2350½, cream soup, ftd.	15.50	17.00	Sauce boat, #2350	55.00	72.50
Bowl, #869/2283, finger, w/6" liner	17.50	20.00	Saucer, #2350	3.00	3.00
Butter, w/cover, #2350, round	175.00	225.00	Saucer, after dinner, #2350	5.00	5.00
Candlestick, #2324, 2"	15.00	17.50	Stem, #870, cocktail	15.00	16.00
Candlestick, #2324, 4"	12.50	15.00	Stem, #870, cordial	65.00	70.00
Candlestick, #2324, 9"	25.00	30.00	Stem, #870, high sherbet	15.00	16.00
Candy jar, w/cover, #2250,			Stem, #870, low sherbet	12.50	13.50
½ lb., ftd.	85.00	110.00	Stem, #870, oyster cocktail	16.50	17.50
Candy jar, w/cover, #2331, 3 pt., flat	65.00	80.00	Stem, #870, parfait	30.00	35.00
Celery, #2350, 11"	15.00	17.50	Stem, #870, water	20.00	22.50
Cheese and cracker, #2368,			Stem, #870, wine	22.50	25.00
(11" plate)	35.00	40.00	Sugar cover, #2350½	75.00	90.00
Comport, #2327, 7½",			Sugar, fat, ftd., #2315	13.50	14.50
(twisted stem)	20.00	22.50	Sugar, ftd., #2350½	12.50	13.50
Comport, #2350, 8"	27.50	32.50	Tray, 11", center handled, #2287	27.50	30.00
Creamer, #2315½, flat, ftd.	13.50	15.00	Tumbler, #5084, ftd., 2 oz.	35.00	37.50
Creamer, #2350½, ftd.	12.50	13.50	Tumbler, #5084, ftd., 5 oz.	13.50	15.00
Cup, #2350, after dinner	25.00	30.00	Tumbler, #5084, ftd., 9 oz.	15.00	16.50
Cup, #2350, flat	10.00	12.50	Tumbler, #5084, ftd., 12 oz.	18.00	20.00
Cup, #2350½, ftd.	10.00	12.50	Urn, small, #2324	70.00	85.00
Egg cup, #2350	30.00	35.00	Vase, #2292, 8"	55.00	65.00

"SPIRAL FLUTES," Duncan & Miller Glass Company, Introduced 1924

Colors: amber, green, pink, crystal

Not many new collectors are starting Spiral Flutes, but those who have done so are finding the going difficult on many pieces. Three items are easily found: the 6¾" flanged bowls, 7 oz. footed tumblers, and 7½" plates; but after that, there is very little found. There is more green available.

	Amber, Green, Pink
Bowl, 2", almond	11.00
Bowl, 3¾", bouillon	15.00
Bowl, 4⅜", finger	6.00
Bowl, 4¾", ftd., cream soup	15.00
Bowl, 4" w., mayonnaise	17.50
Bowl, 5", nappy	6.00
Bowl, 6½", cereal, sm. flange	30.00
Bowl, 6¾", grapefruit	7.50
Bowl, 6", handled nappy	22.00
Bowl, 6", handled nappy, w/cover	65.00
Bowl, 7", nappy	15.00
Bowl, 7½", flanged (baked apple)	22.50
Bowl, 8", nappy	17.50
Bowl, 8½", flanged (oyster plate)	22.50
Bowl, 9", nappy	27.50
Bowl, 10", oval, veg., two styles.	42.50
Bowl, 10½", lily pond	40.00
Bowl, 11¾" w. x 3¾" t., console, flared	30.00
Bowl, 11", nappy	30.00
Bowl, 12", cupped console	30.00
Candle, 3½"	15.00
Candle, 7½"	55.00
Candle, 9½"	60.00
Candle, 11½"	95.00
Celery, 10¾" x 4¾"	17.50
* Chocolate jar, w/cover	210.00
Cigarette holder, 4"	30.00
Comport, 4⅜"	15.00
Comport, 6⅝"	17.50
Comport, 9", low ft., flared	50.00
Console stand, 1½" h. x 4⅝" w.	12.00
Creamer, oval	8.00
Cup	9.00
Cup, demi	25.00
* Fernery, 10" x 5½", 4 ftd., flower box	325.00
Grapefruit, ftd.	20.00

	Amber, Green, Pink
Ice tub, handled	40.00
Lamp, 10½", countess	225.00
Mug, 6½", 9 oz., handled	27.50
Mug, 7", 9 oz., handled	35.00
Oil, w/stopper, 6 oz.	150.00
Pickle, 8⅝"	12.00
Pitcher, ½ gal.	150.00
Plate, 6", pie	3.00
Plate, 7½", salad	4.00
Plate, 8⅜", luncheon	4.00
Plate, 10⅜", dinner	22.50
Plate, 13⅝", torte	27.50
Plate, w/star, 6", (fingerbowl item)	6.00
Platter, 11"	32.50
Platter, 13"	42.50
Relish, 10" x 7⅜", oval, 3 pc. (2 inserts)	70.00
Saucer	3.00
Saucer, demi	5.00
Seafood sauce cup, 3" w. x 2½" h.	22.00
Stem, 3¾", 3½ oz., wine	17.50
Stem, 3¾", 5 oz., low sherbet	8.00
Stem, 4¾", 6 oz., tall sherbet	12.00
Stem, 5⅝", 4½ oz., parfait	17.50
Stem, 6¼", 7 oz., water	17.50
Sugar, oval	8.00
Sweetmeat, w/cover, 7½"	90.00
Tumbler, 3⅜", ftd., 2½ oz., cocktail (no stem)	7.00
Tumbler, 4¼", 8 oz., flat	27.50
Tumbler, 4⅜", ftd., 5½ oz., juice (no stem)	14.00
Tumbler, 4¾", 7 oz., flat, soda	30.00
Tumbler, 5⅛", ftd., 7 oz., water (1 knob)	8.00
Tumbler, 5⅛", ftd., 9 oz., water (no stem)	20.00
Tumbler, 5½", 11 oz., gingerale	55.00
Vase, 6½"	12.00
Vase, 8½"	17.50

*Crystal, $135.00

STANHOPE, #1483, A.H. Heisey Co., 1936 – 1941

Colors: crystal, some blown stemware in Zircon

Stanhope is a Heisey pattern that either you love or you hate. There seems to be little middle ground. The colored insert handles of black or red (round knobs) drive some people to distraction while others think they look great. The T knobs are like wooden dowel rods which act as horizontal handles. If everyone liked the same thing...!

	Crystal
Ash tray, indiv.	20.00
Bottle, oil, 3 oz. w or w/o rd. knob	275.00
Bowl, 6" mint, 2 hdld., w or w/o rd. knobs	15.00
Bowl, 6" mint, 2 pt., 2 hdld., w or w/o rd. knobs	15.00
Bowl, 11" salad	45.00
Bowl, finger #4080 (blown, plain)	5.00
Bowl, floral, 11", 2 hdld. w or w/o "T" knobs	45.00
Candelabra, 2-lite, w bobeche & prisms	135.00
Candy box & lid, rnd., w or w/o rd. knob	160.00
Cigarette box & lid, w or w/o rd. knob	45.00
Creamer, 2 hdld., w or w/o rd. knobs	25.00
Cup, w or w/o rd. knob	15.00
Ice tub, 2 hdld., w or w/o "T" knobs	45.00
Jelly, 6", 1 hdld., w or w/o rd. knobs	20.00
Jelly, 6", 3 pt., 1 hdld., w or w/o rd. knobs	20.00
Nappy, 4½", 1 hdld. w or w/o rd. knob	15.00
Nut, indiv., 1 hdld., w or w/o rd. knob	25.00
Plate, 7"	7.50
Plate, 12" torte, 2 hdld. w or w/o "T" knobs	30.00
Plate, 15" torte, rnd. or salad liner	32.50
Relish, 11" triplex buffet, 2 hdld., w or w/o "T" knobs	30.00
Relish, 12" 4 pt., 2 hdld., w or w/o "T" knobs	35.00
Relish, 12", 5 pt., 2 hdld. w or w/o "T" knobs	35.00
Salt & pepper, #60 top	45.00
Saucer	5.00
Stem, 1 oz. cordial #4083 (blown)	70.00
Stem, 2½ oz. pressed wine	20.00
Stem, 2½ oz. wine, #4083	25.00
Stem, 3½ oz. cocktail #4083	20.00
Stem, 3½ oz. pressed cocktail	10.00
Stem, 4 oz. claret #4083	25.00
Stem, 4 oz. oyster cocktail #4083	10.00
Stem, 5½ oz. pressed saucer champagne	15.00
Stem, 5½ oz. saucer champagne #4083	15.00
Stem, 9 oz. pressed goblet	20.00
Stem, 10 oz. goblet #4083	22.50
Stem, 12 oz. pressed soda	25.00
Sugar, 2 hdld., w or w/o rd. knobs	25.00
Tray, 12" celery, 2 hdld. w or w/o "T" knobs	12.50
Tumbler, 5 oz. soda #4083	20.00
Tumbler, 8 oz. soda #4083	22.50
Tumbler, 12 oz. soda #4083	25.00
Vase, 7" ball	50.00
Vase, 9", 2 hdld., w or w/o "T" knobs	45.00

TEAR DROP, #301, Duncan & Miller Glass Company, 1936 – 1955

Colors: crystal

I still have trouble selling stemware in Tear Drop just as I have trouble finding dinner plates and serving pieces. Even cordials are easily found when compared to finding cordials in other patterns. This is another good starting pattern for beginners. You can buy a lot of it without mortgaging the farm.

	Crystal		Crystal
Ash tray, 3" indiv.	6.00	Coaster/ashtray, 3", rolled edge	7.00
Ash tray, 5"	8.00	Comport, 4¾", ftd.	12.00
Bonbon, 6", 4 hdld.	12.00	Comport, 6", low foot., hdld.	15.00
Bottle, w/stopper, 12", bar	110.00	Condiment set: 5 pc. (salt/pepper, 2	
Bowl, 4¼", finger	7.00	3 oz. cruets, 9", 2 hdld. tray)	95.00
Bowl, 5", fruit nappy	6.00	Creamer, 3 oz.	5.00
Bowl, 5", 2 hdld., nappy	8.00	Creamer, 6 oz.	6.00
Bowl, 6", dessert, nappy	6.00	Creamer, 8 oz.	8.00
Bowl, 6", fruit, nappy	6.00	Cup, 2½ oz., demi	10.00
Bowl, 7", fruit, nappy	7.00	Cup, 6 oz., tea	6.00
Bowl, 7", 2 hdld., nappy	10.00	Flower basket, 12", loop hdl.	110.00
Bowl, 8" x 12", oval, flower	35.00	Ice bucket, 5½"	60.00
Bowl, 9", salad	25.00	Marmalade, w/cover, 4"	35.00
Bowl, 9", 2 hdld., nappy	20.00	Mayonnaise, 4½" (2 hdld. bowl, ladle,	
Bowl, 10", crimped console, 2 hdld.	27.50	6" plate)	27.50
Bowl, 10", flared, fruit	25.00	Mayonnaise set, 3 pc. (4½" bowl, ladle,	
Bowl, 11½", crimped, flower	30.00	8" hdld. plate)	32.50
Bowl, 11½", flared, flower	30.00	Mustard jar, w/cover, 4¼"	35.00
Bowl, 12", salad	35.00	Nut dish, 6", 2 pt.	10.00
Bowl, 12", crimped, low foot	37.00	Oil bottle, 3 oz.	20.00
Bowl, 12", ftd., flower	45.00	Olive dish, 4¼", 2 hdld., oval	15.00
Bowl, 12", sq., 4 hdld.	42.50	Olive dish, 6", 2 pt.	15.00
Bowl, 13", gardenia	35.00	Pickle dish, 6"	15.00
Bowl, 15½", 2½ gal. punch	85.00	Pitcher, 5", 16 oz., milk	50.00
Butter, w/cover, ¼ lb., 2 hdld.	22.00	Pitcher, 8½", 64 oz., w/ice lip	100.00
Cake salver, 13", ftd.	40.00	Plate, 6", bread/butter	4.00
Canape set: (6" plate w/ring, 4 oz., ftd.,		Plate, 6", canape	10.00
cocktail)	25.00	Plate, 7", 2 hdld., lemon	12.50
Candlestick, 4"	9.00	Plate, 7½", salad	5.00
Candlestick, 7", 2-lite, ball loop ctr.	18.00	Plate, 8½", luncheon	7.00
Candlestick, 7", lg. ball ctr. w/bobeches,		Plate, 10½", dinner	32.50
prisms	35.00	Plate, 11", 2 hdld.	27.50
Candy basket, 5½" x 7½", 2 hdld., oval	65.00	Plate, 13", 4 hdld.	25.00
Candy box, w/cover, 7", 2 pt., 2 hdld.	45.00	Plate, 13", salad liner, rolled edge	27.50
Candy box, w/cover, 8", 3 pt., 3 hdld.	50.00	Plate, 13", torte, rolled edge	30.00
Candy dish, 7½", heart shape	22.00	Plate, 14", torte	35.00
Celery, 11", 2 hdld.	15.00	Plate, 14", torte, rolled edge	35.00
Celery, 11", 2 pt., 2 hdld.	18.00	Plate, 16", torte, rolled edge	37.50
Celery, 12", 3 pt.	20.00	Plate, 18", lazy susan	55.00
Cheese & cracker (3½" comport, 11"		Plate, 18", punch liner, rolled edge	50.00
2 hdld. plate)	45.00		

	Crystal		Crystal
Relish, 7", 2 pt., 2 hdld.	15.00	Sugar, 8 oz.	8.00
Relish, 7½", 2 pt., heart shape	18.00	Sweetmeat, 5½", star shape, 2 hdld.	27.50
Relish, 9", 3 pt., 3 hdld.	25.00	Sweetmeat, 6½", ctr. hdld.	27.50
Relish, 11", 3 pt., 2 hdld.	25.00	Sweetmeat, 7", star shape, 2 hdld.	30.00
Relish, 12", 3 pt.	25.00	Tray, 5½", ctr. hdld. (for mustard jar)	11.00
Relish, 12", 5 pt., rnd.	25.00	Tray, 6", 2 hdld. (for salt/pepper)	10.00
Relish, 12", 6 pt., rnd.	25.00	Tray, 7¾", ctr. hdld. (for cruets)	12.50
Relish, 12", sq., 4 pt., 4 hdld.	25.00	Tray, 8", 2 hdld. (for oil/vinegar)	12.50
Salad set, 6" (compote, 11" hdld. plate)	37.50	Tray, 8", 2 hdld. (for sugar/creamer)	7.50
Salad set, 9", (2 pt. bowl, 13" rolled edge plate)	70.00	Tray, 10", 2 hdld (for sugar/creamer)	8.00
		Tumbler, 2¼", 2 oz., flat, whiskey	15.00
Salt & pepper, 5"	25.00	Tumbler, 2¼", 2 oz., ftd., whiskey	12.00
Saucer, 4½", demi	3.00	Tumbler, 3", 3 oz., ftd., whiskey	12.00
Saucer, 6"	1.50	Tumbler, 3¼", 3½ oz., flat, juice	6.00
Stem, 2½", 5 oz., ftd., sherbet	5.00	Tumbler, 3¼", 7 oz., flat, old-fashioned	10.00
Stem, 2¾", 3½ oz., ftd., oyster cocktail	7.50	Tumbler, 3½", 5 oz., flat, juice	6.00
Stem, 3½", 5 oz., sherbet	6.00	Tumbler, 4", 4½ oz., ftd., juice	8.00
Stem, 4", 1 oz., cordial	30.00	Tumbler, 4¼", 9 oz., flat	8.00
Stem, 4½", 1¾ oz., sherry	27.50	Tumbler, 4½", 8 oz., flat, split	8.00
Stem, 4½", 3½ oz., cocktail	15.00	Tumbler, 4½", 9 oz., ftd.	8.00
Stem, 4¾", 3 oz., wine	18.00	Tumbler, 4¾", 10 oz., flat, hi-ball	10.00
Stem, 5", 5 oz., champagne	10.00	Tumbler, 5", 8 oz., ftd., party	9.00
Stem, 5½", 4 oz., claret	15.00	Tumbler, 5¼", 12 oz., flat, iced tea	15.00
Stem, 5¾", 9 oz.	10.00	Tumbler, 5¾", 14 oz., flat, hi-ball	17.50
Stem, 6¼", 8 oz., ale	15.00	Tumbler, 6", 14 oz., iced tea	17.50
Stem, 7", 9 oz.	14.00	Urn, w/cover, 9", ftd.	100.00
Sugar, 3 oz.	5.00	Vase, 9", ftd., fan	25.00
Sugar, 6 oz.	6.00	Vase, 9", ftd., round	35.00

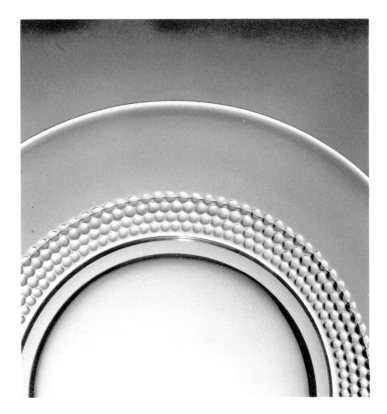

TROJAN, Fostoria Glass Company, 1929 – 1944

Colors: "Rose" pink, "Topaz" yellow; some green seen

Trojan is collected more in yellow than in pink because pink serving pieces are difficult to find. This pattern would be ideal for someone who wishes an abundance of pieces to collect. There are few collectors of yellow Trojan when compared to yellow Versailles or June. This gives less competition and better prices. Trojan is a striking pattern. Check it out!

Having bought several Fostoria collections in the last few years, I can say that clarets are almost nonexistent in any pattern. If you need them, you had better buy them whenever you find them.

	Rose	Topaz		Rose	Topaz
Ash tray, #2350, lg.	50.00	40.00	Ice dish liner (tomato, crab, fruit)		
Ash tray, #2350, sm.	30.00	25.00	#2451	20.00	10.00
Bottle, salad dressing, #2983........	450.00	285.00	Mayonnaise ladle.........................	30.00	30.00
Bowl, baker, #2375, 9"		55.00	Mayonnaise, w/liner, #2375	60.00	50.00
Bowl, bonbon, #2375.....................		13.00	Oil, ftd., #2375	325.00	235.00
Bowl, bouillon, #2375, ftd...........		18.00	Oyster, cocktail, #5099, ftd...........	30.00	27.50
Bowl, cream soup, #2375, ftd.......	27.50	22.00	Parfait, #5099............................	65.00	45.00
Bowl, finger, #869/2283,			Pitcher, #5000	375.00	275.00
w/6¼" liner..............................	40.00	35.00	Plate, #2375, canape	25.00	20.00
Bowl, lemon, #2375	18.00	16.00	Plate, #2375, bread/butter, 6"	6.00	5.00
Bowl, #2394, 3 ftd., 4½", mint......	25.00	22.00	Plate, #2375, salad, 7½"	9.00	8.00
Bowl, #2375, fruit, 5"....................	20.00	18.00	Plate, 2375, cream soup or		
Bowl, #2354, 3 ftd., 6"	30.00	35.00	mayo liner, 7½", ...	9.00	8.00
Bowl, cereal, #2375, 6½"...............	37.50	27.50	Plate, #2375, luncheon, 8¾"	17.50	15.00
Bowl, soup, #2375, 7"	60.00	50.00	Plate, #2375, sm., dinner, 9½"	20.00	17.50
Bowl, lg. dessert, #2375, 2-handled	55.00	50.00	Plate, #2375, cake, handled, 10"	35.00	32.50
Bowl, #2395, 10"	85.00	65.00	Plate, #2375, grill, rare, 10¼"	85.00	75.00
Bowl, #2395, scroll, 10"................	65.00	55.00	Plate, #2375, dinner, 10¼"	65.00	45.00
Bowl, combination #2415,			Plate, #2375, chop, 13"	50.00	45.00
w/candleholder handles, ...	150.00	130.00	Plate, #2375, round, 14"	50.00	40.00
Bowl, #2375, centerpiece, flared			Platter, #2375, 12"	65.00	55.00
optic, 12"...................................	45.00	40.00	Platter, #2375, 15"	125.00	100.00
Bowl, #2394, centerpiece, ftd., 12"	45.00	40.00	Relish, #2375, 8½"........................		15.00
Bowl, #2375, centerpiece,			Relish, #2350, 3 pt., rnd., 8¾"	45.00	40.00
mushroom, 12"...........................	45.00	40.00	Sauce boat, #2375	110.00	95.00
Candlestick, #2394, 2"	18.00	16.00	Sauce plate, #2375	45.00	40.00
Candlestick, #2375, flared, 3"........	20.00	18.00	Saucer, #2375, after dinner...........	10.00	10.00
Candlestick, #2395½, scroll, 5"	60.00	55.00	Saucer, #2375	6.00	5.00
Candy, w/cover, #2394, ¼ lb.........	250.00	225.00	Shaker, #2375, pr., ftd.	90.00	75.00
Candy, w/cover, #2394, ½ lb.........	175.00	135.00	Sherbet, #5099, high, 6"................	25.00	20.00
Celery, #2375, 11½"......................	35.00	27.50	Sherbet, #5099, low, 4¼"	20.00	16.00
Cheese & cracker, set, #2375, #2368.	65.00	60.00	Sugar, #2375½, ftd.	22.50	20.00
Comport, #5299 or #2400, 6"........	35.00	30.00	Sugar cover, #2375½......................	115.00	90.00
Comport, #2375, 7"	45.00	40.00	Sugar pail, #2378	145.00	110.00
Creamer, #2375, ftd.......................	22.50	20.00	Sugar, tea, #2375½	50.00	45.00
Creamer, tea, #2375½.....................	50.00	45.00	Sweetmeat, #2375	15.00	15.00
Cup, after dinner, #2375	45.00	35.00	Tray, 11", ctr. hdld., #2375.............	35.00	32.50
Cup, #2375½, ftd...........................	20.00	18.00	Tray, #2429, service & lemon insert..		200.00
Decanter, #2439, 9"	800.00	750.00	Tumbler, #5099, ftd., 2½ oz.	50.00	40.00
Goblet, claret, #5099, 4 oz., 6"......	110.00	100.00	Tumbler, #5099, ftd., 5 oz., 4½".	30.00	25.00
Goblet, cocktail, #5099, 3 oz., 5¼" ...	30.00	27.50	Tumbler, #5099, ftd., 9 oz., 5¼"	22.50	17.50
Goblet, cordial, #5099, ¾ oz., 4" ...	95.00	70.00	Tumbler, #5099, ftd., 12 oz., 6"......	32.50	27.50
Goblet, water, #5299, 10 oz., 8¼" ...	37.50	27.50	Vase, #2417, 8"	135.00	120.00
Goblet, wine, #5099, 3 oz., 5½"	55.00	45.00	Vase, #4105, 8"	195.00	160.00
Grapefruit, #5282½	52.50	45.00	Vase, #2369, 9"		195.00
Grapefruit liner, #945½..................	47.50	40.00	Whipped cream bowl, #2375	15.00	12.00
Ice bucket, #2375	75.00	65.00	Whipped cream pail, #2378	125.00	110.00
Ice dish, #2451, #2455..................	40.00	35.00			

TWIST, Blank #1252, A.H. Heisey & Co.

Colors: crystal, "Flamingo" pink, "Moongleam" green, "Marigold" amber/yellow; "Sahara" yellow; some "Alexandrite" (rare)

	Crystal	Pink	Green	Marigold Sahara
Baker, 9", oval	10.00	20.00	25.00	60.00
Bonbon	5.00	12.00	17.00	30.00
Bonbon, 6", 2 hdld.	5.00	12.00	17.00	30.00
Bottle, French dressing	35.00	75.00	95.00	125.00
Bowl, cream soup/bouillon	15.00	25.00	32.00	50.00
Bowl, ftd., almond/indiv. sugar	15.00	30.00	37.50	60.00
Bowl, indiv. nut	5.00	20.00	27.50	45.00
Bowl, 4", nappy	5.00	12.00	16.00	17.00
Bowl, 6", 2 hdld.	7.00	15.00	18.00	20.00
Bowl, 6", 2 hdld., jelly	7.00	15.00	18.00	20.00
Bowl, 6", 2 hdld., mint	7.00	15.00	18.00	20.00
Bowl, 8", low ftd.	25.00	35.00	40.00	65.00
Bowl, 8", nappy, grnd. bottom	12.00	25.00	30.00	40.00
Bowl, 8", nasturtium, rnd.	25.00	30.00	60.00	60.00
Bowl, 8", nasturtium, oval	25.00	30.00	60.00	60.00
Bowl, 9", floral	25.00	35.00	40.00	65.00
Bowl, 9", floral, rolled edge	30.00	35.00	40.00	65.00
Bowl, 12", floral, oval, 4 ft.	30.00	40.00	50.00	65.00
Bowl, 12", floral, rnd., 4 ft.	30.00	40.00	50.00	65.00
Candlestick, 2", 1-lite	12.00	25.00	25.00	45.00
Cheese dish, 6", 2 hdld.	5.00	10.00	17.50	20.00
Cocktail shaker, metal top			400.00	
Comport, 7", tall	25.00	60.00	85.00	150.00
Creamer, hotel, oval	25.00	35.00	45.00	50.00
Creamer, individual (unusual)	18.00	35.00	35.00	65.00
Creamer, zigzag handles, ftd.	20.00	30.00	37.50	60.00
Cup, zigzag handles	10.00	25.00	32.00	35.00
Grapefruit, ftd.	10.00	15.00	22.50	30.00
Ice tub	25.00	65.00	85.00	125.00
Pitcher, 3 pint	50.00	110.00	160.00	
Mayonnaise	20.00	40.00	45.00	40.00
Mayonnaise, #1252½	20.00	35.00	45.00	50.00
Mustard, w/cover, spoon	25.00	70.00	80.00	90.00
Oil bottle, 2½ oz., w/#78 stopper	30.00	65.00	85.00	125.00
Oil bottle, 4 oz., w/#78 stopper	35.00	70.00	90.00	135.00
Plate, cream soup liner	5.00	7.00	10.00	15.00
Plate, 8", Kraft cheese	15.00	30.00	40.00	60.00
Plate, 8", grnd. bottom	7.00	12.00	15.00	20.00
Plate, 10" utility, 3 ft.	25.00	30.00	42.00	
Plate, 12", 2 hdld., sandwich	25.00	40.00	50.00	55.00
Plate, 12", muffin, 2 hdld., turned sides	30.00	40.00	55.00	65.00
Plate, 13", 3 part, relish	10.00	17.00	22.00	35.00
Platter, 12"	15.00	40.00	60.00	75.00
Salt & pepper, 2 styles	35.00	65.00	135.00	125.00
Saucer	3.00	5.00	7.00	10.00
Stem, 2½ oz., wine	15.00	30.00	35.00	40.00
Stem, 3 oz., oyster cocktail	5.00	15.00	22.00	25.00
Stem, 3 oz., cocktail	5.00	15.00	22.00	25.00
Stem, 5 oz., saucer champagne	7.00	16.00	22.00	25.00
Stem, 5 oz., sherbet	7.50	12.00	18.00	22.50
Stem, 9 oz., luncheon (1 block in stem)	20.00	25.00	60.00	45.00
Sugar, ftd.	20.00	30.00	37.50	60.00
Sugar, hotel, oval	25.00	35.00	40.00	50.00
Sugar, individual (unusual)	18.00	35.00	38.00	65.00
Sugar, w/cover, zigzag handles	15.00	27.00	40.00	70.00
Tray, 7", pickle, grnd. bottom	7.00	15.00	22.00	25.00
Tray, 10", celery	10.00	20.00	27.00	30.00
Tray, 13", celery	12.00	25.00	37.00	50.00
Tumbler, 5 oz., fruit	4.00	12.00	20.00	25.00
Tumbler, 6 oz., ftd. soda	5.00	13.00	20.00	25.00
Tumbler, 8 oz., flat, grnd. bottom	7.00	15.00	21.00	30.00
Tumbler, 8 oz., soda, straight & flared	7.00	15.00	21.00	30.00
Tumbler, 9 oz., ftd. soda	8.00	16.00	24.00	31.00
Tumbler, 12 oz., iced tea	12.00	25.00	35.00	45.00
Tumbler, 12 oz., ftd. iced tea	15.00	30.00	40.00	50.00

VALENCIA, Cambridge Glass Company

Colors: crystal, pink

A Cambridge pattern often confused with Valencia is Minerva. Note in the pattern shot of Valencia that the lines are perpendicular. On Minerva, the lines meet on a diagonal.

Collectors are beginning to latch onto this pattern. It was not nationally distributed in the quantities of Rose Point or Caprice, but many of the same blanks used for Rose Point are found etched with Valencia. Some of the more unusual and interesting pieces in its repertoire include the covered honey dish, six-piece relish on #3500 12" plate, and the 15" long, three-part, two-handled relish. All of these pieces are highly coveted in Rose Point, but are only beginning to be noticed in Valencia. Pieces in the highly-promoted pattern Rose Point were made in larger quantities than those of Valencia. Since there are thousands of collectors searching for Rose Point, and only a small number looking for Valencia, there is a large discrepancy in price on the same pieces in the two patterns due to demand.

The little metal-handled piece on the right is called a sugar basket by Cambridge. This is similar to Fostoria's sugar pail. Terminology used by the different companies causes collectors problems in figuring out which piece is called what.

	Crystal		Crystal
Ash tray, #3500/124, 3¼", round.	10.00	Relish, #3500/64, 10", 3 comp.	27.50
Ash tray, #3500/126, 4", round	14.00	Relish, #3500/65, 10", 4 comp.	30.00
Ash tray, #3500/128, 4½", round	18.00	Relish, #3500/67, 12", 6 pc.	85.00
Basket, #3500/55, 6", 2 hdld., ftd.	22.00	Relish, #3500/112, 15", 3 pt./2 hdld.	75.00
Bowl, #3500/49, 5", hdld.	18.00	Relish, #3500/13, 15", 4 pt./2 hdld.	85.00
Bowl, #3500/37, 6", cereal	20.00	Salt and pepper, #3400/18	50.00
Bowl, #1402/89, 6", 2 hdld.	18.00	Saucer, #3500/1	3.00
Bowl, #1402/88, 6", 2 hdld., div.	20.00	Stem, #1402, cordial	65.00
Bowl, #3500/115, 9½", 2 hdld., ftd.	35.00	Stem, #1402, wine	30.00
Bowl, #1402/82, 10"	32.50	Stem, #1402, cocktail	20.00
Bowl, #1402/88, 11"	35.00	Stem, #1402, claret	40.00
Bowl, #1402/95, salad dressing, div.	40.00	Stem, #1402, oyster cocktail	16.00
Bowl, #1402/100, finger, w/liner	30.00	Stem, #1402, low sherbet	12.50
Bowl, #3500, ftd., finger	27.50	Stem, #1402, tall sherbet	15.00
Candy dish, w/cover, #3500/103	85.00	Stem, #1402, goblet	20.00
Celery, #1402/94, 12"	30.00	Stem, #3500, cordial	65.00
Cigarette holder, #1066, ftd.	38.00	Stem, #3500, wine, 2½ oz.	27.50
Comport, #3500/36, 6"	27.50	Stem, #3500, cocktail, 3 oz	18.00
Comport, #3500/37, 7"	40.00	Stem, #3500, claret, 4½ oz.	40.00
Creamer, #3500/14	15.00	Stem, #3500, oyster cocktail, 4½ oz.	15.00
Creamer, #3500/15, individual	17.50	Stem, #3500, low sherbet, 7 oz.	12.50
Cup, #3500/1	17.50	Stem, #3500, tall sherbet, 7 oz.	15.00
Decanter, #3400/92, 32 oz., ball	115.00	Stem, #3500, goblet, long bowl	20.00
Decanter, #3400/119, 12 oz., ball	85.00	Stem, #3500, goblet, short bowl	18.00
Honey dish, w/cover, #3500/139	95.00	Sugar, #3500/14	15.00
Ice pail, #1402/52	55.00	Sugar, #3500/15, individual	17.50
Mayonnaise, #3500/59, 3 pc.	40.00	Sugar basket, #3500/13	75.00
Nut, #3400/71, 3", 4 ftd.	50.00	Tumbler, #3400/92, 2½ oz.	15.00
Perfume, #3400/97, 2 oz., perfume	75.00	Tumbler, #3400/100, 13 oz.	20.00
Plate, #3500/167, 7½", salad	10.00	Tumbler, #3400/115, 14 oz.	22.00
Plate, #3500/5, 8½", breakfast	12.00	Tumbler, #3500, 2½ oz., ftd.	17.50
Plate, #1402, 11½", sandwich, hdld.	22.50	Tumbler, #3500, 3 oz., ftd.	14.00
Plate, #3500/39, 12", ftd.	27.50	Tumbler, #3500, 5 oz., ftd.	12.50
Plate, #3500/67, 12"	22.50	Tumbler, #3500, 10 oz., ftd.	14.00
Plate, #3500/38, 13", torte	25.00	Tumbler, #3500, 12 oz., ftd.	18.00
Relish, #3500/68, 5½", 2 comp.	17.50	Tumbler, #3500, 13 oz., ftd.	17.50
Relish, #3500/69, 6½", 3 comp.	20.00	Tumbler, #3500, 16 oz., ftd.	20.00
Relish, #1402/91, 8", 3 comp.	25.00		

VERSAILLES, Fostoria Glass Company, 1928 – 1944

Colors: blue, yellow, pink, green

I have tried to list all of Fostoria line numbers for each piece of Versailles. These numbers can also be used for items listed in June as can the following information.

If you order or ship through ads, you should know the following: liners for cream soups and mayonnaise liners are the same piece; two handled cake plates come with and without an indent in the center and the indented version also serves as a plate for one of two styles of cheese and cracker (both styles are shown in yellow); bonbon, lemon dish, sweetmeat and whipped cream bowls all come with loop handles or bow handles; sugars come with a straight top and a ruffled top, but it is the ruffled top that requires a lid.

Be sure to see page 93 for the Fostoria stems that many people confuse because heights are so similar. Shapes are more important. Clarets are the difficult stem to find with cordials the next most difficult.

	Pink, Green	Blue	Yellow
Ash tray, #2350	24.00	30.00	25.00
Bottle, #2083, salad dressing, crystal glass top	275.00		325.00
Bottle, #2375, salad dressing, w/ sterling top or colored top	350.00	550.00	375.00
Bowl, #2375, baker, 9"	50.00	95.00	55.00
Bowl, #2375, bonbon	15.00	22.50	17.50
Bowl, #2375, bouillon, ftd.	20.00	32.00	20.00
Bowl, #2375, cream soup, ftd.	22.00	27.50	20.00
Bowl, #869/2283, finger, w/6" liner	30.00	45.00	30.00
Bowl, lemon	15.00	22.00	17.50
Bowl, 4½", mint, 3 ftd.	25.00	35.00	25.00
Bowl, #2375, fruit, 5"	17.50	25.00	20.00
Bowl, #2394, 3 ftd., 6"			30.00
Bowl, #2375, cereal, 6½"	22.50	35.00	25.00
Bowl, #2375, soup, 7"	40.00	60.00	40.00
Bowl, #2375, lg., dessert, 2 hdld.	45.00	70.00	40.00
Bowl, #2375, baker, 10"	45.00	75.00	40.00
Bowl, #2395, centerpiece, scroll, 10"	45.00	65.00	45.00
Bowl, #2375, centerpiece, flared top, 12"	35.00	50.00	40.00
Bowl, #2394, ftd., 12"	35.00	50.00	45.00
Bowl, #2375½, oval, centerpiece 13"	50.00	65.00	
Candlestick, #2394, 2"	20.00	22.50	17.50
Candlestick, #2395, 3"	17.50	27.50	20.00
Candlestick, #2395½, scroll, 5"	30.00	40.00	30.00
Candy, w/cover, #2331, 3 pt.	135.00	175.00	
Candy, w/cover, #2394, ¼ lb.			175.00
Candy, w/cover, #2394, ½ lb.			150.00
Celery, #2375, 11½"	35.00	45.00	40.00
Cheese & cracker, #2375 or #2368, set	65.00	85.00	65.00
Comport, #5098, 3"	25.00	35.00	25.00
Comport, #5099/2400, 6"	30.00	45.00	30.00
Comport, #2375, 7"	32.50	55.00	
Comport, #2400, 8"	65.00	95.00	
Creamer, #2375½, ftd.	17.50	22.50	15.00
Creamer, #2375½, tea	42.50	50.00	42.50
Cup, #2375, after dinner	35.00	50.00	35.00
Cup, #2375½, ftd.	17.50	21.00	19.00
Decanter, #2439, 9"	800.00	1,500.00	600.00
Goblet, cordial, #5098 or #5099, ¾ oz., 4"	80.00	90.00	65.00
Goblet, #5098 or #5099, claret, 4 oz., 6"	65.00	100.00	65.00
Goblet, cocktail, #5098 or #5099, 3 oz., 5¼"	25.00	35.00	28.00
Goblet, water, #5098 or #5099, 10 oz., 8¼"	27.50	35.00	30.00
Goblet, wine, #5098 or #5099, 3 oz., 5½"	40.00	60.00	45.00
Grapefruit, #5082½	40.00	65.00	40.00

	Pink, Green	Blue	Yellow
Grapefruit liner, #945½	35.00	45.00	35.00
Ice bucket, #2375	62.50	80.00	75.00
Ice dish, #2451	30.00	40.00	30.00
Ice dish liner (tomato, crab, fruit), #2451	20.00	20.00	10.00
Mayonnaise, w/liner, #2375	35.00	50.00	40.00
Mayonnaise ladle	30.00	40.00	30.00
Oil, #2375, ftd.	325.00	495.00	275.00
Oyster cocktail, #5098 or #5099	22.50	32.50	25.00
Parfait, #5098 or #5099	35.00	45.00	35.00
Pitcher, #5000	265.00	395.00	295.00
Plate, #2375, bread/butter, 6"	4.00	5.00	4.00
Plate, #2375, canape, 6"	20.00	35.00	30.00
Plate, #2375, salad, 7½"	6.00	10.00	7.00
Plate, #2375, cream soup or mayo liner, 7½"	6.00	10.00	7.00
Plate, #2375, luncheon, 8¾"	8.00	12.50	9.00
Plate, #2375, sm., dinner, 9½"	15.00	30.00	17.50
Plate, #2375, cake, 2 hdld., 10"	26.00	37.50	30.00
Plate, #2375, dinner, 10¼"	60.00	80.00	55.00
Plate, #2375, chop, 13"	45.00	60.00	40.00
Platter, #2375, 12"	60.00	75.00	60.00
Platter, #2375, 15"	90.00	125.00	90.00
Relish, #2375, 8½"	30.00	40.00	35.00
Sauce boat, #2375	65.00	100.00	65.00
Sauce boat plate, #2375	20.00	30.00	20.00
Saucer, #2375, after dinner	5.00	7.50	5.00
Saucer, #2375	4.00	6.00	5.00
Shaker, #2375, pr., ftd.	90.00	130.00	85.00
Sherbet, #5098/5099, high, 6"	20.00	27.50	22.50
Sherbet, #5098/5099, low, 4¼"	20.00	25.00	22.00
Sugar, #2375½, ftd.	15.00	20.00	15.00
Sugar cover, #2375½	125.00	160.00	110.00
Sugar pail, #2378	135.00	195.00	125.00
Sugar, #2375½, tea	42.50	50.00	42.50
Sweetmeat, #2375	14.00	18.00	15.00
Tray, #2375, ctr. hdld., 11"	30.00	45.00	35.00
Tray, service & lemon	275.00		200.00
Tumbler, flat, old-fashioned (pink only)	90.00		
Tumbler, flat, tea (pink only)	95.00		
Tumbler, #5098 or #5099 2½ oz., ftd.	32.50	45.00	37.50
Tumbler, #5098 or #5099, 5 oz., ftd., 4½"	20.00	27.50	22.00
Tumbler, #5098 or #5099, 9 oz., ftd., 5¼"	20.00	30.00	21.50
Tumbler, #5098 or #5099 12 oz., ftd., 6"	30.00	45.00	27.50
Vase, #2417, 8"			135.00
Vase, #4100, 8"	125.00	195.00	
Vase, #2385, fan, ftd., 8½"	110.00	175.00	
Whipped cream bowl, #2375	15.00	18.00	13.00
Whipped cream pail, #2378	100.00	145.00	100.00

Note: See page 93 for stem identification.

VESPER, Fostoria Glass Company, 1926 – 1934

Colors: amber, green; some blue

Fostoria's amber Vesper is not as collected as some other colors; but as you can see here, this amber pattern has a multitude of pieces for you to gather! Many pieces are easily found; others will take some patience and searching. Amber Fostoria etched patterns may be the "sleepers" in the Elegant glass collecting field. I've seen gorgeous table settings made with amber glass. Don't sell it short!

I should point out a few of the harder to find items pictured. The amber butter dish is the only one known at this time, so you might want to keep your eyes open for another. Behind the butter is a finger bowl and liner and the sauce boat and liner. Other companies called these gravy boats, but Fostoria always listed them as sauce boats. In the top photo on page 197, two styles of cream soups are shown. The one on the plate is footed while the one to the back of the shakers has no foot.

In the bottom photo on the left is an 8¾" canape plate which is large by most standards. This has a sherbet on the off center ring and was called a Maj Jongg set by Fostoria. They are quite rare. In front of that set is the egg cup and the #2315 moulded grapefruit which also doubled as a mayonnaise. The blown style of grapefruit with the etched liner is shown in the foreground. Some companies called these shrimp dishes. You filled the inside with shrimp or fruit and put ice in the larger container to keep it chilled. Since ice was a valuable commodity in those days, only the well-to-do had these items and that makes for short supplies today.

	Green	Amber	Blue
Ash tray, #2350, 4"	25.00	30.00	
Bowl, #2350, bouillon, ftd.	12.00	15.00	20.00
Bowl, #2350, cream soup, flat	25.00	30.00	
Bowl, #2350, cream soup, ftd.	20.00	20.00	25.00
Bowl, #2350, fruit, 5½"	10.00	12.50	20.00
Bowl, #2350, cereal, sq. or rnd., 6½"	18.00	20.00	25.00
Bowl, #2267, low, ftd., 7"	20.00	25.00	
Bowl, #2350, soup, shallow, 7¾"	18.00	22.00	35.00
Bowl, soup, deep, 8¼"		25.00	
Bowl, 8"	25.00	30.00	
Bowl, #2350, baker, oval, 9"	40.00	60.00	50.00
Bowl, #2350, baker, oval, 10½"	65.00	75.00	100.00
Bowl, #2375, flared bowl, 10½"	30.00	32.00	
Bowl, #2329, console, rolled edge, 11"	30.00	32.50	
Bowl, #2375, 3 ftd., 12½"	35.00	38.00	
Bowl, #2371, oval, 13"	35.00	37.50	
Bowl, #2329, rolled edge, 13"	35.00	37.50	
Bowl, #2329, rolled edge, 15"	40.00	45.00	
Butter dish, #2350		750.00	
Candlestick, #2324, 2"	17.50	22.50	
Candlestick, #2394, 3"	15.00	15.00	30.00
Candlestick, #2324, 4"	15.00	17.50	
Candlestick, #2394, 9"	55.00	75.00	75.00
Candy jar, w/cover, #2331, 3 pt.	90.00	90.00	175.00
Candy jar, w/cover, #2250, ftd., ½ lb.	225.00	150.00	
Celery, #2350	17.00	22.00	30.00
Cheese, #2368, ftd.	18.00	20.00	
Comport, 6"	22.50	25.00	35.00
Comport, #2327, (twisted stem), 7½"	27.50	30.00	45.00
Comport, 8"	40.00	45.00	50.00
Creamer, #2350½, ftd.	14.00	16.00	
Creamer, #2315½, fat, ftd.	18.00	20.00	25.00
Creamer, #2350½, flat		20.00	
Cup, #2350	14.00	15.00	25.00
Cup, #2350, after dinner	30.00	30.00	60.00
Cup, #2350½, ftd.	14.00	15.00	

VESPER, Fostoria Glass Company, 1926 – 1934 (continued)

	Green	Amber	Blue
Egg cup, #2350		35.00	
Finger bowl and liner, #869/2283, 6"	22.00	25.00	35.00
Grapefruit, #5082½, blown	40.00	40.00	65.00
Grapefruit liner, #945½, blown	35.00	35.00	40.00
Grapefruit, #2315, molded	45.00	50.00	
Ice bucket, #2378	60.00	62.50	
Oyster cocktail, #5100	16.00	18.00	30.00
Pickle, #2350	20.00	22.00	30.00
Pitcher, #5100, ftd.	275.00	295.00	475.00
Plate, #2350, bread/butter, 6"	4.50	5.00	10.00
Plate, #2350, salad, 7½"	6.00	6.50	12.00
Plate, #2350, luncheon, 8½"	7.50	8.50	15.00
Plate, #2321, Maj Jongg (canape), 8¾"		40.00	
Plate, #2350, sm., dinner, 9½"	15.00	16.00	20.00
Plate, dinner, 10½"	23.00	29.00	
Plate, #2287, ctr. hand., 11"	22.50	25.00	45.00
Plate, chop, 13¾"	32.00	37.50	60.00
Plate, #2350, server, 15"	45.00	55.00	75.00
Plate, w/indent for cheese, 11"	18.00	20.00	
Platter, #2350, 10½"	30.00	35.00	
Platter, #2350, 12"	40.00	50.00	75.00
Platter, #2350, 15",	75.00	85.00	95.00
Salt & pepper, #5100, pr.	65.00	75.00	
Sauce boat, w/liner, #2350	95.00	110.00	
Saucer, #2350, after dinner	7.50	9.00	15.00
Saucer, #2350	4.00	4.50	5.00
Stem, #5093, high sherbet	16.00	17.50	25.00
Stem, #5093, water goblet	25.00	27.50	35.00
Stem, #5093, low sherbet	15.00	17.00	22.00
Stem, #5093, parfait	30.00	35.00	40.00
Stem, #5093, cordial, ¾ oz.	70.00	75.00	100.00
Stem, #5093, wine, 2¾ oz.	32.00	35.00	45.00
Stem, #5093, cocktail, 3 oz.	25.00	27.50	30.00
Sugar, #2350½, flat		20.00	
Sugar, #2315, fat ftd.	18.00	20.00	25.00
Sugar, #2350½, ftd.	14.00	16.00	
Sugar, lid	160.00	150.00	
Tumbler, #5100, ftd., 2 oz.	30.00	35.00	45.00
Tumbler, #5100, ftd., 5 oz.	15.00	18.00	25.00
Tumbler, #5100, ftd., 9 oz.	16.00	18.00	30.00
Tumbler, #5100, ftd., 12 oz.	22.00	25.00	40.00
Urn, #2324, small	60.00	65.00	
Urn, large	70.00	75.00	
Vase, #2292, 8"	70.00	75.00	110.00
Vanity set, combination cologne/ powder & stopper	195.00	210.00	250.00

Note: See stemware identification on page 93.

VICTORIAN, #1425 A.H. Heisey Co., 1933 – 1953

Colors: crystal, Sahara, Cobalt, rare in pale Zircon

Victorian is another new Heisey entry in this book. Note the colors shown above since these are the only colors that Heisey made in Victorian. If you find pink, green, or amber Victorian in your travels, then you have Imperial's contribution to this pattern from 1964 and 1965. These colors will be marked with the H in diamond trademark, but they were made from Heisey moulds after the company was no longer in business. Imperial also made about ten pieces in crystal, but they can not be differentiated from the original Heisey... and they aren't discriminated against by Heisey collectors.

	Crystal
Bottle, 3 oz. oil	35.00
Bottle, 27 oz. rye	125.00
Bottle, French dressing	50.00
Bowl, 10½" floral	40.00
Bowl, finger	15.00
Bowl, punch	225.00
Bowl, rose	75.00
Bowl, triplex w/flared or cupped rim	80.00
Butter dish, ¼ lb.	65.00
Candlestick, 2-lite	110.00
Cigarette box, 4"	50.00
Cigarette box, 6"	75.00
Cigarette holder & ash tray, ind.	20.00
Comport, 5"	45.00
Compote, cheese (for center sandwich)	17.50
Creamer	25.00
Cup, punch, 5 oz.	10.00
Decanter and stopper, 32 oz.,	50.00
Nappy, 8"	30.00
Plate, 6" liner for finger	10.00
Plate, 7"	20.00
Plate, 8"	30.00
Plate, 12" cracker	75.00
Plate, 13" sandwich	80.00
Plate, 21" buffet or punch bowl liner,	90.00
Relish, 11", 3 pt.	45.00
Salt & pepper	40.00
Stem, 2½ oz. wine	20.00
Stem, 3 oz. claret	20.00
Stem, 5 oz. oyster cocktail	15.00
Stem, 5 oz. saucer champagne	17.50
Stem, 5 oz. sherbet	15.00
Stem, 9 oz. goblet (one ball)	20.00
Stem, 9 oz. high goblet (two ball)	22.50
Sugar	25.00
Tray, 12" celery	25.00
Tray, condiment (s/p & mustard)	150.00
Tumbler, 2 oz. bar	35.00
Tumbler, 5 oz. soda (straight or curved edge)	15.00
Tumbler, 8 oz. old-fashioned	30.00
Tumbler, 10 oz. w/rim foot	20.00
Tumbler, 12 oz. ftd. soda	25.00
Tumbler, 12 oz. soda (straight or curved edge)	22.50
Vase, 4"	22.50
Vase, 5½"	35.00
Vase, 6" ftd.	40.00
Vase, 9" ftd. w/flared rim	65.00

WAVERLY, Blank #1519, A.H. Heisey & Co.

Colors: crystal; rare in amber

This Heisey blank is known more for its use with etched Orchid or Rose than for itself.

	Crystal
Bowl, 6", oval, lemon, w/cover	30.00
Bowl, 6½", 2 hdld., ice	50.00
Bowl, 7", 3 part, relish, oblong	25.00
Bowl, 7", salad	17.00
Bowl, 9", 4 part, relish, round	25.00
Bowl, 9", fruit	20.00
Bowl, 9", vegetable	20.00
Bowl, 10", crimped edge	25.00
Bowl, 10", gardenia	20.00
Bowl, 11", seahorse foot, floral	65.00
Bowl, 12", crimped edge	35.00
Bowl, 13", gardenia	25.00
Box, 5", chocolate, w/cover	60.00
Box, 5" tall, ftd., w/cover, seahorse hand.	85.00
Box, 6", candy, w/bow tie knob	45.00
Box, trinket, lion cover (rare)	600.00
Butter dish, w/cover, 6", square	65.00
Candleholder, 1-lite, block (rare)	120.00
Candleholder, 2-lite	40.00
Candleholder, 2-lite, "flame" center	65.00
Candleholder, 3-lite	65.00
Candle epergnette, 5"	10.00
Candle epergnette, 6", deep	13.00
Candle epergnette, 6½"	10.00
Cheese dish, 5½", ftd.	20.00
Cigarette holder	50.00
Comport, 6", low ftd.	12.00
Comport, 6½", jelly	35.00
Comport, 7", low ftd., oval	40.00
Creamer, ftd.	20.00
Creamer & sugar, individual, w/tray	47.00
Cruet, 3 oz., w/#122 stopper	60.00
Cup	12.00
Honey dish, 6½", ftd.	22.00
Mayonnaise, w/liner & ladle, 5½"	50.00
Plate, 7", salad	6.00
Plate, 8", luncheon	8.00
Plate, 10½", dinner	45.00
Plate, 11", sandwich	18.00
Plate, 13½", ftd., cake salver	60.00
Plate, 14", center handle, sandwich	65.00
Plate, 14", sandwich	35.00
Salt & pepper, pr.	50.00
Saucer	3.00
Stem, 1 oz., cordial	50.00
Stem, 3 oz., wine, blown	35.00
Stem, 3½ oz., cocktail	25.00
Stem, 5½ oz., sherbet/champagne	15.00
Stem, 10 oz., blown	20.00
Sugar, ftd.	20.00
Tray, 12", celery	13.00
Tumbler, 5 oz., ftd., juice, blown	20.00
Tumbler, 13 oz., ftd., tea, blown	20.00
Vase, 3½", violet	45.00
Vase, 7", ftd.	25.00
Vase, 7", ftd., fan shape	40.00

WILDFLOWER, Cambridge Glass Company, 1940's – 1950's

Colors: crystal, mainly; some pieces in color

You will find additional pieces of Wildflower on different Cambridge blanks. I have tried to show the major portion, but (as with other Cambridge patterns) there seems to be a never ending list. You can figure that, like Rose Point, almost any Cambridge blank may have been used to etch this pattern. I have given you the "ball park" to start. Price yellow or gold encrusted items up to 25% higher. Most collectors are searching for crystal!

	Crystal		Crystal
Basket, #3400/1182, 2 hdld., ftd., 6"	25.00	Plate, #3900/20, bread/butter, 6½"	7.50
Bowl, #3400/1180, bonbon, 2 hdld., 5¼"	18.00	Plate, #3900/130, bonbon, 2 hdld., 7"	17.50
Bowl, bonbon, 2 hdld., ftd., 6"	17.50	Plate, #3400/176, 7½"	9.00
Bowl, #3400/90, 2 pt., relish, 6"	17.50	Plate, #3900/161, 2 hdld., ftd., 8"	20.50
Bowl, 3 pt., relish, 6½"	17.50	Plate, #3900/22, salad, 8"	17.50
Bowl, #3900/123, relish, 7"	18.00	Plate, #3400/62, 8½"	15.00
Bowl, #3900/130, bonbon, 2 hdld., 7"	20.00	Plate, #3900/24, dinner, 10½"	65.00
Bowl, #3900/124, 2 pt., relish, 7"	22.00	Plate, #3900/26, service, 4 ftd., 12"	30.00
Bowl, #3400/91, 3 pt., relish, 3 hdld., 8"	25.00	Plate, #3900/35, cake, 2 hdld., 13½"	32.50
Bowl, #3900/125, 3 pt., celery & relish, 9"	25.00	Plate, #3900/167, torte, 14"	35.00
Bowl, #477, pickle (corn), ftd., 9½"	25.00	Plate, #3900/65, torte, 14"	32.50
Bowl, #3900/54, 4 ft., flared, 10"	35.00	Salt & pepper, #3400/77, pr.	35.00
Bowl, #3900/34, 2 hdld., 11"	40.00	Salt & pepper, #3900/1177	32.50
Bowl, #3900/28, w/tab hand., ftd., 11½"	40.00	Saucer, #3900/17 or #3400/54	3.50
Bowl, #3900/126, 3 pt., celery & relish, 12"	35.00	Set: 2 pc. Mayonnaise, #3900/19 (ftd. sherbet w/ladle)	25.00
Bowl, #3400/4, 4 ft., flared, 12"	29.50	Set: 3 pc. Mayonnaise, #3900/129 (bowl, liner, ladle)	30.00
Bowl, #3400/1240, 4 ft., oval, "ears" hand., 12"	45.00	Set: 4 pc. Mayonnaise #3900/111 (div. bowl, liner, 2 ladles)	35.00
Bowl, 5 pt., celery & relish, 12"	35.00	Stem, #3121, cordial, 1 oz.	55.00
Butter dish, #3900/52, ¼ lb.	165.00	Stem, #3121, cocktail, 3 oz.	22.50
Butter dish, #3400/52, 5"	110.00	Stem, #3121, wine, 3½ oz.	30.00
Candlestick, #3400/638, 3-lite, ea.	35.00	Stem, #3121, claret, 4½ oz.	38.00
Candlestick, #3400/646, 5"	25.00	Stem, #3121, 4½ oz., low oyster cocktail	18.00
Candlestick, #3400/647, 2-lite, "fleur-de-lis," 6"	30.00	Stem, #3121, 5 oz., low parfait	30.00
Candy box, w/cover, #3900/165	60.00	Stem, #3121, 6 oz., low sherbet	15.00
Candy box, w/cover, #3900/165, rnd.	50.00	Stem, #3121, 6 oz., tall sherbet	17.50
Cocktail icer, #968, 2 pc.	65.00	Stem, #3121, 10 oz., water	20.00
Cocktail shaker, #3400/175	75.00	Sugar, 3900/41	12.50
Comport, #3900/136, 5½"	30.00	Sugar, indiv., 3900/40	17.50
Comport, #3121, blown, 5⅜"	40.00	Tray, creamer & sugar, 3900/37	15.00
Creamer, #3900/41	12.50	Tumbler, #3121, 5 oz., juice	15.00
Creamer, #3900/40, individual	17.50	Tumbler, #3121, 10 oz., water	18.00
Cup, #3900/17 or #3400/54	16.50	Tumbler, #3121, 12 oz., tea	22.00
Hat, #1704, 5"	135.00	Tumbler, #3900/115, 13 oz.	25.00
Hat, #1703, 6"	175.00	Vase, #3400/102, globe, 5"	35.00
Hurricane lamp, #1617, candlestick base,	135.00	Vase, #6004, flower, ftd., 6"	30.00
Hurricane lamp, #1603, keyhole base & prisms	175.00	Vase, #6004, flower, ftd., 8"	35.00
Ice bucket, w/chrome hand., #3900/671	65.00	Vase, #1237, keyhole ft., 9"	45.00
Oil, w/stopper, #3900/100, 6 oz.	75.00	Vase, #1528, bud, 10"	30.00
Pitcher, ball, #3400/38, 80 oz.	125.00	Vase, #278, flower, ftd., 11"	42.00
Pitcher, #3900/115, 76 oz.	150.00	Vase, #1299, ped. ft., 11"	45.00
Pitcher, Doulton, #3400/141	275.00	Vase, #1238, keyhole ft., 12"	65.00
		Vase, #279, ftd., flower, 13"	75.00

Note: See Pages 210-211 for stem identification.

YEOMAN, Blank #1184, A.H. Heisey & Co.

Colors: crystal, "Flamingo" pink, "Sahara" yellow, "Moongleam" green, "Hawthorne" orchid/pink, "Marigold" deep, amber/yellow; some cobalt

Etched patterns on Yeoman blanks will bring 10% to 25% more than the prices listed below. Empress etch is the most commonly found pattern on Yeoman blanks and also the most collectible.

	Crystal	Pink	Sahara	Green	Hawth.	Marigold
Ash tray, 4", hdld. (bow tie)	10.00	20.00	22.00	25.00	30.00	35.00
Bowl, 2 hdld., cream soup	10.00	16.00	22.00	24.00	28.00	32.00
Bowl, finger	5.00	11.00	17.00	20.00	27.50	30.00
Bowl, ftd., banana split	7.00	23.00	30.00	35.00	40.00	45.00
Bowl, ftd., 2 hdld., bouillon	10.00	20.00	25.00	30.00	35.00	40.00
Bowl, 4½", nappy	4.00	7.50	10.00	12.50	15.00	17.00
Bowl, 5", low, ftd., jelly	12.00	20.00	25.00	27.00	30.00	40.00
Bowl, 5", oval, lemon	7.00	10.00	15.00	18.00	19.00	25.00
Bowl, 5", rnd., lemon	6.00	10.00	15.00	18.00	19.00	25.00
Bowl, 5", rnd., lemon, w/cover	15.00	20.00	25.00	30.00	40.00	50.00
Bowl, 6", oval, preserve	7.00	12.00	17.00	22.00	27.00	30.00
Bowl, 6", vegetable	5.00	10.00	14.00	16.00	20.00	24.00
Bowl, 6½", hdld., bonbon	5.00	10.00	14.00	16.00	20.00	24.00
Bowl, 8", rect., pickle/olive	12.00	15.00	20.00	25.00	30.00	35.00
Bowl, 8½", berry, 2 hdld.	14.00	22.00	25.00	30.00	35.00	50.00
Bowl, 9", 2 hdld., veg., w/cover	30.00	45.00	55.00	65.00	90.00	150.00
Bowl, 9", oval, fruit	20.00	25.00	35.00	45.00	55.00	55.00
Bowl, 9", baker	20.00	25.00	35.00	45.00	55.00	55.00
Bowl, 12", low, floral	15.00	25.00	35.00	45.00	55.00	55.00
Cigarette box, (ashtray)	25.00	60.00	65.00	70.00	80.00	100.00
Cologne bottle, w/stopper	40.00	90.00	95.00	100.00	110.00	135.00
Comport, 5", high ftd., shallow	15.00	25.00	37.00	45.00	55.00	70.00
Comport, 6", low ftd., deep	20.00	30.00	34.00	40.00	42.00	48.00
Creamer	10.00	20.00	20.00	22.00	24.00	28.00
Cruet, 2 oz., oil	20.00	40.00	45.00	50.00	55.00	65.00
Cruet, 4 oz., oil	25.00	50.00	50.00	55.00	60.00	75.00
Cup	5.00	15.00	20.00	25.00	30.00	40.00
Cup, after dinner	7.00	28.00	30.00	35.00	40.00	50.00
Egg cup	20.00	25.00	32.00	39.00	42.00	52.00
Grapefruit, ftd.	10.00	17.00	24.00	31.00	38.00	45.00
Gravy (or dressing) boat, w/underliner	13.00	25.00	30.00	45.00	50.00	45.00
Marmalade jar, w/cover	25.00	35.00	40.00	45.00	55.00	65.00
Parfait, 5 oz.	10.00	15.00	20.00	25.00	30.00	35.00
Pitcher, quart	35.00	55.00	65.00	75.00	125.00	160.00
Plate, 2 hdld., cheese	5.00	10.00	13.00	15.00	17.00	25.00
Plate, cream soup underliner	5.00	7.00	9.00	12.00	14.00	16.00
Plate, finger bowl underliner	3.00	5.00	7.00	9.00	11.00	13.00
Plate, 4½", coaster	3.00	5.00	10.00	12.00		
Plate, 6"	3.00	6.00	8.00	10.00	13.00	15.00
Plate, 6", bouillon underliner	3.00	6.00	8.00	10.00	13.00	15.00

YEOMAN, Blank #1184, A.H. Heisey & Co. (continued)

	Crystal	Pink	Sahara	Green	Hawth.	Marigold
Plate, 6½", grapefruit bowl	7.00	12.00	15.00	19.00	27.00	32.00
Plate, 7"	5.00	8.00	10.00	14.00	17.00	22.00
Plate, 8", oyster cocktail	9.00					
Plate, 8", soup	9.00					
Plate, 9", oyster cocktail	10.00					
Plate, 10½"	20.00	50.00		50.00	60.00	
Plate, 10½", ctr. hand., oval, div.	15.00	26.00		32.00		
Plate, 11", 4 pt., relish	20.00	27.00		32.00		
Plate, 14"	20.00					
Platter, 12", oval	10.00	17.00	19.00	26.00	33.00	
Salt, ind. tub (cobalt: $30.00)	5.00	8.00		15.00		
Salver, 10", low ftd.	15.00	30.00		42.00		
Salver, 12", low ftd.	10.00	25.00		32.00		
Saucer	3.00	5.00	7.00	7.00	10.00	10.00
Saucer, after dinner	3.00	5.00	7.00	8.00	10.00	10.00
Stem, 2¾ oz., ftd., oyster cocktail	4.00	8.00	10.00	12.00	14.00	
Stem, 3 oz., cocktail	10.00	12.00	17.00	20.00		
Stem, 3½ oz., sherbet	5.00	8.00	11.00	12.00		
Stem, 4 oz., fruit cocktail	3.00	5.00	7.00	9.00		
Stem, 4½ oz., sherbet	3.00	5.00	7.00	9.00		
Stem, 5 oz., soda	9.00	8.00	12.00	12.00		
Stem, 5 oz., sherbet	5.00	5.00	7.00	9.00		
Stem, 6 oz., champagne	6.00	16.00	18.00	22.00		
Stem, 8 oz.	5.00	12.00	18.00	20.00		
Stem, 10 oz., goblet	10.00	15.00	20.00	25.00		
Sugar, w/cover	13.00	35.00	30.00	35.00	40.00	40.00
Sugar shaker, ftd.	50.00	95.00		110.00		
Syrup, 7 oz., saucer ftd.	30.00	75.00				
Tray, 7" x 10", rect.	26.00	30.00	40.00	35.00		
Tray, 9", celery	10.00	14.00	16.00	15.00		
Tray, 11", ctr. hand., 3 pt.	15.00	20.00	24.00			
Tray, 12", oblong	16.00	19.00	24.00			
Tray, 13", 3 pt., relish	20.00	27.00	32.00			
Tray, 13", celery	20.00	27.00	32.00			
Tray, 13", hors d'oeuvre, w/cov. ctr.	32.00	42.00	52.00	75.00		
Tray insert, 3½" x 4½"	4.00	6.00	7.00	8.00		
Tumbler, 2½ oz., whiskey	3.00	8.00	10.00	12.00		
Tumbler, 4½ oz., soda	4.00	6.00	10.00	15.00		
Tumbler, 8 oz.	4.00	12.00	17.00	20.00		
Tumbler, 10 oz., cupped rim	4.00	15.00	20.00	22.50		
Tumbler, 10 oz., straight side	5.00	15.00	20.00	22.50		
Tumbler, 12 oz., tea	5.00	20.00	25.00	30.00		
Tumbler cover (unusual)	35.00					

CAMBRIDGE STEMS

1066
11 oz. Goblet

1402
Brandy Inhaler (Tall)

3025
10 oz. Goblet

3035
3 oz. Cocktail

3077
6 oz. Tall Sherbet

3104
1 oz. Cordial

3106
9 oz. Goblet Tall Bowl

3115
3½ oz. Cocktail

210

3120
6 oz. Tall Sherbet

3121
10 oz. Goblet

CAMBRIDGE STEMS

3122
9 oz. Goblet

3124
3 oz. Wine

3126
7 oz. Tall Sherbet

3130
6 oz. Tall Sherbet

3135
6 oz. Tall Sherbet

3400
9 oz. Lunch Goblet

3500
10 oz. Goblet

3600
2½ oz. Wine

3775
4½ oz. Claret

3625
4½ oz. Claret

3779
1 oz. Cordial

HEISEY'S "ALEXANDRITE" COLOR (rare)

Bowl, 12", floral, Twist (1252)	300.00
Candlesticks, pr. (134)	600.00
Cream & sugar, pr., Empress (1401)	425.00
Compote, Albermarle (3368)	160.00
Cup & saucer, Empress (1401)	125.00
Mint, 6", w/dolphin feet, Empress (1401)	165.00
Mayonnaise, w/dolp. ft. & ladle, Empress (1401)	300.00
Plate, 8", Empress (1401)	65.00
Salt & pepper, pr., Empress (1401)	350.00
Stem, 2½ oz., wine, Creole (3381)	180.00
Stem, 2½ oz., wine, Old Dominion (3380)	160.00
Stem, 6 oz., champagne, Old Dominion (3380)	140.00
Stem, 11 oz., water goblet, Carcassone (3390)	90.00
Stem, 11 oz., water goblet, Creole (3381)	160.00
Vase, 4", ball, Wide Optic (4045)	250.00

HEISEY'S "ALEXANDRITE" COLOR (rare)

Ash tray, Empress (1401)..	210.00
Candlesticks, 7", pr. (135)..	350.00
Celery tray, 10", Empress (1401)	150.00
Nut, individual, Empress (1401)..	125.00
Plate, 6", square, Empress (1401)	30.00
Plate, 7", square, Empress (1401)	45.00
Plate, 8", square, Empress (1401)	65.00
Plate, 10½", square, Empress (1401)	175.00
Tumbler, 1 oz., cordial, Carcassonne (3390)..	180.00
Tumbler, 2½ oz., bar, Glenford (3481)..	180.00
Tumbler 5 oz., ftd., soda, Creole (3381)	95.00
Tumbler, 8½ oz., ftd., soda, Creole (3381)	100.00
Tumbler, 12 oz., ftd., soda, Creole (3381)	105.00
Vase, 9", ftd., Empress (1401)..	625.00

HEISEY'S "COBALT" COLOR (rare)

Bowl, 12", Thumbprint & Panel (1433)	160.00
Candlestick, 2-lite, pr., Thumbprint & Panel (1433)	260.00
Candlestick, 6", pr., Old Sandwich (1404)	375.00
Mug, 12 oz., Old Sandwich, (1404)	210.00
Mug, 16 oz., Old Sandwich (1404)	300.00
Mug, 18 oz., Old Sandwich (1404)	290.00
Pitcher, Old Sandwich (1404)	270.00
Salt and Pepper, pr. (24)	250.00
Sign, Cabochon (crystal)	175.00
Stem, 1 oz., cordial, Spanish (3404)	225.00
Stem, 3½ oz., cocktail, Spanish (3404)	90.00
Stem, 5½ oz., sherbet, Spanish (3404)	60.00
Stem, 5½ oz., saucer champagne, Spanish (3404)	85.00
Stem, 10 oz., water, Spanish (3404)	105.00
Tumbler, 10 oz., ftd., soda, Spanish (3404)	85.00
Vase, ball (4045)	150.00
Vase, favor, Diamond Optic (4229)	260.00
Vase, favor, Diamond Optic (4230)	260.00
Vase, tulip, 9", ftd. (1420)	325.00

HEISEY'S "COBALT" COLOR (rare)

Bowl, 11", floral, Warwick (1428)	260.00
Candlestick, 6", pr. (135)	420.00
Candy, w/cover, 6", Empress (1401)	360.00
Cigarette holder, ftd., Carcassonne (3390)	75.00
Plate, 8", Empress (1401)	70.00
Sign, Cabochon (crystal)	175.00
Stem, 6 oz., saucer champagne, Carcassonne (3390)	50.00
Stem, 11 oz., tall, Carcassonne (3390)	100.00
Tumbler, 2½ oz., wine, ftd., Carcassonne (3390)	85.00
Tumbler, 12 oz., soda, ftd., Carcassonne (3390)	75.00
Vase, 7", Warwick (1428)	180.00
Vase, 9", pr., Warwick (1428)	360.00

HEISEY'S "DAWN" COLOR (rare)

Ash tray, 6", square, Prism Square 95.00
Bowl, 6¾", jelly Leaf (1565) 45.00
Butter dish, ¼ pound, Cabochon (1951) 180.00
Creamer, Cabochon (1951) 50.00
Sherbet, 20th Century (1415) 35.00
Sugar, Cabochon (1951) 50.00
Tray, 12", 4 pt. variety, Octagon (500) 300.00
Tumbler, 4", 10 oz., water, Coleport (1487) 30.00
Tumbler, 5¼", 13 oz., iced tea, Coleport (1487) 40.00

HEISEY'S "DAWN" COLOR (rare)

Bowl, 5⅜", berry, Town & Country (1637) 40.00
Bowl, 8½", vegetable, Town & Country (1637) 100.00
Bowl, 12½", salad, Town & Country (1637) 140.00
Cruet, 3 oz., crystal stopper, Saturn (1485) 300.00
Plate, 8⅝", luncheon, Town & Country (1637) 75.00
Plate, 10", dinner, Town & Country (1637) 175.00
Salt and pepper shaker, pr., Saturn (1485) 250.00
Tumbler, 4⅜", 9 oz., Town & Country (1637) 35.00
Tumbler, 5¼", 13 oz., iced tea, Town & Country (1637) 50.00

HEISEY'S EXPERIMENTAL BLUE COLOR (rare)

Sherbet, 5 oz., ALBEMARLE (3368) .... $500.00+ ea.

Note that the top sherbet has a crystal stem with a blue optic top while the bottom sherbet is all blue with no optic. The optic makes the blue seem more pronounced.

HEISEY'S EXPERIMENTAL BLUE COLOR (rare)

Tumbler, 5 oz., ftd. soda ALBEMARLE (3368) .... $500.00+ ea.

Notice the top soda has a blue top and foot with a crystal stem while the bottom left one has a blue top and crystal stem and foot. The bottom right soda is all blue.

HEISEY'S TANGERINE COLOR (rare)

Plate, 8", Empress blank (1401).. 130.00
Stem, champagne, Duquesne blank (3389).. 160.00
Stem, water, Duquesne blank (3389) 190.00
Vase, ivy (4224).. 210.00

HEISEY'S TANGERINE COLOR (rare)

Creamer, Empress blank (1401)... 600.00
Cup, Empress blank (1401) 600.00
Saucer, Empress blank (1401) 200.00
Sugar, Empress blank (1401) 600.00

HEISEY'S ZIRCON (LIMELIGHT) COLOR (rare)

Bowl, 6", hdld., mayonnaise, Fern (1495) 45.00
Bowl, 14", floral, Kohinoor (1488) 1,000.00
Candelabra, Kohinoor (1488) 700.00
Plate, 5", Beehive (1238) 65.00
Plate, 8", Beehive (1238) 85.00
Relish, ftd., hdld., 3 pt., Fern (1495) 350.00
Stem, 9 oz., water, Kohinoor (4085) 120.00
Stem, 5½ oz. saucer champagne, Kohinoor (4085) 80.00
Stem, 9 oz., short water, Stanhope (4083) 95.00
Stem, 6 oz., sherbet, Coventry (4090) 40.00

Other Books by Gene Florence

A publication I recommend:

THE ORIGINAL NATIONAL DEPRESSION GLASS NEWSPAPER

Depression Glass Daze, the original national monthly newspaper dedicated to the buying, selling and collecting of colored glassware of the 20's and 30's. We average 60 pages each month, filled with feature articles by top-notch columnists, readers' "finds," club happenings, show news, a china corner, a current listing of new glass issues to beware of and a multitude of ads! You can find it in the **DAZE**! Keep up with what's happening in the dee gee world with a subscription to the **DAZE**. Buy, sell or trade from the convenience of your easy chair.

NAME _____

ADDRESS _____

CITY _____ STATE _____ ZIP_____

☐ 1 YEAR - $19.00   ☐ CHECK ENCLOSED   ☐ PLEASE BILL ME   ☐ MASTERCARD   ☐ VISA

CARD NO. _____ EXP. DATE _____

SIGNATURE _____

SEND ORDER TO: **D.G.D., BOX 57 GF, OTISVILLE, MI 48463-0008** (Please allow 30 days.)

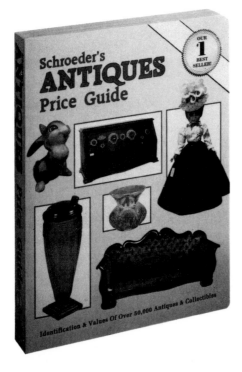